DOING
EXCELLENT
SMALL-SCALE
RESEARCH

SAGE has been part of the global academic community since 1965, supporting high quality research and learning that transforms society and our understanding of individuals, groups and cultures. SAGE is the independent, innovative, natural home for authors, editors and societies who share our commitment and passion for the social sciences.

Find out more at: **www.sagepublications.com**

DOING EXCELLENT SMALL-SCALE RESEARCH

Derek Layder

Los Angeles | London | New Delhi
Singapore | Washington DC

Los Angeles | London | New Delhi
Singapore | Washington DC

SAGE Publications Ltd
1 Oliver's Yard
55 City Road
London EC1Y 1SP

SAGE Publications Inc.
2455 Teller Road
Thousand Oaks, California 91320

SAGE Publications India Pvt Ltd
B 1/I 1 Mohan Cooperative Industrial Area
Mathura Road
New Delhi 110 044

SAGE Publications Asia-Pacific Pte Ltd
3 Church Street
#10-04 Samsung Hub
Singapore 049483

Library of Congress Control Number: 2011945430

British Library Cataloguing in Publication data

A catalogue record for this book is available from
the British Library

Editor: Chris Rojek
Editorial assistant: Martine Jonsrud
Production editor: Katherine Haw
Copyeditor: Sarah Bury
Proofreader: Derek Markham
Indexer: Charmian Parkin
Marketing manager: Ben Griffin-Sherwood
Cover design: Wendy Scott
Typeset by: C&M Digitals (P) Ltd, Chennai, India
Printed by: Replika Press Pvt. Ltd

ISBN 978-1-84920-182-7
ISBN 978-1-84920-183-4 (pbk)

CONTENTS

ABOUT THE AUTHOR

Derek Layder is Emeritus Professor of sociology at University of Leicester, UK. He was awarded a doctorate by the London School of Economics in 1976. Appointed Lecturer in sociology at the University of Leicester in 1974 and promoted to Reader in 1995, he became Professor in 1997 and Emeritus Professor from 2002. He has held several visiting academic positions and has also held honorary visiting appointments at The Australian National University (as a Humanities Research Fellow) and the University of Western Sydney (as Eminent Research Visitor). He taught in the areas of social theory, social psychology, social research methods and the philosophy of social science. He has published numerous academic articles and 11 books. Among his books, in the area of the philosophy of social science he is the author of *The Realist Image in Social Science* (1990), in social theory he has written *Understanding Social Theory* (second edition, 2006), as well as *Modern Social Theory* (1997). On research strategies and methods he has authored *New Strategies in Social Research* (1993) and *Sociological Practice* (1998). He has also written on intimacy, emotion and self-identity, including *Emotion in Social Life* (2004), *Social & Personal Identity* (2004) and *Intimacy & Power* (2009).

PREFACE

This is an introductory guide for those who need to carry out small-scale research. However, it is suitable for a broad readership, including undergraduates, postgraduates and more experienced researchers. I have written it with a view to helping undergraduates with research projects that are part of their degree work. But postgraduates (at master's and doctoral levels), researchers outside academia, and more experienced academics may also find it helpful because it offers an in-depth account of a specific approach to social research.

Instead of describing an exhaustive 'list' of options, the book offers a particular way of doing social research that focuses on how human behaviour is linked to its social contexts. It leads the researcher through the actual process of doing a research project from start to finish, by providing systematic guidelines and advice.

However, the book covers many of the general areas and issues in research, such as: preparation and planning, research ethics, validity, identifying problems and developing research questions, applying techniques of observation, interviewing, documentary sources, blending quantitative and qualitative data, sampling, the use of concepts, coding and data analysis. As such, the book should be useful to those in the following fields and disciplines: sociology, psychology, management and business, health studies and nursing, education, media studies, organisation studies, criminology, social work and social policy, sport and leisure studies, politics and many others.

I have removed all obscure terms and technical issues, in an effort to make it as clear and direct as possible. Most of this attempt at simplification and clarity is fairly self-explanatory. However, there is one issue that deserves some special mention. I often use 'explanation' instead of 'theory' because explanation is a more familiar (and less anxiety-inducing) term. And anyway, theory *is* a form of explanation, so nothing is lost – given my aim of clarity and accessibility. At other times, I use the term 'analytic' or 'analytic issues' to mean roughly the same as theory or theoretical issues.

How to Read the Book: The Plan of Chapters

While each chapter deals with particular aspects of social research, there are two important issues that are treated more generally throughout most of the chapters. First, the ethics of social research – the rules that govern how you should treat your research subjects – which are first discussed at the end of Chapter 1. Other chapters raise ethical issues as they arise from the discussion of particular practices and methods.

Second, the book stresses that the question of validity in social research not only involves ensuring the soundness and defensibility of the data and methods used – including their reliability and accuracy, which is a continuing theme of Chapters 4–6. Just as important is the notion of validity as it refers to the overall logic and structure of research arguments and explanations, as well as the 'conclusions' that are drawn from research findings. These themes are mainly to be found in Chapters 1–3 and 7–9.

As far as the content of particular chapters are concerned, Chapters 1, 2 and 3 'prepare' you for the rest of the book's more conventional description of what is entailed in doing a research project. But these chapters should not be skipped over since they discuss key issues relevant to an understanding of the overall approach.

Chapter 1 offers a more detailed overview of the main elements of the approach – including a brief sketch of six key analytic problems that drive adaptive research. Chapter 2 serves two main purposes. First, it gives a 'flavour' of the kinds of topics or research areas that are appropriate for 'starting' researchers tackling small-scale projects. Second, in discussing some published research, I identify the sort of analytic problems (mentioned in Chapter 1) that underpin them, and how they differ from research topics and questions.

Chapter 3 discusses in more depth how problems and topics are related in adaptive research, and how they influence core research questions. I give this separate and 'advance' treatment because it plays such a crucial role in the adaptive approach. 'Research problems' – as opposed to research topics or research questions – are defined quite differently from conventional introductory texts. This also entails grasping the distinction between conceptualisation and description (and its role in explanation). Mastering the research skills entailed in handling these distinctions is crucial to putting adaptive principles into research practice.

Chapters 4–10 follow a more conventional form of presentation by giving a sequential account of the approach. Chapter 4 covers the main issues in preparing and planning for adaptive research – such as a selective literature review, identifying problems, topics and research questions, and outlining a provisional research design. It also discusses the writing issues and skills essential to the approach, including keeping a Research Log. Chapter 5 focuses on the issue of selecting the most appropriate mix of qualitative methods and strategies for your project. It includes a discussion of the way in which observation, interviews and documentary sources (and the types of data associated with them) are influenced by the analytic 'units' of social life to which they are applied.

Chapter 6 outlines the forms of quantitative data and analysis most suited to mixed strategy research, and suggests ways of integrating quantitative and qualitative data. Chapter 7 describes how to select data samples in adaptive research and the way in which 'problem' sampling offers a way of blending elements of 'probability' and 'purposive' sampling. Chapter 8 examines the importance of both 'orienting' concepts and 'emergent' concepts for adaptive analysis, and outlines the relationships between concepts, coding data and data analysis. Chapter 9 focuses on writing up the research report and how to produce a consistent and reasoned research argument. The mechanics of how to construct an argument are rarely covered in introductory texts, and yet they play such a crucial role in establishing the credentials of excellent research. By way of conclusion, Chapter 10 provides a summary and checklist for the overall approach.

1

OVERVIEW OF THE ADAPTIVE APPROACH

PREVIEW

This chapter covers the following:

- How to choose an appropriate topic for a small-scale project

- The importance of writing as early as possible

- Scientific rigour, validity and the search for explanation

- Understanding the differences between problems, topics and questions

- Constructing a research design

- How to mix strategies and methods

- Data sampling in adaptive research

- How to use concepts in data analysis

- Ethics in social research

- Starting the Research Log

Choosing an Appropriate Topic

This book is designed to help you complete a small social research project. In order to do this to the best of your capabilities, it is important to select a topic that interests and motivates you. It should be 'doable' with the resources at your disposal and within the required time frame. It should be practically manageable while the topic itself should be sharply focused and well defined. Taking on a large and more general topic – say, investigating the effects of government policy on school admissions, or the educational achievements of pupils from different social backgrounds – would invite the criticism that you are being too ambitious. In which case, those who eventually grade your project will have a ready-made reason to find fault with it.

A smaller more focused and well-defined project, such as investigating the rewards and disappointments of friendship at school or your neighbourhood, would not present the same problems. Your efforts and research findings will be automatically tailored to the more limited aims of the project. Whoever grades it will have to judge its merit (its 'adequacy' and 'validity') in relation to these rather modest aims. Thus, right from the beginning you can avoid criticisms of over-ambitiousness or vagueness of aims and objectives. In this respect, it is best to choose a topic that is of great interest to you – perhaps something that directly connects with your daily life. A personal connection like this will naturally help in providing focus and definition to your research project. Also, if you are fascinated with, or gripped by your topic, it is more likely that your enthusiasm will remain high throughout the project. In particular, it will help keep you going when you come up against problems or difficulties.

In Chapter 2 I discuss a range of topics that fit these criteria and hopefully will stimulate your thinking about potential projects. Of course, these are meant simply as *suggestions*, to get you started, they are not meant to restrict your choices. If you are confident about ideas and interests of your own, then by all means pursue them. Of course you should remain open to advice from your supervisor, or advisor, especially if they are going to play some part in marking/grading it. However, it would be unusual for an advisor to *insist* on your concentrating on a particular topic, rather than simply making 'suggestions' about appropriate areas, since the whole point of the exercise is to allow you to demonstrate your ability, make your own choices and display initiative.

The topics discussed in Chapter 2 are well defined and focused as well as being close to everyday experience. In addition, they spotlight what is, perhaps, the central problem issue that underpins all social study. This is the question of how human behaviour *both shapes, and is shaped by*, the wider social environment in which it is embedded. I'll go into this in more detail in the sections that follow, but all the topic examples reveal different aspects of this central issue. Thus, the examples have strong links with key problems and themes in social study. If you are able to weave such themes into your project – and this book is designed to help you with this – your research will be more sophisticated, 'marking it out from the crowd'. Crucially, this will give it an advantage when it comes to the awarding of marks for research excellence.

Deciding on a topic also entails being clear about which ones are best to avoid, especially if you have little experience as a researcher. Although topics close to one's own experiences may be appropriate for small-scale projects, it is of the utmost importance not to let personal views, ideas, opinions and prejudices cloud your thinking. As far as possible research projects must be conducted 'objectively' – that is, freeing them of the personal biases or preferences of the researcher.

Ensuring that personal prejudices and biases do not intrude is probably best served by steering clear of topics or approaches to research that, by their very nature, make it very difficult to maintain a neutral attitude. A good example of this is where research is guided by explicitly 'emancipatory' aims. That is, where the researcher takes it upon him or herself to seek to improve the lot of those social groups who are deemed to get a 'raw deal' from society. Such projects are fraught with difficulty as far as maintaining an unbiased stance is concerned. Problems arise when the researcher identifies with members of social groups that he or she believes to be relatively powerless and has the explicit aim of gathering evidence that will help 'empower' them. Unless handled skilfully and carefully, such an approach runs the danger of being open to the criticism of being politically motivated or partisan. As a result, the validity of such research may be questioned.

A novice researcher should generally avoid research topics that involve him or her making moral judgements about various kinds of behaviour, since these might slant the presentation of research evidence. Due care must also be taken when small-scale research is undertaken with an *evaluative objective* in mind. For example, assessing the efficiency or otherwise of a particular 'social policy' intervention, such as the effectiveness of drugs or smoking 'education' programmes in schools or work, requires a high level of sophistication, care and subtlety not only in terms of the practical aspects of the research, but also in juggling the sensitivities of the various stakeholders.

The Importance of Writing as Early as Possible

Writing should begin as early as possible, even before the serious business of collecting data has begun! From that point onwards writing should be continuous throughout the duration of the research – and documented in your Research Log (see last section of this chapter). In this sense there is no separate writing-up period, which, in conventional terms, comes at the end of a linear sequence of research 'stages'. Writing is an integral and constant 'companion' with this kind of research. When you aren't writing you aren't doing research. Writing is research and research implies writing! There are a number of advantages to be gained from starting to write-up very early on.

Obviously, in one sense, when you begin writing like this, you're not trying to produce the 'final' version of anything. This is partly because having not yet collected the bulk of your data you aren't in a position to draw any conclusions based on them. Another important reason is that whatever you attempt to put down in words at this early stage (such as preliminary chapter or section titles, or contents or notes on your research problem or research design), it is inevitably a *first draft*. But the fact that you are writing from the word go is a way of helping you over the hurdle of writer's block – or more accurately getting over a reluctance to commit yourself to the act of writing in the first place.

Of course, such problems as these can afflict anyone at anytime, but first-time researchers are particularly prone to them, especially if they leave writing-up to the very last minute. Constantly putting it off only increases the pressure on yourself and, in the end, not being able to write can develop into a massive and overblown problem! Making writing an integral part of research at every point eases you into the discipline and skills of writing. By the end, hopefully you become much more accustomed to jotting down your ideas and find writing in general a much less intimidating task.

Beginning to write at such an early stage also prepares you to appreciate the links between thinking and writing, links that are essential to the execution of excellent research. Putting your thoughts and ideas into words and writing them down in a logical form that makes sense to others, as well as yourself, helps clarify your thoughts. Often we assume that the very fact that we *have* thoughts, ideas and opinions on certain matters means that they *must* be reasonably well worked out. However, putting them down on paper often reveals that this assumption is invalid. Thus the process of writing becomes a way of eliminating inadvertent errors and confusions in thinking.

Expressing thoughts and ideas in verbal written form early on in the research process also highlights the links between the act of writing and the development of ideas, concepts and arguments. Familiarity with these discursive aspects of research can only aid you when it comes to defining research problems, shaping research design and constructing explanations. The process of getting ideas down on paper is the best way – indeed the only effective way – of developing and honing them, and making them acceptable for critical evaluation by others. Endlessly thinking them through, without writing them down, only leads to confusion and mental over-load.

Perhaps the greatest advantage to be gained from tackling the writing sooner rather than later is that it makes writing the 'final' research report much easier. In this respect, keeping a 'Research Log' provides you with a record of the procedures and practices you used – including any adjustments in sampling or problem-focus – and links them with your evolving thoughts about the direction and progress of the project. Having a record (the log) that matches what you actually did, against your findings and conclusions as they are expressed in your final report, makes the whole process so much more vivid and transparent. Intellectual honesty, integrity and transparency are highly prized assets when it comes to the evaluation of research. A project that displays these attributes by offering a transparent audit trail will be rewarded by a higher mark or grade.

Finally, developing an attitude towards writing (and re-writing) as an organic part of research and a constant ally (rather than a barrier to be overcome), also allows you to develop the argumentative skills that are so necessary for the communication of your findings to a wider audience – and most immediately, to those who are grading it. All research reports whether they be undergraduate coursework projects or PhD theses, are essentially held together by the force of the arguments you make and the manner in which they are presented.

Each element of the research report is made up of arguments that must be reasoned, coherent and robust. In this respect, each chapter of a thesis or each sub-section of a report is based on, and presented in the form of, a mini-argument. The thesis or report as a whole rests on this patchwork of mini-arguments – but it must also make sense independently of them. It must have its own meta-argument which links all the subsidiary arguments together. A Research Log encourages you to write in a structured and systematic manner, and thus makes you more aware of the need to employ both mini- and meta-arguments, and to develop them with due care and attention.

Scientific Rigour, Validity and the Search for Explanation

Social research requires *scientific* rigour, but what does this mean? This is a big question, but for present purposes we only need to focus on four basic issues.

1 The difference between description and explanation in social research

While description is necessary in social research, it should be regarded only as a stepping stone. The search for answers to the problem-questions that drive the research is the key to scientific adequacy and rigour. Description only scratches the surface of social life by concentrating on how people conduct their lives. For example, a description may provide us with an account of how drug users live out their daily lives, their routines and habits, their pleasures and affiliations. However, social research is required to go further and inquire into *why* people engage in certain kinds of behaviour. What causes them to behave in this manner? How do social influences and pressures – of friends, environment, up-bringing – help shape drug-taking behaviour? In what ways does drug use influence the lives of the users, or those around them, and society in general?

It is the move from the question *how* (or a description of what is happening) to *why* (an explanation or set of reasons for why this is happening) that makes such an inquiry more scientifically interesting. To some extent explanation requires and depends on the preliminary work of description. Thus providing accurate and reliable descriptive accounts of drug-taking behaviour enables the researcher to make the next step and collect evidence and data that may provide reasons (explanations) as to *why* this behaviour is occurring in the first place.

A description may achieve a high standard of descriptive accuracy but for overall excellence small-scale research must *at least* attempt to explain the behaviour under study. The words *at least* are extremely important here. You don't have to come up with a completely comprehensive explanation or 'the last word' on the matter. The point is to organise the research (via its design, methods and forms of analysis) so that it at least attempts to answer some 'why' questions. Even if you only manage to come up with a partial explanation or one that has obvious weaknesses, it will be better than taking the (seemingly) 'safe option' and remaining purely descriptive.

It is important to bear in mind that research excellence depends not only on the successes of a project – whatever they may be. Excellence is often demonstrated by being aware of, and engaging with, potential weaknesses. So even where your project has been less than successful in some (major or minor) respect, it is still possible to achieve excellence. The main requirement is that you show how you have attempted to go beyond description pure and simple.

2 Choosing research methods

Excellent small-scale social research requires adherence to scientific principles and practices which emphasise the search for the explanation of a problem. This differs from a 'pragmatic' approach (Baert 2005; Creswell 2009; Teddlie & Tashakkori 2009), in which methods are chosen on the basis of what is most 'useful' or 'practically expedient' or 'works best'. To the contrary, research methods and strategies should be chosen because they are the most adequate and appropriate for the *problem* than is being investigated. They should be chosen because they help provide explanations of the *problems and questions* that drive the research. Choice of method must also take account of what we know about the main domains of social life and the processes and the mechanisms that produce social behaviour. All these factors help shape research problems and questions.

3 The role of evidence (the data collected) in social research

Evidence – the data collected during the research, such as interview transcripts, documents, the results of surveys, and so on – play a crucial role in supporting explanations that emerge from the research investigation. There are two stages in this process. First, the collection and analysis of data allows the researcher to more accurately describe the phenomenon she or he is investigating. Second, description must be supplanted by a concern with explanation, that is, with the question of *why* the phenomenon is the way it is.

What social influences have caused it to be so? For instance, why is there a greater incidence of certain kinds of criminal behaviour in particular neighbourhoods or, why is drug taking more prevalent in certain kinds of work environment?

Both description and explanation must be firmly anchored in evidence collected during the research. The strength of an explanation is determined by the weight and 'persuasiveness' of the evidence on which it rests. Without such a foundation any proposed explanation will lack evidence to back it up and thus, risks being dismissed as 'speculative'. Conversely, an explanation is *verified* (and thus confirmed) in and through the weight and strength of evidence that supports it.

But there must be a balance between explanation and evidence. Evidence isn't *more* important than explanation. Thus, making sure there is enough evidence to support an explanation must be balanced by a concern with ensuring that the explanation makes sense. Its internal logic must be right. Its conclusions must follow from its initial assumptions. Thus, it is crucial to be sure that the claims the explanation makes, the warrants it draws on, and the arguments that lend it support, are coherent and robust. Claims about evidence and explanation are of equal importance for scientific adequacy and rigour. The *validity* of research involves a constant dialogue between evidence and explanation.

4 The principles of scientific rigour and adequacy

An awareness of the principles of scientific rigour and adequacy should be present in all facets and phases of the research process:

a   The problems, questions and explanations that drive and direct the project

b   The design of the research (based on (a))

c   The methods of data collection

d   The analysis of the evidence (data)

e   The arguments, claims and findings that appear in the concluding report.

In the final written account of the research – the academic report, dissertation or thesis – you should constantly make it clear how the principles in 1–3 above have been worked into your research practices. This is where keeping a written log of your progress is essential, because it ensures that as you go along you make a note of the way in which you attend to these issues. You must make it clear to the reader that you have followed a coherent research strategy (an ordered plan) throughout the research. Even though this plan might be modified during the course of the research, as long as it has been for scientifically justifiable reasons, then there is no problem.

The essential point is to avoid any impression that you were simply reacting in an expedient or convenient manner (the danger of a purely 'pragmatic' approach). By making sure that what you collected and analysed data scientifically, you add to the strength and excellence of your work. The persuasiveness of your findings and conclusions is enhanced by showing how the claims and arguments that you make are supported by the evidence (data) that you have collected.

Research Questions are Problem-Driven

Let us now tease out in more detail the connections between explanations, problems, topics and questions. Social research is literally a search for the best explanation of 'the problem' around which evidence or data is focused. But remember, 'social research problems' are not the same thing as 'topics' or 'areas of interest'. Nor are research problems the equivalent of what are often called 'social problems', such as poverty, unemployment, social inequality, and so on. Research problems address deeper issues about social organisation, social processes and social behaviour. The best quality social research always takes into account that such deeper problems profoundly influence research questions.

There are two types of research question: 'problem-questions' and 'topic-questions'. Problem-questions are most often overlooked in social research but it is important to appreciate that they have a crucial influence on the form and content of 'topic-questions'. In Chapter 3, I discuss in detail six problem-questions that are of great importance for research design. Here I shall introduce them in a preliminary way in order to familiarise you with them early on, and to show how they relate to topic questions.

Six key problem questions

1 *How are a person's self-identity, feelings, ideas and attitudes related to his or her social environment?*

A research project tackling this question might focus on individual's attitudes towards emotional or sexual intimacy in friendships or romantic partnerships, and how they are influenced by TV programmes, films and magazines. Another project might concentrate on whether or not certain individuals, such as those with low self-esteem, are more susceptible than others to drug addiction.

2   *How do people influence each other's behaviour in social interaction – either 'face-to-face' or 'mediated' through texts, emails, mobiles, and so on?*

Consider the following scenario. Two 'friends' meet up and one (or both) reveals for the first time that they find the other attractive. A routine peck on the cheek suddenly becomes a full-blown, passionate kiss, thus changing forever their relationship and their feelings towards one another. The way in which face-to-face interaction can transform people's understandings may thus be the focus of small-scale research. For example, a project could focus on the question of whether mixing with other drug users makes experimenting with different drugs more likely.

3   *How do social settings (such as schools, universities, families, factories, companies, hospitals, and so on) influence the behaviour of those operating within them?*

This question might give rise to a project examining how and why people express emotion and feeling in school, work, family and friendship. Alternatively, a project revolving around drug use might focus on the question 'is the use of certain types of drugs associated with different work settings?' A significant focus for small-scale research projects would be to help map the differences between settings and their effects on social behaviour by concentrating on a particular example – say a school, a university, a religious group, friendship, family or romantic relationships.

4   *How is social behaviour influenced by: (a) social class, ethnicity, gender, age, neighbourhood, region, or politics; (b) cultural values, expectations and institutions (including the media)?*

Such a problem might give rise to research on possible links between drug use and social class, gender or ethnicity. A project on intimacy might explore the extent to which media images of 'romantic love' seep into people's everyday attitudes and experiences.

5   *How does power influence human behaviour and social activity?*

Power is everywhere in social life (although it comes in different 'shapes and sizes', so to speak) and is an especially fruitful theme for small-scale research. Thus, a project on intimacy might centre on the way the balance of control in close relationships determines whether or not they survive in the longer term. A project on drug use could investigate the extent to which users are 'disempowered' by their addiction.

6   *How does the passage of time influence social behaviour?*

A project might investigate changes in intimate relationships over time. Why does the exciting frisson of a new romance begin to fade? Can intimacy deteriorate to the point where the partners are simply 'coexisting' with each other? A project around drug use might explore how long it takes for a user to become addicted, or it might investigate whether drug users' attitudes towards their 'nearest and dearest' change as they spend more time with other users.

Research Questions and Research Design

Unlike problem-questions which are *general* in nature, topic-questions concern *specific* issues about the topic or the area of research interest. So, topic-questions about the family, for instance, might include such things as how particular individuals define their roles, or how family members relate to one another, and so on. Topic-questions about romantic relationships might centre on 'emotional disclosure' and/or the 'commitment' and 'involvement' of partners. Numerous other examples are discussed in the following chapters so I won't dwell on them here. More important at this juncture is to sort out which comes first, problem-questions or topic-questions?

Because of an initial interest in a particular area or topic it is likely that you will also have ideas about the sort of topic-questions you may want to ask, before you even consider the idea of problem-questions. This is OK up to a point – it is one way of crank-starting your particular thoughts on a research project. But you must be willing to at least re-jig, or refine, any topic-questions you may have in mind, after you have decided on your key problem-questions. This is what I mean by the idea that research should be 'problem-driven'. Viewing topic-questions through the perspective of problem-questions acts as a sort of filtering process that gives final shape and focus to topic-questions.

For example, you may be interested in the topic of friendship or romantic relationships which may lead you to pose questions such as, 'how are friendships formed?', or 'why do couples become romantically attached?' In order to give these questions more research relevance and refinement, you need to also ask what problem-questions are pertinent to your concerns? Are you more interested in the way individual's experience friendship or romantic attachments (problem-question 1)? Or in the way friendships or romantic relationships develop through interaction (problem-question 2)? You may, in fact, want to know more about how families, neighbourhoods or schools affect the friendship and romantic choices that people make (problem-question 3).

You might prefer to focus on the way the media – magazines, books, films, internet, music and so on – influence the way people perceive and engage in intimacy (problem-question 4). Questions of power and control may be more compelling, such as 'how are romantic relationships influenced by the power balance between partners' (problem-question 5)? You may wish to explore how ideas about romantic relationships have changed in particular periods of history (problem-question 6). As you begin to decide on your focus, and the problem-questions most relevant to your concerns, you can then refine your topic-questions. As they become more refined and focused, certain tentative answers or explanations may suggest themselves.

Because the design of a project hinges on the development and honing of research questions (both problem and topic varieties) a good amount of time and effort should be given over to deciding what they are *before doing* any actual research. After this essential first step in research design, you will be in a position to decide what kind of data sample you need (how many and what kinds of people, events or documents). The third step, choosing the methods and strategies of data collection, will follow from this, as will the fourth step, choosing the best ways of analysing the data.

It is no good starting out on a research project with only loose ideas, hunches or assumptions about what you are going to do. Research must be systematic, ordered and logical. Developing a research design at the very start provides a framework or template in advance of the research itself, so that it has some planned structure to it. This will help minimise any uncertainties you might have about how to proceed or in dealing with unforeseen or disruptive problems. Of course, deciding on key problem- and topic-questions in advance *does not mean* that you can't change things or be flexible in your thinking and ideas about the project. Thus it is best to regard these things *as preparatory and preliminary* in nature. Once underway, your plans and focus may shift, change or readjust, but having a preliminary focus and design in place will ensure that any changes will be ordered and controlled rather than being 'forced' or ill-thought-out.

Always remember that topic-questions must be 'rinsed' through the filter of problem-questions in order for them to be refined, sharpened and made fully relevant to your research purposes. After this, problem- and topic-questions together provide the key to research design — a coherent overall plan of the research. As problem- and topic-questions become joint parts of a research design they drive the research through its subsequent phases (sampling, methods and strategies of data collection, analysis of data and concluding arguments). The whole sequence then is as follows:

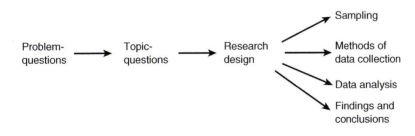

Figure 1.1

Sometimes textbooks give an impression that social research involves a succession of discrete (though related) 'stages' of activity moving in one direction from start to finish – such as design, sampling, data collection, analysis and so on. The researcher completes each successive stage with a 'clean break' before the next is begun. On this view, stages of research are self-contained units related to each other through their succession in time. With the adaptive approach, instead of discrete stages, social research is understood as a continuously unfolding process. During this process various phases of research activity merge into one another as an adaptive response to changes in research circumstances or priorities.

Mixed Design: Mixed Methods and Strategies

With the adaptive approach quantitative and qualitative methods and data are regarded as complementary to each other. In this sense they 'fill out' or 'add to' each other's picture of the social world because they represent or depict fundamentally different aspects of social reality. Quantitative methods are best able to deal with the settings and social contexts of social behaviour while qualitative methods are better suited to dealing with the social dynamics of situations, behaviour and interaction. Although they complement each other in their attempt to explain social phenomena scientifically, the soundness of quantitative and qualitative methods cannot always be judged by exactly the same criteria.

Quantitative methods (such as surveys, questionnaires, 'structured' interviews and observations) are well placed to provide information on such things as: *rates of social incidents or events such as suicide rates* (as in Durkheim 1982); *rates of class or status mobility; birth and death rates; forms of remuneration (salaries and wages); rates of physical and mental illness; indicators of well-being or happiness; the age, gender, class ethnic composition of a population; the extent of equality or inequality between groups; status and consumption patterns (what people spend their money on, and how they see themselves in relation to others).*

Qualitative studies, on the other hand, focus on the dynamic, emergent aspects of social activity. They offer in-depth analyses of specific situations or locations (say a group of friends at school or workers in a restaurant or gangs on the streets). Such studies use observations and interviews to give a detailed sense of how and why people experience what they experience, their relationships and interaction. At the heart of the analysis are the 'central concerns' of the people involved, how they feel (their emotions) about what they are doing, what they want to achieve (their motives and intentions, hopes and fears).

In many cases, qualitative analyses directly complement quantitative studies by providing data on the dynamics of encounters and 'lived experience' that quantitative information cannot directly supply. In other cases, qualitative studies explore areas about which little is known and which may then be 'enhanced' by quantitative data and evidence. However, neither quantitative nor qualitative forms of inquiry are inherently superior. Nor is one more or less scientific than the other. Each form of inquiry taps into, and depicts, different, but complementary, aspects of the social world (social reality).

It follows that to create a full and comprehensive picture of social processes both kinds of study are required. Thus, small-scale researchers must be willing *to draw upon* both quantitative and qualitative methods and data. The phrase to 'draw upon' is of crucial importance. Producing quantitative data from large samples of people is technically difficult, expensive and time-consuming, and thus, usually, beyond the reach of small projects. Thus, small-scale researchers should make use of existing quantitative data sets – such as official government statistics, census data, market research, or surveys originally done for different purposes, to fill out or supplement other kinds of data (see Chapter 6).

Drawing on as many complementary methods, strategies and data resources as possible doesn't require that the researcher be expert in them all. However, researchers must have *some awareness* of the broad range of possibilities. The main point is to avoid the limitations imposed by having an overly rigid and detailed knowledge of just one method or area of analysis.

Flexible Sampling: Using Your Imagination

As well as flexible designs and mixed strategies, the adaptive approach also favours the flexible and constructive use of data samples (of people, events, settings and documentary materials). This raises some initial difficulties when it comes to blending and integrating quantitative and qualitative data, because quantitative data (as in surveys) are closely associated with fixed samples (and fixed designs). However, in Chapters 5 and 6 in particular, I suggest some ways in which quantitative and qualitative data may be combined, while also using flexible sampling strategies

Flexible sampling expands the range of creative interventions the researcher can make during the research and allows him or her to monitor newly collected data in order to respond to it on an emergent basis. However, this doesn't mean that it involves any less rigorous (scientific) planning and preparation than with a fixed research design (such as a survey or experiment).

In adaptive analysis the initial phases of research require a 'conventional' sample chosen on the basis of the main research problems and questions. Sampling only enters into a 'flexible' phase once the research is underway. Thus, only after the collection and analysis of data has indicated possible benefits of a shift in the sample base can the original sample be added to or modified.

In this sense the sample is increased or decreased according to the development of your overall research arguments and the explanations they support. The idea here is that the 'explanation' (of the research questions driving your research) doesn't just 'pop up' out of the blue, so to speak. It emerges cumulatively during the course of the research. Thus, continuous sampling aids the emergence of this explanation.

For example, say you began studying romantic relationships and were focusing mainly on how the interpersonal dynamics of the partners creates truly satisfying intimacy. Your initial sample of interviewees might be mainly composed of couples in 'successful' long-term relationships. However, while interviewing the couples you come to realise that in order to fully address the problem you need to compare those in your sample with individual's whose relationships have failed. That is, in order to show how and why some relationships have remained successful and satisfying, you also need to identify the breakdown points in failed relationships. This kind of comparison will enable you to define more exactly the reasons why the successful relationships are indeed successful.

Had the initial sample provided the basis for an adequate explanation of the dynamics of successful romantic relationships, then you would proceed with the research on that basis. However, because it became apparent that 'other' evidence (data) was needed, the decision was taken to extend the sample to address this problem. In this manner, the research is kept moving forward productively. The researcher keeps asking the question 'what sort of evidence do I need to provide answers to, and explanations of, my research problem?' There is no automatic assumption that the initial sample will provide such evidence.

What Does the Evidence Show: Concepts and Data Analysis

Data, information or empirical evidence that has been brought together during the course of a specific research project must be deciphered in certain ways. The 'facts' do not literally speak for themselves although, in fact, they may seem to imply particular interpretations. Data analysis is a means of clarifying the implications of the data for understanding and explaining the main research problems and questions. This link between data analysis and explanation, which itself depends on reasoning and argument, is crucial for the execution of excellent research.

Here the importance of *concepts* comes to the fore, because it is the forming, using and storing of concepts that allows reasoning and argument to proceed (Magee 1997). Understanding the relations between concepts and observations is essential for excellent research. Chapter 8 clarifies what concepts are and how they are used in social research. In particular, the chapter spells out how concepts relate to research experience and the coding and analysis of data (Layder 1998; Rose 1984).

Concepts can be used in two main ways. First, there are what might be called 'ready-made' concepts, which have been constructed and established through social research and analytic discussion. Since they are already in regular use, they can be used to identify and explain patterns in data or evidence. For example, the concept of 'emotional labour', originally formulated by Hochschild (1983) to help explain the 'sympathetic' behaviour of airline flight attendants (particularly 'service with a smile'), could be used to throw light on encounters between an array of other service personnel and their clients – for example, sales assistants and customers, hospital staff and patients, pupils and teachers, or students and professors.

At the same time, analysing data from these areas may make it apparent that the concept of emotional labour itself should be extended, elaborated or changed so that it may be applied in different contexts. This revelation would be a significant contribution, and a very worthy research finding or conclusion. Alternatively, the concept might even be extended to reveal important aspects of the interpersonal dynamics of romantic relationships – providing a non-commercial comparison.

Social research is also concerned with 'emergent' concepts. These are especially important for areas where there are only few established concepts. They are also essential where existing concepts fail to fully capture or depict what is indicated by data from an ongoing study. For example, in my study of power and control in intimate relationships (Layder 2009), the concept of 'emotional labour' served as a useful initial 'marker' and starting point for thinking about the role of emotions and feelings in close relationships. This 'background' idea fed into my thinking while scrutinising data from interviews with couples about their everyday behaviour. I asked analytic questions such as 'what is going on here?', and/or 'what is the best way of characterising (and thus understanding), certain types of intimate relationship?'

In order to convey the inner texture of different relationships, I came up with the distinction between 'energising intimacy games', in which there is a dynamic, emotional rapport between partners, as compared with 'deficit games', which are emotionally flat, and where partners drain each other of psychic energy. For one of the deficit games, I came up with the concept of 'emotional withholding' to depict the way partners try to maintain (some) control over a relationship by being emotionally elusive. These concepts have some link with 'emotional labour' but they also radically depart from it, by opening up new ground in terms of their content and applicability.

For first-time researchers a note of caution is called for because developing emergent concepts requires more skill and creativity than in employing ready-made or 'established' ones. In order to develop emergent concepts a researcher must have confidence and experience in handling conceptual materials, and making connections between data and concepts. Such confidence must be solidly grounded otherwise either confusion will set in, or it will lead to inadequate, 'flaky' concepts. The most solid grounding for this kind of confidence is that gained from first-hand experience. Of course, for the first-time researcher such experience will be in short supply, although this should not necessarily deter him or her from making an attempt at conceptual innovation. However, it must be remembered that developing an existing concept, or shaping a new one as a result of data analysis, is double-edged. When it is done well, it is a clear marker of research excellence. When it is done badly, it may deflect attention from other strengths that the project may possess.

Ethics in Social Research

All social research requires adherence to ethical principles that govern the conduct of researchers and are instrumental in safeguarding the rights and well-being of research subjects. Different areas of study and their professional bodies in the UK, such as the British Sociological Association, the British Psychological Society, the Medical Research Council, and the Economic and Social Research Council, have developed approved sets of ethical guidelines (the same is true of other countries). It is important to be aware of the relevant code of ethics as it applies to your project and area of study. As far as possible researchers are expected to adhere to such guidelines and any departures from them must be justified and argued for as an integral part of your project.

Also, there are ethics committees whose approval must be sought and obtained before embarking on certain kinds of research, particularly those involving sensitive topics or issues such as in health or medicine. But your own university or college might have its own ethics approval committee, which must be satisfied as to the integrity of your research and the practices and methods it entails before you would be allowed to get started. You must take care to be aware of such 'local' committees and the standards which their approval requires. If in doubt, consult your supervisor. While each area of study or professional body may have its own special requirements, their respective guidelines share many common elements and I shall summarise the main ones here. More particular advice is to be found at the relevant points in the chapters that follow, and more detailed discussions may be found in many methods texts (for example, Bell 2010; Bryman 2008; Denscombe 2002; Homan 1991; Smith et al. 2009).

Varieties of informed consent

The principle of *informed consent* is central to ethical guidelines in general. Both research staff and research subjects must be fully informed of the purposes and methods of the research and the potential uses to which it may be put. Social researchers should not exert pressure on people, or manipulate them into becoming involved with a project. Participants should be informed about what their participation entails and any 'risks' should be pointed out (ESRC 2005). It should be made clear that participants have a right to withdraw from the research at any time if they change their mind, and should be reassured that such withdrawal will have no negative consequences for them. Vulnerable people, such as the elderly, children under a certain age, those with learning difficulties, patients in hospital or people with mental illnesses, or addictions to alcohol or drugs, require great care and sensitivity over the issue of informed consent. Sometimes relevant guardians or caretakers may also need to be informed and written consent forms may be required.

There are some situations where it is not feasible to ask for consent, or even to ensure that people know they are being studied for research purposes, for example, public situations, or where 'covert' or 'unobtrusive' observations are being made, or with people you meet by chance – as in the case of 'directed', but 'casual' conversations (see Chapter 5). In such cases, asking for consent might have the effect of ruining the spontaneity and sincerity of the subject's responses. This is because their awareness of participating in a research project may lead to unnatural or artificial responses. Sometimes it can lead participants to attempt to please the researcher by 'anticipating' the sort of behaviour the researcher is looking for.

In other cases, obtaining full and wholehearted consent is unrealistic since there is a fine line between persuasion or inducement on the one hand, and milder forms of coercion on the other. In this respect, the extent to which people feel free to say no is crucial, especially where power relations are involved in influencing the decision. As Denscombe (2002: 188) observes, the difficulty of gaining consent that is 'completely voluntary' is acknowledged in some codes of ethics. Thus the notion of 'adequate consent' is often embraced as a more practically realistic ethical principle. It certainly measures up more squarely to the reality that there are degrees of both reluctance and enthusiasm in potential participants when making decisions about consent.

Research approaches based on flexible and 'emergent' (rather than fixed or rigidly pre-structured) designs raise the issue of how far initial consent remains valid, or in place, as the research proceeds and develops. Since the adaptive approach is based on structured but flexible research designs, this issue is moot. In particular, if the progress of the project is such that new data samples are required or existing samples need topping up (although this is not always the case), then it might be better to regard consent as potentially renewable, and subject to constant negotiations between the researcher and research subjects.

Protecting participants' interests

As a researcher you should at all times take great care to protect your research participants from physical and mental harm – and this is especially important in relation to vulnerable people. Participants' 'interests' include quite a number of issues. For instance, you should avoid asking potentially distressing questions in interviews (or questionnaires) and, of course, this requires at least a modicum of sensitivity as well as the ability to empathise with others. You shouldn't be intrusive or invade the privacy of participants. Also, you must respect participants' autonomy, including the right to withdraw their cooperation at any point. You must treat participants with consideration and respect, and manifestly demonstrate fairness in your dealings with them, such that you are not seen to be giving benefits or rewards to some rather than others.

At all times, you should take the utmost care not to puncture participants' self-esteem or expose them to ridicule or embarrassment. Also, apart from refraining from undue pressure in obtaining their consent to take part in your project, you should not mislead participants as to the purpose of the research or what you intend to do with the findings or the data you collect. That is, you should never use deliberate deception in your routine dealings with research participants.

Confidentiality and anonymity

Informed consent needs to be backed up by assurances of confidentiality and anonymity for participants. Information gathered by a researcher on specific places, people or organisations should not be disclosed to anyone else other than co-researchers on the same project. This ensures that the information cannot be traced back to the originating sources. Denscombe illustrates this point with the following example: 'It would be unethical to feedback views expressed during an interview with one person to her colleagues in subsequent interviews – unless, that is, some specific agreement had been reached on the point' (2002: 180).

A guarantee of anonymity is about protecting the identities of participants and reinforces the principle of confidentiality. To ensure anonymity, researchers typically use 'pseudonyms', that is, alternative or fictitious names to protect the real names and identities of people, places and organisations. Bell (2010) stresses that the promise of anonymity should really stand up, and thus great care should be taken with research data and information because 'if you invent a pseudonym or a code it still might be easy for readers in the know to identify the individual or institution concerned' (2010: 50). So promises of confidentiality and anonymity should not be made lightly and might even require the shredding of interview transcripts, questionnaires and records once the research is completed.

One aspect of confidentiality and anonymity that is rarely mentioned, but which is clearly of moment for the adaptive approach, concerns the project's broader objectives and level of analysis. Adaptive analysis emphasises the need to go beyond mere description and to engage in explanation. As subsequent chapters make clear, explanation is achieved through the use of concepts and rational arguments. In this sense, conceptualisation advances beyond description and is expressed in more general abstract terms which are independent of specific times, places and people. The centrality of conceptualisation, rather than description, for the adaptive approach helps in the effort of making data and information anonymous and confidential. This is because in the final analysis, the approach is not concerned with providing descriptions of specific (and therefore, identifiable) individuals or groups, but rather with revealing the underlying patterns of social behaviour and the general principles that explain them.

Your Research Log Begins Here!

What is a Research Log and how does it differ from a research diary?

Research diaries

Many textbooks on research methods discuss the use of 'diaries' in research and there are two forms that such diaries can take. The first is when a researcher asks particular individuals, selected from the data sample, to keep diaries of their experiences, usually according to instructions from the researcher, so that they may eventually be drawn upon as research evidence. The other type of research diary is used by the researcher him or herself as a means of keeping a record of various issues relevant to the research project in question. These are usually straightforward records of such things as: general references and specific literature searches, lists of contacts and addresses, dates and times of appointments for interviews, addresses of useful websites, and so on (Hart 2009). In short, this kind of diary is a permanent record (and thus, place of safekeeping) for a miscellany of bits and pieces of mainly 'practical' information relevant to the research.

The Research Log

By contrast, a Research Log is a way of recording a rather different, but quite specific set of issues related to the development of the research over time. The log consists of regular written entries or 'discussion pieces' which concentrate on particular issues. These might include mini-debates (with yourself – as researcher), memos about alternative approaches or courses of action, self-critiques, raising or posing questions about best practice, proposed solutions to problems, and so on. Each entry should correspond to a key element of the research process and concentrate on problems of strategy and implementation encountered along the way. Eventually these discussion pieces will cover the whole span of the project.

Your Research Log will be your constant companion throughout the whole journey of your research project and will help you make strategic decisions along the way. By enabling you to rehearse arguments and present your findings, it will also help in the preparation of the final research report. You should begin your log immediately by responding to the points in the checklist below about issues covered in this chapter with *short* notes that comment on, or attempt to answer, the questions and issues they raise. At this stage your comments will be tentative and preliminary and should remain brief. You should feel free at this point to express any uncertainties and anxieties because the notes are simply for your own private consumption. Nonetheless, the log will act as an essential means of clarifying thinking, and in helping you to develop ideas about the project.

As you progress with the research you will be able to revise and restructure your ideas, making lengthier and more accurate notes based on what you actually do, or did, at various points in time. Supplementary and additional questions and issues arise from each chapter, so, as you read through the book, your thinking should develop and become more sophisticated. Eventually, the log will become an invaluable resource which will be the basis on which you will be able to construct your final report.

Checklist for Research Log Notes

Write preliminary notes on the following:

- Reflect on possible topics – are they appropriate and why?

- What is your research problem?

- What is the link between research questions and research design?

- What is the most appropriate mix of strategies and methods?

- How will you select samples and sampling units?

- What concepts are relevant?

- How will you code and analyse data?

- What is your overall research argument?

- What are you attempting to explain?

- What are the major ethical considerations relevant to your project and how will you tackle them?

2

FINDING A TOPIC & A RESEARCH PROBLEM

PREVIEW

This chapter covers the following:

- Choosing suitable topics and identifying research problems
- Researching celebrity culture
- Researching body, health and lifestyle issues
- Researching gyms and fitness centres as social settings
- Researching popular culture and popular music
- The McDonaldization of society
- Settings, McDonaldization and problem-questions
- Researching intimacy, friendship and interpersonal relations
- Researching love-life, sex and romance: intimacy and couples

Faced with the necessity of doing a small-scale research project first-time researchers often find that the very first hurdle – choosing an appropriate topic and research problem – is, in itself, a daunting and somewhat dispiriting task. 'Where to begin?', 'what shall I do?', 'what's my problem?' are all questions that pose particular difficulties. This chapter is designed to help out with this sometimes perplexing task by discussing examples of possible research topics that fit easily with the adaptive approach. I must make it clear, however, that the examples discussed *are not meant* to represent the whole range of topics or areas. In this sense, the chapter is not intended to limit or constrain your eventual choices in any way. Obviously, if you have strongly held ideas that lie outside the scope of the examples mentioned here, then you will pursue them regardless of what I say – although it is essential that you first check with your supervisor that he or she thinks it is an appropriate and viable choice before you commit to anything.

Generally, the discussion is meant to both stimulate and structure your thoughts and ideas about potential projects and the research strategies you will need to carry them through. In particular, this chapter highlights the importance of identifying a *research problem* that will give your project shape, direction and a scientific basis. In the previous chapter, I described six key problem-questions and discussed the importance of the distinction between problem- and topic-questions. Thus, in the examples in the following discussion I focus on the main problem-questions they explore. I hope that this will familiarise you with the issue of research problems and their importance more generally. Even more importantly, I hope it will make it easier for you to understand and define your own research problems and the sorts of questions they raise.

Researching Celebrity Culture

Some of the most widespread influences in modern society are linked with various aspects of culture. Here I shall focus on 'celebrity culture' and 'popular culture' (which to some extent overlap). I shall also discuss 'body culture', which links up more broadly with health and lifestyle issues. It is hard not to have some experience of 'celebrity culture' in the modern world for it seems to dominate virtually all aspects of the mass media (see Rojek 2001, 2011; and Rowlands 2008, for broad-ranging discussions). Its influence is mostly derived from the 'entertainment' industries, such as films, video, popular music, fashion, sports, and so on, but includes artists, writers, even some socialites and politicians. It is expressed in human form through celebrities from different fields – 'pop stars', 'reality TV personalities', sports stars, fashion models, celebrity 'presenters' (of TV news and entertainment programmes), and entertainers such as comedians. The influence of celebrity culture is not simply confined to the stars themselves, but also includes their fashion choices, lifestyles, intimate partners, which are such a prominent feature of the 'gossip' sections of tabloid newspapers and glossy celebrity magazines.

If we begin to think about the topic of celebrity culture and how it influences society and social behaviour in terms of the *problem-questions* (sometimes referred to as PQs) outlined in Chapter 2, a number of distinct research possibilities suggest themselves. For instance, PQ 1 is concerned with how personal identity is formed in relation to social influences and thus suggests a research focus on whether (and how) people 'hang', or base their own self-identities on particular celebrities – using them as role models for their behaviour and self-images. Such an investigation would focus on the extent to which individuals (chosen, say, from a sample of your friends and family) convey images of themselves based on their favourite celebrity (or celebrities). Do they mimic their behaviour, using idioms or catch phrases? Do they adopt similar mannerisms, styles of fashion, make-up, tattoos or body piercings?

This general theme could be explored from an almost endless variety of viewpoints. For example, you might choose to focus on one particular age group. Alternatively, you might compare two (or more) age groups to investigate whether there are differences or similarities between them. Of course, you could choose to focus on how individuals are influenced by their social class background, neighbourhood, gender or ethnicity. For instance, do men and women respond in different ways to celebrity culture?

You might choose to base your study on observations and interviews, and supplement this with documentary sources such as books on or about celebrity, or even by analysing celebrity magazines. On the other hand, a concentration on documentary sources would reveal more about the way celebrity culture is transmitted by magazines, newspapers, and so on. In this sense your research interests may be guided by a combination of problem-questions. For instance, the question of individual or personal identity (PQ 1) might be combined with a focus on how TV or publishing companies and celebrity culture shape people's attitudes and behaviour more generally. To what extent are people 'free' to reject or resist such influences? Are fears about the general 'dumbing-down' of cultural life, educational standards and so on, or the erosion of 'high' or 'elite' culture, overstated?

Rojek (2001) suggests there are three main types of celebrity. First, there are those who possess 'ascribed' celebrity because they are born into a family that is already famous. Members of the royal family are examples of this, as are, to a lesser extent perhaps, the offspring of existing celebrities in the sense that being, say, the son or daughter of the Beckhams, or Tom Cruise and Katy Holmes, confers a sort of celebrity. Second, there is 'achieved' celebrity, those who, entirely through their own efforts, have made outstanding contributions in particular fields – such as eminent scientists, politicians, sports stars, pop stars, dancers, opera singers. Finally, there are those that Rojek calls 'celetoids', who become famous because they have been singled out by the mass media for special attention. This type includes reality TV personalities (such as Jade Goody or Jordan, 'Katy Price'). These individuals have no particular abilities or achievements to speak of, they are simply famous for being famous, that is, for being 'themselves' or media personalities.

The recent proliferation of the latter celetoid type of celebrity has generated rather controversial questions about their purported influence on young people and society in general. For example, it has been claimed that as a consequence of such influence, young people today have unrealistic expectations that all their efforts (no matter how minor or trivial) should be rewarded. Has the influence of such celebrities (or celetoids) led to an unhealthy obsession with and/or craving for fame and adulation? More generally, is the undue influence of celebrity culture responsible for diverting attention from high standards and hard work? Have they been replaced with an obsessive concern with superficial glamour, 'trivia' and mediocrity?

It will be recalled that problem-question 5, centres on the nature of power in social life and its influence on social behaviour. With regard to celebrity culture, this poses a series of questions, such as: Do celebrities 'possess' or 'have' power? If they do, over whom do they wield it? Do they have social influence? What is the difference between power and social influence? What is an 'elite' and how is it applicable to the study of celebrities? Do celebrities, as a group, constitute a cohesive 'elite', or do they form several overlapping elites? Are they a status grouping? Clearly, problem-questions that centre on these issues are concerned with tracing the connections between social status, influence, power and elites. Without doubt these are very important problem-questions that could become the driving focus of a social research project.

A crucial concept closely related to power is that of 'charisma' and this very much applies to celebrities. The sociologist Max Weber used the concept of charisma to describe a type of power based on the unique (extraordinary) psychological qualities of an individual (such as mesmeric powers of persuasion, oratory or inspirational leadership qualities – possessed by both Hitler and Churchill). Recently, charisma has been adopted more commonly in everyday usage. People frequently describe particular individuals as 'charismatic'. Clearly many celebrities possess charismatic qualities. A relevant research question is 'to what extent do charismatic qualities contribute to celebrity status and power? Is charismatic power essential to making the transition from celebrity status to political power and influence? The cases of Ronald Reagan, the former US President, and Arnold Schwarzenegger (who became Governor of California) are good examples of this kind of transition, since they first came to public attention as Hollywood film stars.

Problem-question 6 concerns the manner in which social life and social organisation change over time. In relation to this you might be interested in whether or not celebrity culture in the present era has changed as compared with previous generations (1930s, 1950s or 1960s). Has it become more or less influential? What are the reasons for this? Cashmore (2006) has drawn attention to the growth of media outlets to understand the role of celebrity today. In contrast, Rojek (2001, 2011) emphasises the emotional component of modern celebrity culture – the emotional attachment people have to celebrities or the misplaced sense in which they feel they are connected to them or 'know' them. He also points to some of the ways in which celebrities and celebrity culture has filled the void left by the decline of religion in the modern world. People turn to celebrities to inform their own beliefs and help them to make lifestyle decisions and choices.

Researching Body, Health and Lifestyle Issues

The question of celebrity influence overlaps with other questions about the influence of popular culture on lifestyle choices (smoking, use of drugs and alcohol, clubbing) their health effects, and the body-image issues associated with them. These, in turn, are linked with other social phenomena, such as the growth in rates of anorexia, particularly among (younger) females (although men are also affected), or the increased use of gyms by certain age groups of both men and women. Such topics or areas are very fruitful sites for small-scale research projects and can be approached from a wide variety of viewpoints.

Clearly, for instance, there are links between celebrity culture – in this case prominent fashion models – and social anxieties about body images generally. In particular, there are concerns about young girls and women becoming obsessed with being very slim or 'thin' (sometimes referred to in the media as the 'size zero' problem). Connected with this is the so-called 'slimmer's disease' or anorexia nervosa – although doing a viable study specifically on anorexia might be difficult because of ethical issues about intrusion, privacy and consent.

However, a suitable small-scale project might focus on the broader issue of 'eating control' among samples of women (and men) of varying ages (perhaps comparing them with each other). Such a study might focus on personal identity, exploring how particular 'life careers' ('psychobiographies') influence an individual's control over their food intake or dietary choices (PQ 1). Alternatively, the emphasis might be on how interaction with peers affects attitudes towards food and control over eating (PQ 2). Further, the primary research emphasis might be on *informal* settings, such as coffee bars, night clubs, fan clubs or internet chat-rooms, as compared with more *formal* settings, such as schools, university, work, religious institutions, and so on (PQ 3).

Equally, a study could focus on the role of family or religious values and expectations and/or media portrayals in shaping attitudes towards food and eating behaviour (PQ 4). The question of power (PQ 5) could involve exploring feelings of powerlessness (or empowerment), and how control of eating and level of food intake is linked to retaining a sense of personal control (over one's own life and over others – and thus lessening other people's control and influence over you).

Finally, the way in which the passage of time influences social life may become the primary focus of investigation (PQ 6). Here, documentary sources might show how attitudes towards eating and body-images have changed over time. This could be done by comparing different periods *within* the twentieth century, or making comparisons over larger sweeps of historical time. The time element could also be investigated by examining changing social attitudes over individual lifetimes, or of the changing circumstances of particular social classes, gender, or ethnic groupings.

Exactly the same considerations for projects on food, personal control and eating disorders could be relevant to the topics of smoking, alcohol consumption and drug use. Thus the lifestyle, health and risk-taking implications of these types of activity might throw light on any of problem-questions 1–6. Of course, these activities (particularly drug-taking and alcohol use) require ethical dilemmas to be resolved before undertaking any such project. A researcher must be aware of the potential personal dangers that she or he may face, particularly if forms of observation or interviewing are being considered as possible methods of data collection. Even if ideas about potential topics seem exciting and interesting, they should be avoided if there is any hint of personal danger.

Researching Gyms and Fitness Centres as Social Settings

Activities such as the use of gyms and fitness centres link up with lifestyle and body-image topics, and could be treated in a similar fashion (Smith 2001, 2008; Smith and Stanway 2008). An interest in body-image and body sculpting is clearly related to the question of personal identity, but also to dieting, drug taking (for example, steroids), and so on. Interestingly, studies of gyms or fitness centres draw attention to a particular kind of social setting, in which people's behaviour is socially organised and regulated. The same is true of cafés, restaurants, bars and airports.

Thus for the staff, a gym or leisure centre is a work organisation in which they are paid employees, contracted to work by the management and owners. They relate to each other as work colleagues, although some have more authority to give orders. As staff members, however, they regard gym users as 'customers' (or clients) who require instruction in how to use the facilities (the exercise machines and dressing rooms). On the other hand, the customers (clients or users) regard 'health clubs', gyms and fitness centres as leisure settings (even though they often involve strenuous exercise or 'work-outs'). They regard the staff as fitness 'advisors' who are there to help them achieve their personal goals of fitness, health or body-image. In this regard, the staff must be adept at people skills and 'emotional labour' (Hochschild 1983), by being sensitive to users' emotional and psychological needs.

In this sense the setting of the gym represents an interface between a work environment (from the staff point of view) and a leisure/exercise environment for users. Understanding how these two facets coexist alongside each other could be tackled in a variety of ways in the context of a small-scale research project. For example, as far as staff are concerned, relevant questions are: To what extent do they develop their own 'working culture'? How do they deal with their workloads at times of pressure? How do they deal with management demands? How do they regard users? From the user viewpoint, relevant questions are: How do they get value for money for the service they are offered? To what extent do they regard staff as 'helpers' or 'hinderers' to their exercise or body-image goals? How friendly do they perceive the staff to be?

But a project could also focus on interactions between staff and customers (PQ 3), either with a view to identifying possible points of tension or conflict, or to focus on the ways in which they achieve a smooth working relationship. The concept of 'emotional labour' might be of use here for investigating more specific topic-questions. For example, how successful are staff members in their dealings with customers? Do they display empathy and emotional intelligence (Goleman 1996)? Are customers satisfied with the service they receive? Do they feel that service could be improved? Do staff and customers employ different types of emotional labour?

Researching Popular Culture and Popular Music

The area of popular music is fertile ground for potential small-scale research projects. For instance, the structure and dynamics of (rock) bands could be studied from three main viewpoints. First, it could be studied in a fairly distanced or objective sense from the viewpoint of the interested observer. Second, it could be approached from the slightly more 'involved' standpoint of a committed 'fan'. Third, the study could be conducted from a 'members' or participants point of view (the sociologist Howard Becker, studied jazz musicians as a member of a jazz ensemble; Becker 1963). As long as you are able to guard against subjectively biased judgements, group membership can provide valuable insights for a researcher. However, seeing beyond personal involvement and treating the subject matter of the research with a degree of detachment is essential.

The sorts of problems and questions you can investigate also vary considerably. You might be interested in the lyrics of pop songs for what they can reveal about various aspects of society. What are the predominant themes of the lyrics and how are they expressed? You might study the ways in which group members relate to one another and how this affects their creativity (Sawyer 2003a, 2003b). You may wish to focus on how fans relate to each other (in concerts or fan club meetings). You may prefer to concentrate on the relationship between fans and the artistes that are the 'targets' of their admiration. For instance, what kinds of relationships do fans think they have with particular artistes, and why?

Ian Inglis has produced some interesting studies in the area of popular music, especially in relation to The Beatles. For example, in one study he examined the lyrical content of love songs written and performed by The Beatles (Inglis 1997), and compared them against a typology of love styles originally proposed by Lee. Lee (1977) identifies six love styles: (serious) romantic love; playful love (as a game involving flirting and flattery); caring love (as in friendship); love as a practical arrangement; obsessive or possessive love; and finally, unselfish love (as compassion for others). By comparing the lyrics with these 'styles of loving', Inglis was able to classify different Beatles songs according to the love styles to which they corresponded. On this basis he was able to make some general observations about changes in lyrical content over time.

One of Inglis's findings was that the lyrical emphases of Beatles' songs changed over several years. For instance, during the years 1962–5 there were a high proportion of love songs (97 per cent) as compared with the years 1966–70, in which songs about love declined to 32 per cent of their total output. Also, during the earlier period the two predominant styles of love that characterised the songs were serious romantic love and love as a game. This was in stark contrast to the period 1966–70, in which there was a significant decrease in songs with these themes and an increase in the themes of caring and unselfish styles of love. Having demonstrated this, Inglis offers some reasons why this rather abrupt and marked transformation occurred in the group's lyrical renderings of love. He drew on published accounts of The Beatles' personal experiences and changes in perception (of themselves and others) in order to account for these changes.

In another study centred on The Beatles, Inglis (1998) takes a quite different research tack. He focuses on the group's early history and specifically on the fact that they replaced their original drummer, Pete Best, with Ringo Starr (Richard Starkey) in the weeks immediately before they achieved their first big successes. By piecing together evidence from published accounts of this period in the group's development and analysing it in terms of the dynamics of informal groups, Inglis offers some possible explanations as to why Best was replaced as The Beatles' drummer.

He focuses on the question of group 'solidarity' and why the cohesiveness of group members may vary. Inglis considers several different possibilities, the first of which concerns the issue of deviancy. Was Best expelled from the group because the other three Beatles didn't think he 'fitted in' with them in terms of image, attitude and behaviour (style of dress, hairstyle, drug taking, and so on)? Second, Inglis considers the question of status conflict. Was Best deliberately ousted because the other Beatles resented his greater attractiveness? Third, he examines whether Best's perceived incompetence as a drummer was the reason behind his rejection. Finally, he examines the possibility that the others considered Best a liability because of some, as yet undisclosed, reason.

Inglis's analysis relates to problem-question 2, which centres on the dynamics of face-to-face interaction or 'situated activity'. The factors affecting group cohesiveness (that Inglis explores in relation to The Beatles) are among a range of factors included in problem-question 2. Aspects of problem-questions 5 and 6 are also covered in Inglis's study. For instance, issues of power and status (PQ 5) are directly relevant to the sacking of Pete Best. Was Best ousted because he was too popular/attractive or because he was considered a liability by the others? Either way, this would alter the balance of power in the group. Was the sacking caused by conflict between group members about the relative status ranking of individuals? Finally, although the passage of time (PQ 6) was not given special attention in this study, it is of great importance in understanding what social interaction means to those involved.

The McDonaldization of Society

The McDonaldization of Society is the title of a book by George Ritzer (2011), in which he examines the ways in which many of the principles underlying the organisation of the McDonald's fast-food industry have influenced numerous other modern social settings. In this respect, Ritzer's book offers a fund of potential research topics that are eminently suitable for the approach I am outlining here. Ritzer first makes the point that the basic principles of organisation underlying McDonald's were first suggested in the work of the German sociologist Max Weber in his account of the process of rationalisation (Weber 1964). Weber noted the proliferation and growing importance of rational systems (like bureaucracies) in the modern world, and Ritzer points out that this is directly reflected in the organisation of McDonald's fast-food restaurants.

Based on its spectacular success, the McDonald's business enterprise has also spread its influence far and wide in modern societies. This, Ritzer calls the process of McDonaldization, in which the McDonald's model has been used and applied (to varying degrees) to virtually every other sector of society. Thus settings and organisations far beyond the restaurant business, such as education, work, travel, leisure-time activities, dieting, politics, and the family, have been deeply influenced by the process of McDonaldization. One of the larger questions Ritzer wants to address is whether this process is inexorable and if its effects will insinuate themselves into every aspect of society and our lives. Also, he wants to challenge the assumption that rational systems are as rational as is frequently claimed by their advocates. In this respect, Ritzer is keen to map out some of the irrational features of McDonaldization.

The four basic dimensions underlying the McDonald's model (and which are integral to Weber's model of bureaucracy) are efficiency, calculability, predictability and control. First, McDonald's aims to provide the most *efficient* means of producing and serving food, by using an assembly-line production of burgers, standardising the 'filling' and maximising the throughput of customers. Second, McDonald's offers food and service that can easily be *quantified and calculated*. Thus it claims to offer better value for money (creating the impression of getting more food, more cheaply) as well as seemingly saving customers the time and effort of preparing their own meals. Third, McDonald's offers *predictability* in so far as the customer knows that the food will be the same (the same standardised shapes and sizes) at any time and any place – in short, there will be no surprises. The final dimension, of *control*, is exemplified by the rigorously trained and supervised workers, the use of non-human technology to replace human beings (wherever this is possible). Customers are controlled through lines (queues), limited menus and options, and uncomfortable seats which 'encourage' diners to eat quickly and leave.

Part of Ritzer's overall argument is that these 'rational' principles can be observed to a greater or lesser degree in other types of setting or organisation, and this adds up to the general McDonaldization of modern society. For instance, Ritzer notes that efficiency and calculability are very prominent features of gyms or modern health clubs. In these settings exercise machines are specialised to efficiently increase fitness in specific areas of the body. Thus running machines increase cardiovascular fitness, while weightlifting machines increase strength and muscularity. Another efficiency associated with these machines is that you can do other things while exercising, such as read, listen to music, watch television, and so on. Also, the exercise machines offer high levels of calculability, keeping you informed of how many miles you have run, the level of difficulty achieved and the number of calories burned (Ritzer 2011: 48).

The efficiency of the 'people moving' mechanisms of McDonalds (maximising the flow of people to, through, and out of the restaurant) can also be observed in modern amusement parks such as Disneyland. For instance, once in the park, 'visitors find themselves on what is, in effect, a vast ... conveyor belt which leads them from one ride or attraction to another' and then, via 'cars, boats, submarines, planes, rocket ships or moving walkways' they are 'moved through and out of the attractions as quickly as possible' (Ritzer 2011: 51). In the educational system, particularly in American universities, the pressure towards efficiency can be seen in the tendency to adopt machine-graded, multiple-choice examinations. One-to-one examination by professors was deemed too labour intensive and inefficient, as was the subsequent method of essay examination, which was also too time-consuming. Thus now there is a preference for multiple-choice, computer-graded examinations that maximise efficiency.

Ritzer goes on to point out that the whole educational system (and this applies not just to the USA), including primary and secondary schools, colleges as well as universities, are highly bureaucratised, since bureaucracy (as Max Weber observed) is the model for rationalisation and efficiency.

Although Ritzer (2011: 56) argues that bureaucracy has been replaced by McDonald's as the model of rationalisation, 'it remains a structure designed to efficiently handle large amounts of work'. In this respect, while the amusement park 'can be seen as a people-moving machine, bureaucracy can be viewed as mechanism for the efficient moving of paper and, more recently, computer-generated information'. As Ritzer says, 'this is the case in educational bureaucracies, but it is also true of bureaucracies in a wide range of institutions' (2011: 56).

Settings, McDonaldization and Problem-Questions

Many of the issues Ritzer raises in relation to the general process of the McDonaldization of society resonate with much of what I have said about appropriate small-scale research topics. In particular, the *organisational* characteristics of different kinds of social settings are of especial relevance. All the examples relevant to the issues raised by McDonaldization, such as fast-food restaurants, shopping malls, amusement parks, schools, colleges, universities, medical centres, gyms, health clubs, hotels, travel-package holidays, regular restaurants, pubs and clubs, sports and so on, are all examples of what I have referred to as 'social settings'. As such, any proposed small-scale research project based on any of these topics areas would almost automatically demand a focus on problem-question 3. That is, a concern with the manner in which human social behaviour is influenced by the particular kind of social setting in which it takes place and whether and how these influences compare with those of other settings.

As I have already suggested, social settings are uniquely placed in terms of problem-questions because they are at the intersection of social and psychological influences. While the organisational characteristics of social settings influence behaviour and interaction, they also act as a conduit for wider social influences, such as class, gender and ethnicity, economic factors, values, expectations, and so on. At the same time, they filter and process the psychological inputs of individuals. In this sense settings are 'gathering points' for a diversity of social and psychological influences, which makes them fruitful sites for many kinds of research projects. Potentially at least, a research project could focus on *any* of the key problem-questions, although it is best to focus primarily only on one, or a few, problem-questions at any one time (three, at most). This is probably the best way of achieving (and retaining) clarity and direction in your project.

Bearing these cautionary points in mind, Ritzer's study suggests some productive small-scale projects. For example, how do particular social settings 'encourage' certain kinds of behaviour or types of social interaction? Ritzer points out that in many fast-food outlets, interaction between customer and counterperson is brief and routinised. Staff offer fake friendliness and false camaraderie in order to lure customers and keep them coming back (2011: 85) and this raises the issue of 'emotional labour' (Hochschild 1983). This concept refers to 'emotional displays' that employees are required to perform as part of their jobs. In the case of McDonald's and similar enterprises, Ritzer argues that such displays create the 'illusion of intimacy', but in reality the effect is to corrupt and degrade intimacy (2011: 113).

This is part and parcel of what Ritzer considers to be a dehumanising aspect of fast-food restaurants. Minimising contact between customers and employees by ensuring the fleeting nature of their relationships means that even regular customers are not able to develop long-term personal relationships with counter staff. Such impersonal and anonymous relationships are heightened by the fact that employees are trained to interact with customers 'in a staged and limited manner' (2011: 133). In turn, customers may feel that they are dealing with automatons rather than fellow human beings. Thus, argues Ritzer, fast-food restaurants greatly restrict the possibility of genuine fraternisation between customers and employees and that this dehumanisation is part of the overall irrationality of a 'supposedly' rational organisation.

A small-scale research project might 'test out' some of Ritzer's observations. The findings of such research might endorse Ritzer's overall conclusions and, in itself, this would be a valuable contribution – especially if it was done carefully and thoroughly. Another approach might attempt to add to, or supplement, Ritzer's findings. For example, your study might suggest ways in which employees or customers resist or overcome the constraint on developing genuine relationships. Or you may wish to compare the customer–employee relationships described by Ritzer in his study of McDonald's, with those in other kinds of settings. Although other settings may be similar to fast-food restaurants, others still will be markedly different. By carefully choosing your comparison setting you may produce some unusual and interesting results. For example, although a school or college might seem, at first sight, quite dissimilar to fast-food outlets, such a comparison might prove instructive.

Ritzer himself stresses that universities are bureaucratic in nature (perhaps increasingly so), and in this respect they display some rather irrational features. For instance, because of the huge factory-like atmosphere of some universities, many students and faculty members experience it as dehumanising, feeling as though they are automatons 'to be processed by the bureaucracy and the computer, or even cattle being run through a meat processing plant' (2011: 142). The dehumanising experience is heightened by masses of students, large impersonal dorms (halls of residence), and huge lecture classes which make it difficult to get to know other students. Large lectures and tight timetables make it difficult to get to know professors on a personal basis. Grades are generated by computers from multiple-choice exams and they are often posted in an impersonal fashion by social security number rather than the student's name. In sum, says Ritzer, 'students may feel like little more than objects into which knowledge is poured as they move along an information-providing and degree-granting educational assembly line' (2011: 142).

Clearly, Ritzer's observations could be used as a rich source from which potential research projects could emerge. To what extent do schools or universities produce such dehumanising experiences in students? What are the key causal factors? Are there other, more pleasurable aspects of student life that alleviate the dehumanising tendencies? Do students recognise the causes of such experiences? How do individuals psychologically deal with the impersonality of life at university? The difference between the formal and informal aspects of the organisation of schools or colleges may be important in explaining satisfaction or dissatisfaction among students. For example, the formal aspects of school or college organisation may be the main source of impersonal rules and procedures, while various informal (unofficial) practices – engaged in by both students and faculty – might mitigate any more unpleasant effects.

Researching Intimacy, Friendship and Interpersonal Relationships

The commonplace nature of friendships, family or romantic partnerships makes them aptly suited to form the basis of small-scale research projects. This is seen most clearly if we compare study in this area with one in an organisational setting such as school, a club or a university. Various 'gatekeepers' control access to such settings and must be happy with the objectives of the research and the personal integrity of the researcher before giving their consent to the study. At one extreme, gatekeepers may be 'deliberately obstructive' or overprotective. However, the simple fact that there is an extra layer of permission to be sought makes the whole thing rather trickier, especially if the gatekeeper has to obtain the permission of yet others before making a decision.

The study of intimacy and interpersonal relationships isn't usually affected by such problems. Personal knowledge of potential research subjects can make obtaining a suitable sample of individuals to study much easier. Of course this doesn't mean that you won't encounter problems. Individuals might not wish to be research subjects for many reasons (including the fact that you personally know them) and you must respect their right to refuse to participate. If they do wish to participate, then there are ethical issues to consider. You must treat any information they divulge with great care and avoid unnecessary invasion of their privacy. Also, you should take care not to disclose their identity.

As a possible focus for a research project, friendship is particularly interesting since it plays an important part in everyday life (Allan 1989; Brain 1976; Duck 1992). Many of the things that underpin friendship are taken for granted and remain unexamined – which raises a number of intriguing questions. How, and in what sense, do friendships differ from family relationships? In what ways are friendships different from romantic or sexual partnerships? Are there different kinds of friends? Why do some friendships last for long periods of time while others fall by the wayside?

A study of friendship (Spencer and Pahl 2006), based mainly on interviews, led the authors to distinguish between different types of friendship. In 'simple friendship' the friends play well-defined and rather limited roles, and can be usefully distinguished from 'complex friendships', which are multifaceted and based on different clusters of qualities and roles (2006: 65). There are four types of simple friendship. '*Associates* share a common activity' (such as a club or a sport), *useful contacts* exchange information and advice, *neighbourly or favour friends* help each other out, and *fun friends* socialize together' (2006: 61). Spencer and Pahl point out that the key to simple friendship is that it is limited to one main form of interaction.

There are also four types of complex friendship. *Helpmates* are solid dependable friends who socialise together and help each other out, but do not act as confidants or offer emotional support. *Comforters or rocks* do much the same as helpmates but also give each other emotional support. In fact, it is the friend's sympathetic qualities that are particularly valued. *Confidants* are involved in the disclosure of personal information, although these relationships vary in their degree of intimacy – that is, the degree to which issues or secrets are shared. In this regard, people sometimes distinguish between friends who are trustworthy and those who are indiscreet (2006: 69). The final type of complex friendships are what the authors call *soulmates*. They are friends who confide, provide emotional support, help each other out and enjoy each other's company. They feel they are 'on the same wavelength' and that they know each other inside out; they are emotionally bonded and strongly committed to each other.

Typologies, like this of friendship, are very useful ways in which research can be given direction and organisation (see Layder 1993, 1997) by stimulating and identifying research problems. For instance, a small-scale project might test out the usefulness of the types identified by Spencer and Pahl. Do they throw light on newly collected data or data gathered for some other purpose (say, interviews with romantic partners)? New research might lead to a revision or modification of the assumed characteristics of a particular type identified by Spencer and Pahl. In any case, a typology can be used as a resource for developing research plans and designs.

One aspect of friendship that Spencer and Pahl's study does not address is how personal (self)-identity is constructed and develops within friendship. Of course, Spencer and Pahl recognise that psychological factors are important in friendship, especially in relation to differences in individual's emotional vulnerability, feelings, ability to trust and so on. However, PQ 1 – how personal identity is forged from the interplay of psychological and social factors – is not a central part of their analysis. In this regard the concept of 'psychobiography' usefully captures such influences as they unfold over time and space (see next section).

Also, friendship is a good vantage point from which to consider problem-question 2, the influence of social interaction in shaping the meanings that people give to their (situated) behaviour. A research project might investigate the way in which individuals develop and maintain their friendships through different types of interaction. This raises the issue of whether there are differences between real face-to-face friendships and those that are conducted through internet chat-rooms, *Facebook*, and so on. It also taps into the debate about whether there is a link between an increase in feelings of loneliness and the proliferation of internet 'friendships' (*The Times* 2009).

Another crucial component of friendship concerns problem-question 5, the influence of power and control on social behaviour (Layder 2009). Friendships are not only *webs of interconnections* between individuals, they are personal relationships, and are experienced differently by the individuals concerned. This brings us to the fascinating role of power and control in friendship. In order to understand this it is necessary to focus on interactive interchanges between friends and to treat personal relationships as constantly evolving and changing over time (PQ 6).

Researching Love-Life, Sex and Romance: Intimacy and Couples

The same considerations that apply to studying the experience of friendship also apply to other kinds of intimate relationships, such as those of love, sex and romance. For instance, how 'couples' experience their personal relationships is essential to understanding the nature of intimacy in the modern world (Layder 2009). This involves such things as the impact of the relationship on personal identities, including the effects of the partner's 'games' and 'habits' on their emotional satisfaction. Equally important are the dynamics of power and control in personal relationships. Evidence of this is present in examples of interview-based research on couples, such as Reibstein (1997), Miller (1995) and Marshall (2006), which lend support to the idea that modern intimacy is complex and variable.

Reibstein (1997), for instance, stresses that successful, happy relationships are those in which the partners place a concern for protecting each other at the centre of their lives. She argues that this is beneficial because it allows partners to be psychologically dependent on each other. Such relationships don't automatically 'work', nor are the partners guaranteed satisfaction. They have to continually deal with the problems that arise from 'day to day rubbing along together'. Delicate negotiations are required so that their respective needs for protection can be met.

Marshall (2006) concentrates on the question of how partners sustain intimacy after the initial 'honeymoon' passion has waned. He suggests that after this initial passion there is typically a transition to what he calls 'loving attachment', in which couples must continuously accommodate their differences and weaknesses and grapple with the complexities and practical demands of life (such as work and having children). If a couple is unable to develop 'loving attachment', the relationship may be transformed into what Marshall calls 'affectionate regard'. With this kind of love we care for someone but don't feel as though our destiny is entwined with theirs in the same way as loving attachment. According to Marshall, this corresponds to the 'I love you but I'm not in love with you' syndrome. In such relationships there is a loss of communication and a tendency to drift apart emotionally and physically, often resulting in 'polite sex' rather than intimate love-making.

On the basis of his own research, Miller (1995) argues that modern intimacy is characterised by 'emotional terrorism', or the struggle for power in relationships, and that this has severely compromised the myth of romantic love and the idea of the binding force of love in intimacy. Without going into detail about Miller's argument and the evidence on which it is based (see Layder 2009 for a detailed discussion), it underlines the importance of the theme of power and control in the understanding of intimacy. Clearly also, the work of Reibstein, Marshall and Miller provide a fund of possible research problems and questions. For instance, Reibstein's work prompts the questions 'to what extent does successful intimacy rely on the psychological dependence of the partners?' Marshall's work raises the question of the usefulness of the notions of 'affectionate regard' as compared with 'loving attachment' in characterising different kinds of intimacy. Miller's rather provocative notion of 'intimate terrorism' raises the question of whether it accurately describes modern relationships in general.

Based on such evidence, I developed a typology of intimate relationships. Among other things, it is intended to throw light on the different phases that personal relationships may undergo over time. It also suggests an explanation of why some relationships remain intense for long periods of time, while others tend to deteriorate – sometimes, perhaps, never to be revived. When a close relationship is on the wane, it progresses through different phases as the intimacy itself becomes less intense. Thus a loving relationship might start out as 'dynamic intimacy', in which partners have a high level of trust, emotional investment and commitment to one another, and communicate openly and honestly. However, if their intimacy loses quality, it may become 'episodic' or 'semi-detached', whereby trust, commitment and disclosure become narrowed and distorted in various ways. When partners remain together even though their intimacy has seriously eroded, they may engage in role-play to preserve a public image of themselves as remaining 'close'. This 'pretence intimacy' is the end of the road for many relationships.

The above suggests interesting starting points for thinking about potential small-scale research projects that are practical and manageable, but also points to important research problems and the research questions they raise. The main problem-focus would appear to be on self-identity and personal relationships in everyday life. However, friendships or sexual/romantic partnerships also reflect the influence of larger structures, values and cultural ideas. For research on intimacy, it is important to take account of the reciprocal influence of macro and micro features of social life.

The study of power raises particularly interesting research questions. Power appears in different forms, shapes and sizes according to whether we are dealing with individuals, interactions, settings, or wider social contexts. The various forms of power can be measured in different ways as reflected in observations, interviews and documents. Different types of power are embedded in, and interweave with, macro and micro levels of social life.

For example, in friendship or romantic/sexual relationships, personal power is crucial. Partners may have badly mismatched personalities or clash about what they want or need from a relationship (security versus excitement, for instance). Such incompatibilities may create psychological barriers that may prove difficult to overcome. In this sense individual or personal power will decisively influence the long-term success or failure of an intimate relationship. But it is also clear that in personal relationships individual (subjective) power blends almost imperceptibly into interactional power and control. The way in which the power and control of the partners affects their daily life feeds into their longer-term emotional, psychological and sexual satisfaction.

Personal and interactional power are also constrained and shaped by their immediate settings (such as work, school, university, leisure) as well as wider factors, including gender, social class, ethnicity, neighbourhood, family upbringing, social values, media, and so forth. In this sense, we conduct our personal relationships, and judge them, through the lens provided by these wider social influences.

In short, intimacy (and personal relationships of any kind) offer plentiful opportunities and rich possibilities for first-time, small-scale researchers. For instance, there are interesting research questions concerning the role of gender in personal relationships. To what extent does a person's gender influence their intimate behaviour (Way 2011)? Do men and women use language differently in everyday conversations? Cameron (2007) discusses many of these and associated issues, and challenges some of the views of Deborah Tannen (1992, 2002), John Gray (1992) and Baron-Cohen (2004). In particular, she questions whether the available evidence supports the idea that there are essential differences in men and women's use of language and communication. She suggests that much behaviour is influenced by the roles, relationships, expectations and obligations that both men and women are required to play in particular contexts. The roles that we are required to play '*as* men or women vary from one situation to another, and our linguistic behaviour reflects that variation'. In many cases the important differences in linguistic behaviour are differences between women and women or between men and men, not between men and women (Cameron 2007: 51).

Final Comments

In the foregoing discussion I have attempted to give a flavour of some of the possibilities of small-scale research projects. As I said at the beginning, my intention is not to limit your choices or substitute for your own imagination. Rather, the examples I've chosen are meant to stimulate your own thoughts on possible topics and ways of approaching them! I've also tried to underline the importance of distinguishing between research *problems* and *topics*. One of the most common and glaring omissions in social research, particularly among first-time researchers, is a proper understanding of research problems and an appreciation of the distinction between 'problem-questions' and 'topic-questions'. Certainly, if you can demonstrate that you are aware of this crucial distinction and take it into account in your own project, it may transform what might have otherwise have been a fairly 'ordinary' project, into an excellent one.

3

DEVELOPING QUESTIONS FROM RESEARCH PROBLEMS

PREVIEW

This chapter covers the following:

- What is problem-driven research?

- The difference between problem-questions and topic-questions

- Research questions and research design

- Key problem questions

- Developing and refining research questions

- Defining the range of topic-questions

- Shaping specific topic-questions

- Limiting the number of topic-questions

- Deciding on core research questions

- Tightening up research questions

The adaptive approach taps into the unfolding nature of the research process by flexibly responding to unanticipated data, evidence, concepts and ideas. However, in many other respects it is quite unlike the model of 'unfolding' research described by Punch (2008: 22–7). One fundamental difference is that it stresses the need to develop and hone research questions right from the word go – before data collection – in order to inject shape and direction into a project. But another difference is that it centralises the idea of research as problem–driven. Many methods texts stress the importance of research questions (Blaikie 2009; Creswell 2009; Punch 2008) for providing early structure to a project. However, there is no mention of the role of (explanatory) problems in framing the initial design of a project, providing its ongoing practical impetus, and influencing how it unfolds in the longer term.

These two characteristics – structured questions in advance of data collection and its problem-driven nature – have a close and very special relationship. Thus the central problem-focus of a research project importantly shapes and influences the research questions that underpin the overall research design. This chapter examines exactly what is involved here, and how it is achieved in the context of particular projects. But other, more basic issues are covered, such as: what is a research problem? How does a problem differ from a topic? What is problem-driven research? What is the role of research questions? How does a problem-focus influence the development and refinement of research questions?

Problem-Driven Research

From the adaptive perspective it is important to make a distinction between '*research problems*' and '*research topics*'. This is because in the methods literature, 'problems' and 'topics' are frequently regarded as synonymous, and thus the two words are used interchangeably. For example, Blaikie (2009: 46) suggests that 'research topics can also be stated in the form of a research problem to be investigated'. Many other authors simply omit to talk about research problems altogether. However, in the present context it is of the utmost importance to think of 'problems' as quite different from 'topics' since the distinction has a general bearing on the unfolding of research projects. Furthermore, the distinction has a particular role to play in the development of research questions. First, let us clear up the issue of what a research problem is.

Social problems

A 'research problem' must not be confused with what is commonly referred to as a 'social problem'. A 'social problem' indicates a state of affairs that is deemed to be unsatisfactory – say, an increase in knife or gun crime, or in divorce rates – which is thought, by government or policymakers to be in need of rectifying by some legal or policy intervention.

Research problems

A 'research problem', by contrast, is more analytic and centres on how different dimensions of society (or constituent features of social life) combine and 'work' together. These sorts of problems can be said to be *explanatory problems* because some aspect of the operation and functioning of society is in need of explanation. (They are also sometimes referred to as 'analytic' or 'theoretical' problems.)

Research topics

A research 'topic' is much more specific and empirical. It focuses on discrete areas of social activity in society. Topics centre on specific types of activities, such as work, leisure/entertainment, family, intimacy and personal relationships, crime, bureaucracy, and so on. They focus on the nature of the social relationships between those people operating within the sphere of activity in question.

Research problems and research topics each provide a focus on different aspects within the same research project. As such, they also raise different kinds of research questions about what is going on in the specific sphere of activity that is the subject of the research.

What is the difference between problem-questions and topic-questions?

The following preliminary definitions indicate the differences between these types of question.

Topic-questions are specific and descriptive.

Problem-questions are general and explanatory.

Let me illustrate these by discussing a specific example of research on universities. What is said here is not limited to the example of universities. Exactly the same could be said of many other examples – schools, hospitals, health clubs, fast-food restaurants, cafés, night clubs, gangs, and so on.

With universities, topic-questions would target the issue of the differences between individual universities. Since there are many universities, all of which their own specific characteristics, a factual description of any particular university will enable us to distinguish it from others, say in terms of its physical size and campus layout, the number of students it has, how popular it is, its academic status as compared with others, and so on. Thus topic-questions would focus on the particular descriptive details that emphasise differences between universities.

On the other hand, problem-questions would ask 'why are universities structurally similar to each other?' Thus an important question for social analysis is 'what is it about a particular organisation that enables us to identify it as a university in the first place? What general characteristics make a university distinguishable from, say, a fast-food restaurant or a hospital? To answer this we have to move away from individual differences and ask 'what characteristics do all universities possess? Among other things, we could point to: their educational role in society; the existence of groups of students and teachers (lecturers and professors) and the transmission of knowledge between them; age-graded learning; the capacity to award examination certificates, and so on. Such characteristics serve to categorise particular organisations as universities.

Since problem-questions are concerned with the general characteristics shared by all universities, it is not necessary to focus on individual differences.

In summary

Topic-questions focus on the variations in social organisation produced by people and their activities, at specific times and places. Topic-questions, therefore, focus on 'what', 'how' and 'when' questions and, as a consequence, they are more concrete and empirical in nature. Thus they are:

Particular, Concrete and Empirical,

Vary in terms of Time, Place, People,

Descriptive.

By contrast, *problem-questions* focus on patterns of social organisation and activity that do not vary from time to time, place to place, or people to people. As a consequence, they are more abstract and conceptual in nature. Thus they are:

General, Abstract and Conceptual,

Independent of Time, Place and People,

Explanatory.

Research Questions: Problems, Topics and Research Design

More detailed examples of the differences between problem- and topic-questions will appear as the discussion proceeds. Before this, however, let me briefly underline what is involved in problem-driven research by spelling out the links between problems, topics, research questions and research design.

The important point is to develop some core research questions which will serve to define the nature, scope and objectives of the research, and thus give it clarity and momentum right from the start. However, I have emphasised that research questions themselves result from the combined influence of a problem-focus and a topic-focus. Thus research questions are a definite mixture of problem- and topic-questions. The importance of research problems, in providing a focus for a project and in influencing research questions, is essential, although frequently neglected. Figure 3.1 summarises the links between the different elements.

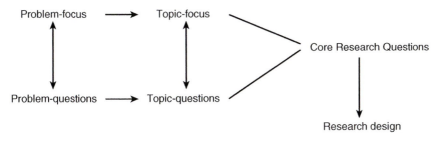

Figure 3.1

A problem-focus provides the starting point and driving impetus of the project. It ties the research to explanatory objectives and thus moves it beyond an exclusively descriptive account. Of course, good descriptive and informational elements are also essential and targeted by the topic-questions. Thus, research questions result from a combination of problem- and topic-questions. *However, 'problems' have a dominant role within this 'mixture' in so far as they shape and influence topic questions.* The result is expressed in the core research questions, and I shall explain how this is achieved further on in the discussion. Once the core research questions have been decided, you are then in a position to take the next step, which is to outline a research design (dealt with more fully in the next chapter).

Problems, Topics and Research Questions

This section focuses on how problem-questions help to define and refine topic-questions and how they are linked with particular kinds of data or evidence. What exactly should you be looking for? What data or evidence do you need in order to throw light on the issues raised by your research problems and questions? What sources of evidence are most useful? The discussion proceeds by examining each of the six key problem questions introduced in Chapter 1. As such, each of the questions deals with an important social domain.

The format of the discussion is the same for each problem. First, the core problem focus is stated and followed by a short discussion unpacking its implications for research. Then, in order to bring out their differences, several related problem- and topic-questions and themes are identified for comparison. This format gives the reader an impression of the relationship between the two types of question and the skills required in formulating good research questions.

Take especial notice of what happens in switching from thinking about problem-questions to topic-questions. There is a shift from the general, abstract level of problem-questions, to the more particular, level of topic-questions. As you try to envision problem-questions in empirical terms, the more you ask 'what sort of data, information or evidence is relevant to these problems and issues?' Conversely, to check the relevance of topic-questions against a particular problem-focus, it is necessary to take the opposite journey from the particular to the general, and so on. It is this continual movement back and forth, between the different levels and types of question, which enables the researcher to decide on research questions.

Key Problem-Questions

1 Self-identity and life careers (domain of psychobiography)

The core problem-focus:

How are a person's self-identity, feeling, ideas and attitudes related to his or her social environment?

The relationship between an individual and society – or between subjective experience and social organisation – is one of reciprocal influence. As 'individuals' we are never completely separated from social contact and involvements with other people. We are 'automatically' entangled in a fairly complex array of social relationships, ranging from the more 'durable' ones with family, friends, colleagues and neighbours to the more 'transient', with fellow travellers, strangers, passers-by, ticket sellers, and so on. However, each of us tends to see ourselves – and are seen by others – as a unique individual with a distinctive 'self' or 'personal identity'. Clearly, self-identity is to some degree influenced (formed and shaped) by social involvements and influences, although it isn't completely moulded by them. Individuals always have some freedom from social influences, pressures and constraints and are able to react to and creatively shape their own destinies.

Each of us has a unique personal history of social involvements as we pass from childhood to adulthood, while ongoing life experiences endow us with unique personality traits, capacities and behavioural responses. For instance, individuals have different levels of confidence, security and self-esteem which in turn, determine their capacity for love, how they get on with others, and how resentful or content they are with their lot. Such individual differences are manifested in how sociable we are, how skilled at conversation, our ability to sympathise with others or read their emotions, to deal with the misfortunes or successes that life has to offer, and so on. Each person has a repertoire of feelings and behavioural responses that are specific to them as an individual person.

In short, everyone has a psychobiography (or life career) that traces changes and continuities in personal identity as we make our way through life (Layder 1993). Psychobiography maps the interplay between private thoughts and feelings and social experiences and involvements over time.

Problem-questions

1 What is the 'subjective' career of the self over time as a person engages in certain social activities and involvements?

2 What feelings, motivations and experiences are associated with particular spheres of activity?

3 To what extent do psychological and social influences shape human behaviour?

Topic-questions

1 What subjective careers are associated with: (a) crime (robbery, violence, shop lifting, fraud, drug dealing, homicide); (b) work; (c) illness; (d) marriage; (e) personal relationships?

2 What motivates people to become involved in drug taking or alcohol or petty theft? Do individuals' perceptions of the meanings of these activities and meanings change over time?

3 Why do individuals feel entrapped or fulfilled by marriage, partnerships and friendships?

4 Why do individuals resent the authority others hold over them at work?

5 What are a person's ambitions at school, college, work or in personal life?

2 Social interaction (encounters) (domain of situated activity)

The core problem-focus:
  How do people influence one another's behaviour in social interaction?

We encounter each other in everyday life at school, at work, during leisure or relaxation periods, on the street, on public transport, and so on. Sometimes these encounters are between strangers, at other times with people we know very well. Most encounters are face to face, although in the modern world they are often 'mediated' by mobile phones, texts, the internet, and so on. Face-to-face interaction produces *emergent* characteristics which affect the behaviour of those involved (Goffman 1983). For example, individuals tend to 'present' themselves in particular ways so as to impress, persuade, help or manipulate others. Also, those present in encounters create and share 'local' meanings. Thus, what is said in an encounter may only be completely understandable to those present since bystanders or outsiders may not be privy to its special meanings. Finally, there are social rules about the appropriateness of certain kinds of interactive behaviour, such as standing at a certain distance from a speaker, allowing them appropriate conversational turns, and not needlessly embarrassing or unmasking them.

Problem-questions

1 What is the nature of the encounter? Is it transient, as with a stranger on public transport, or is it part of a linked series of encounters over time, as with family members, friends or work colleagues?

2 In what kind of social setting does the encounter occur? How does it affect the encounter? Is it a *formal* setting, such as at college, school, work, or is it an *informal* setting, such as between family and friends?

3 What meanings and rules are created and shared by the participants?

4 How are the self-identities of the participants influenced by the dynamics of the encounters?

Topic-questions

1 Do encounters on public transport and in shopping malls differ from those at work, school and university? How do they differ from encounters between friends and family members?

2 Do conversations with friends differ from those between acquaintances?

3 Why are some individuals excluded from encounters, or from their real meanings and business? Are there 'rules' of inclusion and exclusion?

4 What is the nature of interaction between customers in shops, restaurants, cafés? Does the size of such establishments make any difference to the quality of the interaction?

5 Is there tension and conflict in encounters between customers and staff in a particular fast-food restaurant or a gym?

6 Does gossip help cement bonds between friends or lovers?

7 How and why do people support others in conversations? How and why do they attempt to undermine others?

3 The influence of social settings (domain of social settings)

The core problem-focus:
  How do social settings (for example, schools, hospitals families or companies) influence behaviour and activity?

Social interaction always takes place within specific social settings, but 'interaction' and 'settings' are very different kinds of phenomena. Social interaction has a transient, evanescent quality and depends on the comings and goings and matching up of particular people. Social settings have a more durable quality and, over time, give rise to *routine patterns* of interaction. In this sense they have an *already established* pattern of social organisation. Some settings are formally organised with positions of power and authority, as in bureaucratic organisations like banks, hospitals, factories, industrial companies even schools and universities. Other types of setting are more loosely and informally organised, such as family or friendship networks, gangs and criminal sub-cultures. Nonetheless, they are socially organised in terms of roles, expectations and values.

Problem-questions

1 How does the type of social setting influence behaviour and social activity? What are the significant differences between formally organised and informal settings?

2 How do established *social practices* within settings affect behaviour? What roles or social positions are there? How is power and authority organised within the setting?

3 How do people become attached and committed to particular settings? How are social relationships organised within settings?

Topic-questions

1 How is a particular factory, hospital, school, religious sect or fast-food restaurant socially organised? Is there a hierarchy of power, authority and control? How does this organisation affect social behaviour and activity?

2 In what ways are family ties or friendship networks socially organised? What sort of bonds are there in such settings? How do people become committed and attached to them? What are the general rules and expectations of friendship?

3 Are relations between customers and staff in fast-food restaurants fleeting, alienated and artificial? If they are, why is this so?

4 What range of emotional expression is expected of flight attendants, school teachers or social workers in their respective work settings? Do these settings fulfil creative, emotional or spiritual needs?

5 Do families fulfil or thwart emotional needs?

6 Do factors associated with class, ethnicity, gender or age influence the organisation and operation of particular settings?

4 The wider social context (domain of contextual resources)

The core problem-focus:

How is social behaviour influenced by (a) social class, ethnicity, gender, age, neighbourhood, region or politics and (b) cultural values, expectations and institutions?

Society as a whole stretches beyond the boundaries of particular fields of activity. In a society-wide sense, money, property, possessions, status and power are organised and distributed between social groups in terms of structural factors such as class, ethnicity, gender, age, and so on. The forms of inequality so created profoundly affect people's life experiences and their subjective responses expressed in feelings, attitudes, values and expectations. The central, political and economic institutions of a society also promote values, ideas and ideologies that encourage or discourage certain forms of behaviour. Thus the macro context of society impinges on particular spheres of activity by shaping their social settings and influencing values and attitudes in everyday life.

Problem-questions

1 How do class, gender, age and ethnicity affect intimacy, drug taking, leisure and sport, educational experiences, and so on?

2 In what sense is the political, religious and economic situation relevant to the focus of the research project? How do such factors influence social behaviour?

3 In what ways do values, expectations and ideology encourage or discourage certain forms of behaviour?

4 How do social media shape values and imagery?

Topic-questions

1 Are women (or ethnic minorities) treated differently in the workplace?

2 Why and how do some people suffer harassment or bullying on the street, in clubs or in school?

3 Are some social groups discriminated against in the educational system? What role do financial inequalities play in such cases?

4 How do people deal with fear caused by gang violence or paramilitary violence or terrorism?

5 Power and social activity (dimension of power)

The core problem-focus:
How does power influence social activity?

Power can be found everywhere in social life, although it takes different forms and affects people's lives and behaviour in different ways. With *individual or subjective* power a person's physical and psychological attributes enable him or her to wield varying degrees of control and influence over others. Situational dynamics are also important because the power that an individual possesses tends to vary from situation to situation (*situational power*). A chief executive officer of a multinational company may be powerful in the workplace, but oppressed and put upon in her or his personal life. An ordinary member of the public may perform an extraordinary act of bravery, and so on. Occupational positions in work settings often have a quota of power and authority so that individuals holding these positions exert control over co-workers (*positional power*). Finally, there is power deriving from a group's position in the wider (macro) structure of society (*structural power*). Inequalities of power between various groupings are based on unequal distributions of resources.

Problem-questions

1 What are the main differences between types of power in social life? How do they operate and what is their domain of influence?

2 In what ways do different power types influence social behaviour and activity?

3 How is interpersonal power shaped and moulded by subjective power and structural power?

4 On what kinds of resources are particular forms of power based? Is power visible, direct and upfront or concealed, indirect and behind the scenes? Is power benign or exploitative?

5 What does it mean to say that particular groups are relatively powerless or powerful?

Topic-questions

1 Are certain individuals 'natural' leaders and why? What qualities do they possess? What personal and social resources do they draw upon?

2 How does the balance of power in a relationship affect the quality of intimacy in romantic and sexual partnerships?

3 Does holding a position of power and control at work make it difficult for a person to be friends with co-workers who are subject to their authority?

4 Are lower-class children less likely to succeed in the educational system?

5 Do men have more power than women?

6 Temporality and history (dimension of time)

The core problem-focus:
How does the passage of time influence social behaviour?

The elapsing of time has several kinds of effects on social activity depending on which element of social life we focus upon. For example, self-identity is not a fixed 'essence'; it develops over an individual's lifetime and continues to do so as new experiences imprint themselves on the psyche. Situated social interaction is shaped by the duration of an encounter which, as we have seen, may be brief and one-off (as with strangers on a train or aircraft) or part of chains of encounters (Collins 2005) over successive periods of time (like those with loved ones). Social settings not only have organisational 'histories' of their own, but often operate according to their own defined rhythms of time. Finally, there is the larger sense of the passing of time, the vast sweeps of history which not only mark out specific epochs, but also transitions between types of society (such as that between feudal and capitalist society). All these different senses of time impinge on social life and thus influence it in different ways.

Problem-questions

1 How does the passing of time influence the study of individuals, encounters, settings and contexts?

2 How is social behaviour influenced by different 'constructions' of time?

Topic-questions

1 Do individuals base their self-images on past experiences or their aspirations?

2 Does intimacy inevitably erode over time? What roles do familiarity and habituation play in personal relationships?

3 How does a person's status within a group change over time?

4 Have conceptions of romantic love changed in the last two centuries? Do present ideas about romantic love bear any resemblance to earlier ideas?

Distinguishing between Problem- and Topic-Questions

This concludes the discussion of the key problem-questions. Hopefully, you will now be able to spot the 'problem' and 'topic' elements in research questions. You need to feel confident in handling both, and in being able to think about, and organise, your efforts in these terms. As I said earlier, moving in your mind from problem to topic elements (and back again) requires a shift in thought processes – a shift from fairly abstract and general considerations to more concrete and empirical issues, and vice versa. Importantly, you need to be able to do this fairly rapidly and easily in order to extract most benefit.

Unless you are very lucky and are naturally gifted in this regard, honing such skills takes a lot of practice, and no little experience. However, careful study of the examples in the previous discussion will help to make you aware of what is required and also, perhaps, inspire you to develop research questions for your own project.

Developing and Refining Research Questions

Although research questions are derived from a mixture of problem- and topic-questions, the problem-driven nature of the approach means that problem-questions will have an important influence on shaping and refining topic-questions, and thus on how you finally decide on the core research questions.

Given that problem-questions play this large and crucial role, you must ensure that any prior fascination you may have with a particular topic does not get in the way of this process. If your interest in the topic itself develops into an obsession or fixation, then it can be a problem. Remember, a key component of excellent research is to demonstrate your awareness of the importance of a problem-focus for the overall shape and scope of topic-questions.

Having your attention fixed exclusively on topic issues is more likely to happen at the beginning of a research project when your objectives and purposes are less well developed or pinned down. Nevertheless, this can be a distraction and, if not dealt with, can linger on to haunt you all the way through the project. If you recognise that you are only, or mainly, dealing with topic-related issues, you must shift tack. Otherwise, you will be in danger of losing sight of important research aims and objectives. You must stand back and ask 'what is my problem?' Then ask 'what are my problem-questions?' Once you have a definite problem-focus – and the problem-questions that go with it – you can switch your attention back to topic-related issues.

In the following sections I describe how to develop and refine research questions by using research problems and problem-questions as filters and shapers of topic-questions.

Defining the Range of Topic-Questions

The most basic issue in this regard concerns understanding how problem-questions define the parameters of topic-questions. We can see the mechanism at work here when we examine what happens if we change the problem-focus of a research project, but keep the same topic area. Generally speaking, a change in problem-focus requires a change in the focus and relevance of topic-questions. This can be observed in the following hypothetical example of two research projects focusing on the same topic area, gym or health club use, but with each project tackling it from the point of view of a different problem-focus.

(A)

The first project focuses on the social interaction between staff and users of a gym or health club (problem-question 2).

In this respect the relevant problem-questions are:
How does interaction between staff and users influence their perceptions of, attitudes and behaviour towards each other? Is their interaction characterised by tension and conflict, or by harmony and cooperation?
Relevant topic questions might be:
How successful are staff members at dealing with users? Do members of staff show empathy and sensitivity with users and their problems? Are staff able to adapt to changing user demands? How do staff members perceive users? Do users find staff officious and reluctant to assist, or pleasant and helpful? What are the most frequent complaints about staff? Do users' backgrounds or goals affect their relations with staff?

(B)

The second project centres on the self-identities and body images of users.

This shift in problem-focus raises a different set of problem-questions:
How is self identity shaped and developed through social involvements over time, with significant others, and through the influence of social background (occupation/ class gender, ethnicity).

The shift in problem-focus requires a corresponding shift in relevant topic-questions:

How frequently do particular individuals attend the gym/health club? For what reasons do they attend – appearance, fitness/health, weight loss, social contact? Does social background influence goals and aspirations? Do users wish to alter their self-image? Do they want to be more attractive or socially sought-after (say, by shedding fat or gaining musculature)? Does gender play a role?

Comment on examples

Clearly, because the problem-focus in each of the above examples is different, a correspondingly different range of topic-questions is required. This is because the *relevance* of the topic-questions *is defined in and through the lens of the problem-focus and problem-questions.*

Having said this, however, it is important to note that while both the problem- and topic-questions change, their general nature remains the same. That is, in both examples the problem-questions remain abstract and conceptual because they refer to *general characteristics* – which don't vary, regardless of which particular gym or health club you choose to study. Topic-questions remain more focused on particular, concrete and empirical aspects. They are centred on 'factual' details and information about the particular club you are studying, separating it out from other gyms and health clubs. In this sense, the relevance of topic-questions is tied to particular empirical settings.

Defining and Shaping Specific Topic-Questions

In the two examples of research on gyms/health clubs it is clear that when the problem-focus changes the *range* of relevant research questions must also change. However, this range includes many possible topic-questions so the list must be narrowed down to more specific questions depending on their importance to the problem-focus. The relevance of particular topic-questions can only be decided upon in the light of your problem-focus.

Topic-questions need to be fine-tuned by filtering them through the lens of your problem-focus and problem-questions. This will ensure that they really 'hit the mark' in terms of your overall research aims and objectives – what you want to investigate and what you want to explain. Allowing the problem-focus to refine and shape topic-questions means that it is more likely that they will target data/information/evidence pertinent to the problem itself, and not simply the topic.

For example, if your problem-focus is on the dynamics of interaction in fast-food restaurants or universities, there is quite an array of possible topic-questions that could be of relevance – perhaps too many for comfort! However, if you refine your problem-focus to an interest in the *quality of interaction*, say, *between* staff *and* customers in a fast-food restaurant, or *between* professors *and* students in a university, this will narrow down relevant topic-questions. For example, your main topic-questions would need to centre on the purposes served by the interaction and to what extent it is smooth and sincere as opposed to being strained and artificial. You would be less concerned with issues about stresses and strains *among* restaurant staff or *among* students. Thus the range of relevant research questions would be narrowed down. Filtering topic-questions through a problem-focus helps align your main research questions with the most relevant data and greatly increases your chances of collecting the best evidence.

Limiting the Number of Topic-Questions

A problem-focus also imposes a limit on the number of topic-questions that are pertinent. First-time researchers are often confused by the potentially endless number of questions (or issues) that can be investigated. It often seems that the more you think about a topic, the more questions you come up with, all of which seem important. However, as the potential questions multiply, the more confused you become about which are the most important. Anxiety and uncertainty are likely to creep in.

Having a problem-focus offers a way around such difficulties because it helps limit your main research questions to a relatively stable core. As a result, it reduces the tendency to think endlessly of new topic-questions. The only topic-questions that matter are those that relate directly to the problem-focus. Realising that *not everything is relevant* alleviates the nagging feeling that you might have missed out something important. A sure way of focusing only on research questions that are directly relevant to your 'current' research objectives is to ask whether a particular topic-question throws any light on your research problems.

The word 'current' here is important because, at this time, it is best not to regard objectives as absolutely fixed or permanent. The adaptive method stresses the benefits of an unfolding approach in which research questions *may* change, shift or gradually transform in the light of incoming evidence as well as evolving ideas about how to analyse and interpret this evidence. So the process of refining and limiting research questions is *designed to provide structure and momentum at the very beginning of the project.* And while the structure may remain relatively unchanged throughout the project, this is not inevitable. In many cases, subsequent changes in problem-focus and topic-questions will be required.

Deciding on Core Research Questions

Core research questions will consist of some problem-questions and some topic-questions. By formulating core questions and writing them down as succinctly but accurately as possible (as notes in your Research Log), you can confidently let them front-up your research design. It is crucial to throw out any questions that are marginal to your concerns. Reduce them to the bare minimum otherwise they will clutter up your mind and impede the progress of the research. Be ruthless, but keep a note of *everything* you discard, including notes and ideas as well as discarded questions, in your Research Log. You may change your mind later on and want to use the material after initial data collection analysis has begun. It may become apparent that discarded questions and thoughts still have some relevance to the project.

Tightening up Research Questions

Finally, having settled on your core research questions you should then go about reviewing them with an eagle eye, making sure that they are expressed as accurately, appropriately and as economically as possible. Every word counts and, crucially, a single word can have the power to draw your attention either to or away from seemingly small details that may later take on much greater significance. It is important, therefore, to be sure from the outset that your research questions convey as closely as possible what they are meant to convey (White 2009).

Final Comments

This chapter has emphasised the importance of developing and refining core research questions from a problem-focus. The problem-driven character of the approach ensures that it will have at least some explanatory (as well as descriptive) objectives, which are essential for achieving research excellence. Settling on core research questions also gives the project a definite structure right from the start. But this does not in any way compromise the unfolding or emergent character of the approach. Rather, it merely guards against the confusion that can result from starting out with an unstructured 'wait and see' approach. The adaptive method ensures that any subsequent unfolding will take place smoothly and effectively because it does so in relation to a stable point of reference.

Remember the following. Setting up core questions in advance of data collection doesn't mean you are limiting the capacity of the research to let issues emerge. You are not predetermining the answers to these core questions. At the beginning of the research 'answers' are, as yet, merely unfulfilled potentials. They are 'open' in the sense that they are formulated from the interplay between incoming evidence/data and its analysis. Shifts and transformations in core research questions can happen at any point during the project, after data collection has begun, and are a natural part of the research process.

Checklist for Research Log Notes

- Make sure you know the difference between 'problem-' and 'topic-' questions.

- Make sure you know the links between problems, topics, research questions and research design.

- What is your research problem?

- What is your topic?

- How does your problem-focus help you to develop and refine research questions?

- Keep a note of all discarded material (such as rejected research questions) – they may be important later on.

4

PREPARATION & PROJECT DESIGN

PREVIEW

This chapter covers the following:

- Topic selection and accessibility
- The purpose of a selective literature review
- Summarising work on the topic or area
- The selective review as a creative process
- Developing research questions
- Stating your contribution and making your case
- The writing habit
- Writing to clarify thinking
- Writing 'back to front': creating structure
- Sectioning: Titles, headings and sub-headings
- Interlocking sections or chapters
- Producing the research proposal
- Preparing and planning – a time-saving sequence

This chapter discusses preparation for small-scale research using the adaptive approach. The first section focuses on choosing a topic in the light of practical considerations of accessibility, personal safety and ethical issues about 'professional' integrity. The second section concentrates on the need to consult previous research on your chosen topic or area. By engaging in a selective literature review you will be able to identify exactly what your project will contribute in the way of understanding and knowledge. It will also enable you to target the main ideas, methods, concepts and strategies that are of central relevance to the project. Finally, it will be of decisive help in identifying the differences between topic- and problem-questions.

The third section concentrates on the benefits of starting to write up the research from the earliest possible moment. Filling in a Research Log on a regular basis can kick start the writing process and give it a momentum that may enable you to avoid writer's block during the research. This section also describes how writing is the most effective method of clarifying your thoughts as you grapple with hands-on issues as the research unfolds. The fourth section describes what is involved in constructing a research proposal and how keeping a Research Log helps you do this. A proposal offers a preliminary statement of what you intend to do in the project and the way you will go about it, but it may also come in useful later in the research by serving as a 'first draft' of your final report.

Topic Selection and Accessibility

There are several senses in which *accessibility* is relevant in selecting a topic for small-scale research. First, a topic may be accessible in the sense of being 'convenient' or 'near to hand'. For instance, research projects on celebrity or popular culture, on school or college experiences, or on family or friendship issues are part of everyday life, and thus do not require you to stray too far in order to find potential sources of research data. In fact, relevant evidence and information is all around you, in the form of newspapers, magazines, films, videos, radio, photographs, and so on.

Also with more accessible topics, such as friendship, romantic relation-ships, or school or college experiences, it is less likely that you will be exposed to personal danger. Obviously, some topics pose more threats than others. For example, violence or the threat of violence is always a possibility when investigating street gangs, knife crime or drug taking. Of course, this is a matter of degree, and you would be wise to think through in advance any possible problems that might compromise your personal safety.

The same is true of topics that raise difficult ethical issues. As a first-time researcher, it is best to choose topics and/or problems that do not involve challenging ethical issues, such as disguising your identity in order to study a particular group or deceiving your research subjects in order to gain infor-mation or data. Securing the informed consent of those you wish to study should be a guiding principle of your research plans and practices. Anything that directly compromises this principle, or in any way challenges your integrity as a researcher, should be avoided.

What is your research problem? Preliminary thoughts

To produce an excellent research project it must address a clearly defined analytic problem. In choosing a topic, therefore, it is paramount that you begin thinking as early as possible about exactly what 'problem' you are concerned with, how it relates to your topic and the difference between 'problem-' and 'topic-' questions. Getting this sorted out at the very beginning will pay dividends in terms of the eventual smooth running of the project and the sense of confidence you will gain from the clarity it brings. Most importantly, sorting it out now will ensure that your project will be set up properly right from the word go.

Working out the relationships between your topic and problem will enable you to identify and clarify your main research questions and thus help you to construct a 'preliminary plan' – a research proposal or the design of your project. Such a plan will aid you in deciding which methods and strategies to use to collect data, what sort of findings to anticipate, and how you hope to analyse and interpret them.

The Selective Literature Review: Consulting Previous Research

Having chosen a topic, a research problem and a set of research questions, the next step is to undertake a selective literature search and review. Like most others, the adaptive approach stresses the importance of a literature review, although different aspects are given special emphasis. I shall not be dealing with the nitty-gritty practicalities of library searches for articles in academic journals, books and reviews. Descriptions of the best ways of tackling such tasks can be found in many introductory texts (see Bell 2010; Kane 1990). Instead, the following discussion concentrates on the nature and purpose of a literature review as it applies to adaptive research.

A selective search and critical review

I want to stress the idea that a literature search should be *selective*. You are not trying to find and read absolutely everything that has ever been written on the subject/topic or that might be generally relevant to it. It is very tempting to keep on reading and tracking down more and more seemingly relevant information on the assumption that you are simply being conscientious or thorough. Unfortunately, in fact, this is not generally how it works. More often than not the very opposite happens. The more you read, the more you convince yourself that you don't know enough – and can never know enough – about all the relevant information, possible approaches, ideas, concepts, and so on. Getting into the state of mind of 'never knowing enough' and consequently seeking out more and more reading material can be fatal. Such an attitude inevitably leads to confusion, uncertainty and lack of confidence, even before you have really got going.

This happens because you are attempting to assimilate and organise too much information all at once. It doesn't work because these things can only be done slowly, and incrementally, by seeing how each bit of information fits in with the concerns of the project. So instead of producing greater wisdom and increased confidence, reading too much too early on will create confusion, anxiety and chaotic thinking. In turn, this may lead to a 'paralysis of the will', in which you keep putting off the decision to actually get started.

It is therefore important to place a limit on the amount you read before you actually do start, and keep strictly to these self-imposed limits. Keep reminding yourself that you can extend your search and reading later on, when you are looking for specific things, such as gaps in understanding, missing information, or checking up on certain ideas or concepts. Remember also that, in principle, a literature search and review can, and should, continue throughout the research, right up to writing the final report. There is no compelling need to complete everything beforehand or all at once.

Another possible consequence of not being selective is writer's block – even before you've started writing! More than anything else, I want to stress that actually starting to write, and getting into a regular habit of writing, as early as possible is probably the most important factor in helping you to carry through a research project to its completion. Acquiring the habit of writing requires some effort, but is absolutely invaluable because it de-clutters the mind. It can bring greater clarity to your thinking, particularly if you are overloaded by 'non-selective' prior reading! So being 'choosey' about what you read initially will actually pay dividends. Remember also that your search should be specific and strictly focused. The only things that matter are those central to your immediate concerns. In this sense your focus should be defined by the issues raised in the following sections.

Summarising Work on the Topic or Area

A central reason for a literature review is to show that you are aware of the 'key' or most important work already done on the area. So although you don't want to delve too deeply or cover absolutely everything, you cannot afford to miss out references to pieces of influential research that are directly linked to your topic or problem. Clearly, your own research will have to take this work into account even if you intend to be critical of some aspects of it – if, for example, you know that it has failed to consider crucial evidence.

Apart from showing that you know the key research in the area and its significance, you must examine it with a view to identifying the reasons why your own project matters. In this sense you are using existing research as a template against which to measure the worth of your own research. The end result of such a review should be that you are able to state what is distinctive about your own research project, why it is necessary, and how you intend to achieve what you set out to achieve. In short, you will be defining your intended 'contribution to knowledge' in relation to your chosen topic and problem. This will become an essential part of your research design.

Your selective review should contain three essential components:

1 It must *summarise the key pieces of existing research* in terms of the leading concepts, theories, methods, strategies and approaches that they have employed.

2 It must also include *a critical evaluation* of each of the above so as to identify exemplary or strong points of the research as well as any gaps or problems. In so doing you will be describing how your own project will attempt to develop, build on, rectify or go beyond particular features of this previous research.

3 Finally, the review should target the relevant ideas, concepts, methods and strategies that you intend to use in your own research.

The Selective Review as a Creative Process

Although a selective review is essentially focused on an already established body of research knowledge, it should not be thought of as an unexciting and 'uncreative' process through which you simply familiarise yourself with other researchers' ideas. By being selective in a literature review you avoid closing down your imagination. Some authors (for instance, Glaser 2001: 84) downplay the importance of a literature review on the grounds that it might stifle a researcher's 'openness' and ability to think 'afresh' about the topic or area. As a result, she or he will be less likely to develop new ideas or novel ways of thinking about particular research questions and problems. According to Glaser (2001), a likely consequence of this is that further on in research – perhaps in the data gathering or data analysis phase – you will be tempted to 'force' data or evidence to 'fit in' with ideas, concepts or forms of explanation that are really not suitable and which do not properly 'fit' the evidence or data.

Certainly, a literature review must not become an obsession. Nor should it become a justification for imposing a straitjacket on your thinking or the way you analyse data. You should approach the literature review in a critical manner and avoid the temptation to slavishly adhere to 'received views' and preconceived ideas. However, having said this, there are *many more* potential dangers associated with *not* undertaking a literature review.

The main danger, of course, is that you are likely to overlook useful and important ideas that are already out there! In so doing, you will miss the chance of being able to feed these ideas into your own thinking and help firm-up or shape your own 'original' ideas. In this respect, it is particularly important to be aware of the way in which other researchers have used evidence, concepts and explanatory approaches.

Another danger of by-passing a literature review is that you will fail to benefit from the experiences of earlier researchers, the problems they encountered and how they dealt with them. Clearly, being forewarned and forearmed through a careful reading of their work is an insurance against potential problems and pitfalls that may arise in your own research!

Using a literature review to help construct or develop your own research project is not the same as rigidly sticking to an inflexible framework. Rather, it is a means of deciding which conceptual resources you can use in your own work. For example, on the basis of a literature review you may decide that a concept that has been used in previous studies is not appropriate for your own research. Knowing this can make it easier to decide on or develop your own ideas because you will have a clearer idea of which sorts of concepts you want to avoid and which would be more suitable. Or you may decide that some alteration or modification of the original concept would be a good 'starting point' for your project. The fact that you have the original concept as a baseline or template to work from can make this easier. Regardless of whether you reject the concept outright or attempt to remodel it, you will be involved in a creative process.

In this sense it is important to appreciate the potential creativity that is involved in a literature review. Immersing oneself in the 'received' literature does not necessarily limit thinking, stifle the imagination or act as a block to creativity. The point of a literature review should be to feed the imagination rather than shut it down. The cumulative nature of social scientific research means that it often builds on (extends or modifies), previous research, even though sometimes this may also involve a critique or rejection of it. Therefore, it should be assumed that previous research will or might have some relevance to new investigations. Of course, you must avoid slavishly reapplying received ideas in a new project. Thus all concepts must be critically evaluated in order to justify reapplication in their original form. The uncritical application of received concepts indicates both a lack of imagination and a failure to follow sound scientific principles.

Appropriately done, a literature review familiarises you with existing concepts, problems and questions associated with a particular topic or area. A truly creative approach to research harnesses the potential of *received* ideas and concepts *while at the same time* leaving room for *emergent* ideas and concepts. If we were to rely exclusively on one or the other of these, then we would be limiting possible sources of knowledge. But we should not turn our backs on accumulated knowledge and ignore the rich fund of existing concepts and data at our disposal.

Developing Research Questions

In dealing with the difference between topic- and problem-questions in the previous chapter I underscored the crucial role it plays in planning and doing excellent social research. However, it should not therefore be assumed that this issue should be settled once and for all *prior to* a selective review. Knowing the difference between topic- and problem-questions, and being able to spot them in pieces of published research, is not necessarily the same as defining those that are pertinent to your own specific project. In this sense you must use the selective review to sort through and spot potential topic- and problem-questions, and to refine and firm up your choices about the key research questions that will drive the research and underpin its design.

Stating Your Contribution and Making Your Case

Apart from identifying the most compelling reasons why your research project is important and why it is necessary, a selective literature review will also help you to decide on the most appropriate methods and strategies. This is required as part of established research protocol and will feed into your research design as well as the final report. But a statement of purpose is also extremely useful in a purely practical sense. If you can sum up your key aims, purposes and objectives in a short statement (and the more vivid and evocative this is, the better), then you will have a constant reminder of the exact nature of, and reasons for, your research. As such, you will be able to recall this 'summary' statement whenever you feel uncertain, confused or anxious. Your sense of direction and confidence will soon return if you have access to this reminder of your core statement of purpose.

The Writing Habit

As I mentioned previously, it is essential to start writing as soon as possible, and keeping a Research Log is an ideal way of developing the discipline and habit of writing. However, beginning to write very early on – even before you've started to collect data – directly challenges the 'intuitive' feeling that the writing comes later in the process. Thus it is very often the case that first-time researchers assume that the best practice is to leave the writing until the end of the research, after all the data has been collected, presented and analysed. This might also seem the most 'logical' and 'common sense' way of proceeding. But this is where intuition and commonsense can be very misleading.

Just as reading too much (in a literature review) may inhibit writing, so too can collecting too much data be a block to writing. Again, the problem often stems from information overload and the confused thinking that follows from it. Trying to hold too much information (including abstract thoughts and concepts) in your mind all at once leads to an inability to sort through the chaos which builds up over time and eventually makes you fearful of committing your thoughts to paper. As a consequence, even if you do manage to start, you will probably be unhappy when your first attempts seem less than 'perfect'. To remedy the obstacle of 'perfectionism', you must simply start writing! This is slightly easier if you assume that it will be a first draft which you will revise when required. Getting into a routine and habit of writing is by far the best way of overcoming the feeling that you must get your thoughts 'clear' before you start, and thus running the risk of never starting at all (Becker 1986).

Writing to Clarify Thinking

I agree with Wolcott (2001: 21) that 'the conventional wisdom is that writing reflects thinking', but actually it is the other way round. In this sense, 'writing is thinking' or at least 'a form of thinking' (Becker 1986). As Wolcott points out, 'writing is a great way to discover what we are thinking, as well as to discover gaps in our thinking' (Wolcott 2001: 21). But why is this so?

First, writing is a discipline that forces us to order our thoughts in a manner that others can understand. In so doing, we are also forced to refine them by getting rid of ambiguities that we weren't necessarily aware of, and which only become apparent when we try to write them down. Also, writing forces us to attend to the rules of grammar and syntax required to sequence our thoughts and present them in complex forms (like phrases and sentences). By laying out ideas in more complex and ordered ways, we become conscious of the need for logical and sequential coherence. Creative thoughts often float around the mind in a half-baked form. They deceive us into thinking they are fully-formed and definite until, in trying to write them down, we find that they were in fact unclear or confused. It is the act of writing them down that identifies any confusion and points the way to eventual clarity.

Writing Back to Front: Creating Structure

The conventional wisdom that writing reflects thinking depends on the idea that thoughts proceed in some predetermined, logical sequence. But this is an illusion. In fact, in order to arrive at a coherent conclusion you must already have in mind at least a general impression of the sort of conclusion that would be acceptable and appropriate! In this particular sense you are in fact working back to front, in order to simultaneously make progress in a forward direction!

Exactly the same is true when it comes to constructing an overall plan of a research project. Some measure of control is achieved – and thus uncertainty is minimised – by setting out with some idea of where it is you want to end up, and what the intervening steps will be. In this sense, filling in a Research Log provides this kind of structure. The main 'constituents' or 'phases' of the research process are known in advance and thus they provide a ready-made plan for writing up the research.

In this manner you can truly begin to write 'back to front' by completing a preliminary or first draft of what you imagine will be the overall sequence of the research before you have even begun collecting data. Working this way is not 'fixing', 'forcing' or 'predetermining' anything. It is merely ensuring that you have an organisational blueprint (of the elements applicable to all research) that you can work from. The details, the methods and data collecting strategies you use, your actual findings and your interpretation of them, and so on, will be filled in as you go along. As a result, what you anticipated at the beginning will change somewhat as the actual research unfolds. However, the basic structure, as evidenced by your Research Log, will remain the same throughout.

Writing with the end product in mind

When acquiring a routine of writing, you need to consider what your end product will eventually be. In fact, your 'final research report' will actually be one of the following:

- an extended (research) essay

- a dissertation

- a masters or doctoral thesis

- a published article

- a book

- a monograph.

Although the role, length and intellectual standard of these distinct forms of report vary considerably, they all have a similar basic structure. One of the main differences between them is the length of the units or segments in which their informational content is expressed. Extended essays or articles are shorter pieces which are organised in terms of 'sections', while the longer reports, such as a PhD theses or books, are organised in terms of 'chapters'. Although 'sections' and 'chapters' may differ considerably in size, they perform similar jobs in that they communicate individual segments or components of the research. Thus, all research reports, large or small, are required to contain similar segments (whether they are written as sections or chapters) which deal with each of the key elements of the research process. These are:

1 Purpose and objectives

2 Research design

3 Methods and strategies

4 Presentation of findings

5 Analysis and interpretation of data

6 Conclusions and implications

Sectioning: Titles, Headings and Sub-Headings

Although these key elements are common to all research, you, of course, are free to decide exactly how you describe each individual segment. Thus, you should pay special attention to asking questions such as 'how many sections do I need?' 'How many headings and sub-headings shall I work with, and what will be their content?'

You also need to decide the exact wording of headings and sub-headings as soon as possible because the names or labels you give them are short-hand, condensed evocations of the content. Playing around with different possibilities for the headings and sub-headings can be useful in stimulating your ideas or evoking new ways at looking at things. It is also an important way of reminding you of what is relevant for particular sections (the issues, the arguments, the evidence, and so on).

What is true for individual sections is perhaps even more so with regard to your 'main title' – that is, of the whole research report. Deciding on a title, or at least a *working* title, right from the word go can firm-up your thoughts about the overall purpose and objectives of the research. Tackling this early on allows you to keep coming back to it and reminding yourself of the essence of the project. Of course, being relatively sure of your overall title will also make it easier to decide on sectional headings and sub-headings.

Interlocking Sections or Chapters

It is important to make the proposal, research design or final report, hang together as a whole. It is the key to producing a coherent and robust account of the project. This can be achieved by remembering that the 'sections' or 'chapters' must interlock with each other. They must be able to 'lean on' and give mutual support to each other in terms of their logic and arguments. A fairly common problem, which not only affects first-time researchers but also more experienced PhD candidates, is a tendency to treat each section or chapter as independent and discrete, as if each unit of discussion has little in common with the one before or the one after. Now, while it is important that each unit is internally consistent, logical and sound, it must also play a part in achieving an overall cumulative argument.

Because of the *inter*dependence of the key elements, attention must be paid to the manner in which the individual units hang together and interlock with each other. The writing in each section or chapter must, in itself, be internally consistent and logical, but it must also flow into the next (and subsequent ones) in terms of arguments, themes and issues. In addition, to some extent it must also refer back to the previous sections. In this sense there must be a manifest chain of continuity in the discussions as they spread from unit to unit. Thus the *transitions or joins* between particular sections or chapters are in special need of care and attention. Transitions should not be abrupt, as if the subject were being changed completely. There needs to be a 'smoothing-over', in which themes and issues are blended together in a gradual change of emphasis.

Producing a Research Proposal

A research proposal is a statement of intent that is required and evaluated by others; it is needed in order to describe and justify the main purpose of your project. As with the above advice, you need to construct a proposal by saying something about each of the key elements of the research – in points 1–6 above. You should already be making notes in your Research Log so you can use these as a basis for your research proposal. Basically, you need to make fairly brief, informative comments and observations with regard to the following issues and elements as you anticipate they will pan out.

1 You must outline the *purpose and objectives* of the project in relation to the most relevant existing research. You need to reflect on the relevance of specific concepts or methodological approaches and how they can best be used, developed or modified.

2 You need to comment on issues pertinent to *research design*. Specifically, you must say how the design has evolved from a double focus on an

analytic problem and an empirical topic, and the research questions that follow from them.

3 You need to say something about which data collection methods and strategies you anticipate using, as well as the *sampling units and strategies* you intend to employ.

4 You need to comment on the kind of findings, data, information or evidence that you anticipate you will gather and how you intend to *present and organise* them.

5 You must anticipate, at least in a preliminary manner, the way in which you intend to *analyse your data* (findings, information or evidence).

6 You must convey your thoughts on the sorts of *conclusions and implications* that might result from the project.

The same basic structure (i.e. the six key elements that form the *proposal*) will also serve as (and thus become) your *research design* once you have firmed up some of its more provisional aspects.

Preparing and Planning – A Time-Saving Sequence

This chapter has emphasised the time- and energy-saving aspects that come from early planning and preparation. The discussion has traced the following sequence of decisions and activities:

Although this sequence seems to offer an obvious starting point and an obvious end point, the different elements and activities frequently overlap with each other so that the sequence is not rigidly fixed or unidirectional. Thus, once the process is started you may find yourself dealing with several of the elements at the same time, as well as shuttling back and forth between them. For example, firming up your 'research questions' might easily become an aspect of your 'selective literature review', or even your 'proposal' or 'research design'. The main common element that runs through all them all is the need to acquire a writing habit as quickly as possible. This is built

| Topic selection | Research questions | Selective review | Early writing | Research proposal | Research design |

Figure 4.1

into the idea of a Research Log, which is a continuous record of your attempts to deal with the tasks and problems involved. By adhering to the general principles described in this chapter, you will gain direction and focus in your research project – a clear sense of what you are doing and how you are going to do it. At the same time, you will be preparing the ground for the later, concluding parts of the project, such as writing the final report.

Checklist for Research Log Notes

- How accessible is your topic?

- Use a selective literature review for summarising previous work and as a creative way of developing research questions.

- Identify your main contribution and make a compelling case for your project.

- What steps will you take to acquiring the writing habit? How will drafting and redrafting material help to integrate the different elements of your project?

- Reflect on the ways in which writing down thoughts and ideas may aid in their clarification.

- Be aware of how the method of writing 'back to front' can help solve many practical and organisational problems.

- Make sure you know the importance of creating 'structure' through the use of titles, heading and sub-headings.

- Why is it vital that 'individual' sections or chapters should interlock with each other to create an overall argument?

- Why do the proposal and design constitute 'key' elements of research? How can your Research Log notes contribute to their construction?

5

QUALITATIVE DATA & MIXED STRATEGIES

PREVIEW

This chapter covers the following:

- Problem-driven strategies and methods
- Directed observation and observational roles
- How and what to observe: problem-focused and refined observations
- Note-taking: recording observations
- Directed interviews and conversations
- Recording interviews
- Documentary sources
- Personal documents
- Secondary analysis of qualitative data
- Explanatory frameworks
- Enhancing validity: triangulating methods and data

The adaptive approach is problem-driven rather than methods-driven. That is, methods or strategies of data collection are adopted and used in order to throw light on specific problems and topics rather than because of some predetermined commitment to specific methods or type of data (qualitative or quantitative) as representing the 'best way' of approaching a topic or tackling a problem. The adaptive approach is about gathering empirical data which will throw light on the nature of the principal social domains and the key analytic or problem–questions with which they are linked – as outlined in Chapters 1 and 3. The problem-driven nature of the approach means that it is compatible with both quantitative and qualitative data. In this respect the approach can be linked with three main types of research design. These are:

- purely qualitative research

- purely quantitative research

- mixtures of quantitative and qualitative research.

First, this chapter presents the main qualitative strategies and methods that can be used (either singly or mixed with quantitative methods) to explore and collect data about social domains. By contrast, the next chapter focuses on the way in which quantitative data and methods may be used to gather data on social domains – again, either alone or in conjunction with qualitative data.

Mixing Qualitative Strategies and Methods

The four main sources of qualitative data and methods of collection examined here are:

- directed observation

- directed interviewing

- documentary sources

- secondary materials.

Even though these all give rise to forms of qualitative data, it is important to make as many investigative 'cuts' into the data as feasible in the circumstances. In this way the different strategic or methodological cuts will interlock and support each other. Observations will act as both a check on interviews, and/or documentary and secondary materials. Conversely, documentary materials and interviews will serve as a check on the reliability, accuracy and validity of your observations or evidence gathered from secondary sources. The more data you gather from different sources, the more robust will be your overall findings, because evidence that is not confirmed or corroborated by one of the methods will be gradually sifted out. By complementing each other, this mixing of methods will also provide a more rounded and complete picture of the social processes under investigation.

Of course, because you are not concentrating exclusively on one particular method, you must be careful to share out your energies between the different methods you do use. However, by trawling qualitative data from several different methods and sources you are gaining more reliable data as well as a better overall understanding of the problem and topic under investigation.

The exact balance of different qualitative methods and sources of data you decide to use will depend on the particular circumstances of your project. Time or budgetary constraints, gaining access to events or activities, obtaining the consent of interviewees, and so on, will all affect the extent to which different methods and sources can be called upon. So bearing these considerations in mind, once you have a problem, a topic and some research questions, it is best to decide, as far in advance as possible, what range of data is available to you – what sort of opportunities there are for observations and interviews, and what sort of documentary sources or secondary material will be most relevant. In turn, this will determine which is the best combination of methods and sources of data appropriate to your project. For example:

- interviews with observations, supplemented by secondary material, or

- documents with interviews supplemented by observation.

As these examples show, all qualitative methods or data sources may not be equally significant. As a result, some will be used in a supplementary manner to support the data from the 'main' sources. To avoid potential confusion, where possible it is probably best to decide these issues in advance of actual data collection. However, this is not a cast iron 'rule'. Decisions about including more, or different, sources of data may be reasonably made later in the research, if it becomes apparent that they are necessary or would greatly enhance the project.

Of course, the idea that you should use as many sources and methods of data collection as possible is only something to be 'aimed at', and is not an absolute requirement. In fact, it is better to concentrate on particular combinations that are specifically tailored to the needs and circumstances of your project. In any case, the amount (and spread) of data alone do not completely determine the value (or excellence) of your project. Obviously, it might only be possible to draw from a minimum of sources, but you should aim for two at least so as to ensure some cross-checking of data. In this case, the strength of your project will depend on what you do with the data in terms of the conclusions you are able to draw from them, and how much light they throw on your research problems and questions.

Directed Observation

The general nature of directed observation

Unlike 'interviewing', 'observation' requires that you 'stand away' from the social behaviour or activities that you are attempting to observe and try to see and hear what is actually going on. By observing, you are attempting to gather relevant information in order to understand what people are doing (and perhaps saying to each other) as they go about their business. This is very different from interviewing, where the researcher asks direct questions of the participants about the meaning of their activities. With observation you are not relying on what people say about what they are doing, which might, to some extent, be exaggerated or biased. Rather, you are relying on your own independent account. In this sense observation can be a good check on what interviewees say, while interview data itself can be an effective way of checking the accuracy and veracity of observations. Thus having some elements from each data source in a research project gives the findings and conclusions a firmer basis.

The main kind of observation I recommend here is 'directed observation'. This can be distinguished from what is generally referred to as 'systematic observation' and occasionally termed 'structured observation' (Martin and Bateson 1993). With these latter, a list or inventory of items is decided upon in advance of the research and acts as a schedule for specially trained observers who make a note every time they observe one of the items. This kind of systematic observation is closely associated with psychological studies. For example, Flanders' Interaction Analysis Categories system (Flanders 1970) has been used to build up a picture of classroom activity by recording at 25 second intervals the behaviour of teachers and children according to various predetermined categories, such as when a teacher is praising a child or when pupils are reacting positively or otherwise to the teacher. As can be imagined, systematic or structured observation is especially suited to the generation of quantitative data measuring how much of what kind of interaction events and items of behaviour are observed during the period of the research.

It is unfortunate that these forms of observation have hijacked the terms 'systematic' and 'structured', because although directed observation differs very considerably from them in many respects, it is just as systematic and structured. The main difference is that directed observations are not constrained in advance by operating with predetermined ideas about which detailed items of behaviour are to be observed and counted as evidence. While the researcher is directed by the 'problem-relevance' of what he or she observes, there is much more leeway for the researcher to judge which instances of observed behaviour are relevant. With directed observation the researcher is not trying to catalogue or classify behaviour and ultimately give it mathematical and quantitative precision. Instead, the researcher is trying to interpret and understand what he or she observes, in the whole context of the lives of the people being observed. The observer is attempting to imaginatively reconstruct the meanings that people are giving to their behaviour as they interact with others. In this sense they are trying to make the lives and behaviour of those observed intelligible in terms of qualitative, interpretative data.

Observational roles and vantage points

Before saying more about how directed observation works and what specific kind of data it is directed at, we must consider the types of observational role that can be taken up during observational research. Many methods textbooks contrast systematic or structured observation with what they term 'participant observation'. This contrast seems to imply that participant observation is somehow 'unstructured' or less 'systematic', and as I have already intimated, directed observation must not be seen in this way. The associated implication that it is somehow less 'scientific' than observations that are quantifiable should also be resisted for reasons that will become apparent later in the discussion.

Another major difference is that directed observation does not require the researcher to conceal his or her identity or in any way deceive informants about her or his true research interests. Thus, directed observation is unlike 'complete participant observation' in which the researcher 'becomes' a member of the group studied for the period of the research in order to observe them in a covert manner. In any case, the kinds of topics that require this kind of disguised participation are peculiarly difficult for the first-time researcher to contemplate because they pose large ethical problems (about informed consent) and may also involve physical danger.

Another marked difference from participant observation is that while directed observation requires fairly close contact with a group of people (whose activities are the focus of the research), it does not generally require the researcher to 'become' one of these people or to really 'participate' in their social worlds. Thus, the term 'participant' does not really capture what the researcher is trying to do, which is to get close enough to the activity so as to be able to make sense of it and to understand it while at the same time retaining some degree of detachment.

There may be some rare instances in which directed observation will involve your genuine 'participation' as a researcher. For example, if you happen to be doing temporary/vacation work, and using this as a basis for a research project, say, into fast-food restaurants, or if you were studying friendship or intimacy and drawing on some of your own contact networks. But even in these cases the most important part of your role as researcher concerns your ability to make relevant observations, not the fact of your involvement in the activities you are studying. In this sense, some degree of 'detachment' is necessary for you to make relevant observations

As a directed observer, then, your identity as a researcher is openly recognised in so far as you have gained the full informed consent of those involved. In this sense you are engaging in a kind of 'shadowing' of particular individuals, or a group, in which you bear intimate witness to their routine activities (Czarniawska 2007). Although you should aim to develop sustained and trusting relationships with informants over time, your role as researcher will mean that your relationships and contacts should not limit your ability to investigate as widely as possible. In fact, you must be able to move around freely and observe the most interesting aspects of behaviour and interaction. So the directed observer role is a delicate balance of involvement and detachment, in which you have passionate commitment and interest in particular informants, while retaining a modicum of critical distance and detachment which allows you to view things relatively objectively.

Finally, what does the 'directed' part of the term 'directed observation' mean? This involves a double meaning of the word 'directed'. The first refers to what the observations are *directed by*, while the second meaning focuses on what the observations are *directed to*. I shall go into this in more detail in a later section but here it is important to point out that the first meaning of 'directed' refers to the fact that your observations should be led, informed, and thus 'directed', by your problem- and topic-focus, and the research questions to which they give rise. This is what gives structure and organisation to your observations and makes the whole process systematic. The observations are not simply open-ended – you are not trying to observe absolutely everything. Instead, your attention is focused, you are looking for particular things – those that bear some relevance to your research problem and research questions.

The second meaning of 'directed' refers to the fact that observation should be seen in conjunction with alternative sources of data and information, in this case, interview material. Thus, in this sense, your directed observations can be understood as preliminary explorations as to the 'lay-of-the-land', so to speak, in which you develop ideas, hunches and insights into 'what is going on' in the research site. Your observations lead you to 'read' the meaning of the interaction and behaviour you are witnessing with a view to checking this out later, and elaborating on it through directed interviews with key informants. So a pivotal purpose of directed observation is to identify individuals who might potentially act as useful informants in so far as they might enlighten you on key issues for which you need corroboration, or which you have found puzzling, or are in need of further explanation.

Thus, the function of directed observation is either to supplement prior interviews or to be supplemented by later interviews. Of course, once you have done some interviewing your findings will feed back into any further observations you may make and thus there will be continual, reciprocal influence between observation and interviewing. This ensures systematic cross-checking of data and evidence as well as offering the chance to develop insights and analytic ideas that would add solidity to a project and undergird the veracity of its findings.

Of course, the same sort of cross-checking can occur if you begin data collection with directed interviews, and there is no necessary reason why you should begin with observation. In such a case, the interviews would help you arrive at preliminary ideas that can be checked out through subsequent directed observation. But whichever you start with, the whole point of the process is to achieve the reciprocal interweaving of insights and evidence brought about by the shuttling to and fro between observation and interviews.

How and What to Observe

The first, and probably the most pressing, problem is to reduce the range and scope of observational 'events'/phenomena that are potentially available. You must make the assumption that not everything is of importance otherwise you'll easily become overwhelmed by the sheer volume of observational phenomena that could command your attention. You can reduce potential overload by organising your observations in terms of either 'problem-focused' or 'refined' observations. 'Problem-focused' observations are directly linked to the six problem questions described in Chapters 1 and 3. 'Refined' observations are more closely tailored to the specific research questions that underlie the project.

Problem-focused observations

These are six observational categories corresponding to the key problem-questions. They are: settings; interactions; individuals; context; power; and temporality. In what follows power and temporality are dealt with in the context of the discussion of the other four, while in the later discussion of interviews and conversations, they are dealt with separately.

Settings

We begin with social settings as the main frame for research observations since all social activity – and thus all social research – takes place against the backdrop of a specific type of setting. In this sense, the setting is the location of specific events, sites and social activities arising from the intersection of individuals (their lives, careers, personalities and behaviour) with their day-to-day social interactions. Many settings, such as schools, universities, hospitals, gyms, sport clubs, night clubs, restaurants, shops, factories and bureaucracies, are easily identifiable because they are 'formally' organised. Other settings, such as family and friendship groupings or relationships based on romantic love and sexuality, are more informally organised and thus perhaps less 'identifiable' as settings. Nonetheless, they too are organised in terms of social roles, positions expectations and values. Yet other kinds of settings are halfway between these two, in such fields of activity as the arts, performance and entertainment. As potential research sites, what they all offer are opportunities for observation in terms of typical events and locations.

The central activities in many settings might appear to be located within a single site but it is important to determine whether there are important sub-sites, how many there are, and which ones you want to observe (this of course includes listening to, or overhearing, conversations). For example, studying the work routines of hospital nurses would entail making decisions about which wards to observe, whether you should stay at one nurse's station or move around, whether and which meetings you should attend, where you should eat and have coffee, and so on. Roughly the same sorts of questions would be required if you were studying the staff in a fast-food restaurant. Should you observe their front-of-house behaviour with customers only, or should you mix socially with them at break times or even out of work? Which are the best locations for observing what is going on and overhearing conversations?

The decision to include or exclude particular sites as observational units is important. Certain places might yield different kinds of information because people tend to behave differently in front of different 'audiences'. Of course, decisions about which sites to use depend on other factors, such as 'accessibility' and the extent to which they allow you, as researcher, to be as unobtrusive as possible. Another crucial factor here is whether or not you are successful in gaining permission from key personnel or gatekeepers to move freely around all the relevant research sites.

As far as 'events' are concerned it is necessary to ask yourself – (probably based on preliminary inquiry) which kinds of events are most pertinent to your research concerns. Broadly speaking, events can be classified as continuous, regular (recurrent) or irregular. Many 'formally organised' settings have their own routines and rhythms (Burgess 1984). For instance, activities in hospitals are punctuated by visiting hours, meal times, staff meetings, shift changes, and so on. In schools, there are assemblies, break-times, staffroom interaction as well as classroom interaction. It is as important to sample routine events as it is to observe the more unanticipated or extraordinary ones, such as crises or emergencies.

In more general terms, it is crucial to think about how the setting of the research is socially organised. Particular locations, sites and events can yield information about the nature of the setting in this respect. For example, is there a formal authority hierarchy? How many steps in the hierarchy are there? Is there a flat or steep system of authority positions? What are the official titles of the positions in the hierarchy? Who has power and control over whom? With regard to more informal settings, is there a status structure and system of expectations about role behaviour? In intimate settings, how are relationships regulated? Do lovers and friends exert power and control over one another? What form does this take? All these questions make good subjects for observation, conversations and interviews.

Interactions

Interactions represent the 'main business' of social life as it is enacted in particular sites and locations of social settings. When two or more people come into contact with each other in social settings they are doing a number of things, such as:

- trying to establish or maintain bonds with each other on a personal or official basis through the exchange of conversation, gestures, emotional signals (such as facial expressions and talk about feelings and sensitive topics)

- exchanging practical information crucial for the performance of their tasks, jobs or roles within settings

- creating meaningful exchanges of information about attitudes and feelings towards others – as friends, colleagues, authority figures, employers, customers, and so on

- communicating their authority or power over others or, conversely, their subordination or lack of control over their situation

- establishing or maintaining control over others, based on gender, ethnicity or class, formal position or status, or through personal qualities such as strength of character, attractiveness, and so on

- communicating feelings and emotions about the (personal or work) situation in which they find themselves, or their personal circumstances, or about the other people with whom they are interacting.

Observing interactions in which some of the above are present is crucial for 'getting a feel' of what is happening in a setting. Of course, it may not be possible to simply observe such things, so you must also rely on what you overhear as well as your own conversations and interactions within the setting. As a directed observer, you rely on making close contacts with key informants and establishing trusting relationships with them. This may require that you guarantee them a level of confidentiality, even though they know you are engaged in research and not 'socialising' for the sake of it.

In work settings it is important to distinguish between interactional matters that are part of personal relationships between colleagues and friends and those that have to do with the work itself. These formal and informal aspects of social relationships are often closely bound together in daily encounters between those working in the setting. As such, social interactions in these kinds of settings are often complex combinations of instrumental or practical elements, as well as more emotionally toned ones. It may thus be more difficult to 'read' or interpret the different aspects and levels of

Doing Excellent Small-Scale Research

communication taking place. In more personal settings, such as friendship, family, romance and sexual ties, encounters are to a greater extent formed around diffuse emotional commitments and relationships.

Individuals

Opportunities for the observation of individuals – as well as for direct contact with them – are crucial for establishing what they think and feel, independently of what they say and do, in the company of others. That is, you will have to rely on having one-to-one contacts and conversations with key individuals in order to get at underlying attitudes and feelings which they may prefer not to express publicly. What do you need to know about individuals?

- Who they are and what position or role they hold within the focal setting? In a work setting this may be a formal position of authority, while in 'informal' settings individuals have more leeway to 'negotiate' and create the roles they play with each other in their relationships (such as dominant or passive, understanding, protective, supportive or jealous and undermining, and so on).

- What kind of person are they? What sort of personal power do they have? For example, a charismatic personality or physical attractiveness, or the ability to charm and/or persuade others? What do they lack in terms of personal power? For instance, an inability to empathise with others or to get them on side, a lack of confidence or self-esteem, tactlessness, lack of sensitivity or excessive egotism?

- How have they got where they are? How has their life career unfolded? What motivates them to do what they do? Is the work they are doing what they would wish to do? Is it temporary or permanent work? Is it fulfilling and enjoyable or alienating, boring and a drudge? If the research is about intimacy, you need to know how the individual 'understands' his or her relationships. What views, conceptions of, or attitudes towards love or romance do they have? What do they mean by friendship? What do they expect of a partner?

- What is their self-image and self-identity? How do they deal with social situations? How do they see themselves? How do they think others regard them? Are they aware of their own limitations and shortcomings as well as their strengths?

Of course, many of the above questions cannot be gleaned simply from 'detached' observation. They depend on you, as researcher, establishing fairly close relations with specific individuals and sharing sometimes quite personal information with them. Also, such information is generally imparted over time, when levels of trust have been built up gradually. Thus conversations with, and observations of, such informants must be gleaned sensitively, subtly and should not be forced or rushed.

Context

The wider social context of the setting and the interactions is of critical importance even though its influences may seem vague or remote. It is essential to be aware of the way in which social factors such as gender, ethnicity or class make themselves felt in the situations or events you are observing. Some, but not all, work settings are rife with sexist, racist and homophobic practices, and the discrimination, abuse and bullying that often go with them. Clearly, the wider political and economic climate can influence the working atmosphere and labour relations of particular work settings.

In more informal settings, wider values and ideologies (say, about love and romance, or the nature of family relationships and the morality of friendship) play a prominent role in people's attitudes and social behaviour towards others. The historical development of such values, ideas and ideologies may thus play an important role in present-day issues of trust and commitment, particularly as they are represented in magazines, films, music, newspapers books, and so on.

Refined observations

While problem-focused observations have a general link with problems common to all research, 'refined' observations are more sharply and intensely focused on a specific project. Thus, for example, if your project is centred on the nature of customer and staff relationships in a setting such as a fast-food restaurant or a gym or health club, then your observations will be structured by the research questions behind the project. In this case your research questions would be focused on two issues. First, how the setting itself influences the nature of the staff–customer relationships and, second, how customers and staff interact with each other Thus 'interaction' and 'settings' are the observational categories of most use because of their relevance to your research questions. If the project is centred on the body-image issues of gym or health club users, the main observational areas of interest would be 'individuals' and 'settings', and so on. Whichever of the six general observational categories are of greatest relevance to your research problem and research questions will become the principal areas of interest for you as a researcher, and thus provide a basis for further, more refined observations.

This focusing-in has two principal effects. The first is to yield more sharply defined and more accurately targeted data or information. Second, it makes the researcher aware of gaps in knowledge and information. On these two counts, focusing on more refined questions prompts the researcher to say 'I must find out more about that' or 'I don't really understand what is happening here'.

In this sense, *refined* observations have a close link with *directed* interviews with key informants. That is, refined observations can help suggest questions that may become part of a semi-structured interview schedule. They are thus an important ingredient of your overall investigative strategy. Once you have set up a series of interviews in tandem with directed observation, then the two strategies can operate in parallel with each other, promoting continual feedback. Thus refined observations generate further questions, while directed interviews might suggest new lines of observational inquiry.

Refined observation and interviewing intermesh to form a continuous process of data cross-checking – or *triangulation*. Once underway, the intermeshing allows the researcher to confirm (or disconfirm) data, and the conclusions that may be drawn from them.

Note-Taking: Recording Observations

Observations can only be reliably committed to short-term memory. Impressions of incidents and events fade rapidly, so it is best to try to record them as they happen or as soon as possible thereafter. However, of course, making *mental notes* of things as they happen is essential if you are later to make a more permanent record of them. In this sense you are directing your conscious mind to remembering things you observe – events, things said, conversations, the physical character of the setting, and so on.

However, alongside these mental notes, it is also important to make a more permanent record of your observations while you are still in the field. Thus, when you get the chance you must jot down your thoughts and observations as soon as possible. Depending on circumstances and the types of relationship you have with informants, your note-taking should be either conspicuous or inconspicuous. For example, if you feel that others would find it inappropriate or would object, then you should try to be as discrete as possible. On the other hand, if you feel that those you are studying expect and/or understand why you would want to take notes, then you can even ask them what they think about what you have written. Nevertheless, *jotted notes* should be made *in situ*, at convenient (or inconvenient) times and places such as at coffee breaks, in restrooms, cars and hallways.

Finally, and perhaps most importantly, you should make *full field notes* at the end of a day's observation. These will summarise in full detail what you have jotted down in abbreviated form during the day. But at the same time, you will be 'filling out' these notes with other facts and incidents recalled once you have time to reflect on your field observations. Writing such notes requires personal discipline and commitment since it must be done on a regular basis as soon after the relevant events as possible. Memory fades rapidly. To wait more than a day would involve forgetting and thus losing a massive amount of material.

The full field notes are a chronological account of what is happening in the setting, what the concerns of the main actors are, and how they deal with one another. However, the notes should also include an account of your own involvement in the setting. You must be reflexive in your accounts of observations, in the sense of considering how your own involvement has impinged on the behaviour of others, and the assumptions you are making about what people are doing and saying. Overall, the notes should consist of running descriptions of events, and people, things heard and overheard, conversations among people, conversations with individuals, accounts of observed activities and incidents, and so on.

Field notes should not be confused with entries in your Research Log. While some of the things you write in field notes might eventually make their way into your Research Log, they will take on a different form. Field notes should mainly consist of the raw, unanalysed evidence you have gleaned from observations or interviews. Entries in your Research Log will consist of more reflective and 'worked on' thoughts about the meaning of data and the concepts and arguments that will help to explain them.

Directed Interviews and Conversations

Many of the considerations applying to directed observation are also relevant to directed interviews and conversations, for they too are significantly influenced by research problems and questions. Of course, with interviews you are not relying on independent observational accounts garnered from your experiences in the field. Instead of adopting the somewhat 'detached' stance of observer, you enter into a genuine dialogue with specific individuals in order to find out what they reckon they are doing, how they feel about it, and why they are doing it. And, in the same sense that interviews act as a check on observations, observations themselves provide a means of checking the truthfulness and accuracy of what people say in interviews.

What I am calling 'directed interviews' (I'll deal with conversations separately) can be distinguished from 'structured interviews' associated with quantitative methods of research (such as questionnaire surveys). In these, interviewees are asked to choose from a range of pre-formulated answers to pre-structured questions. The interviewee has no freedom or leeway to answer questions in the way she or he wishes. Rather, the questions and the range of possible answers are determined in advance by the researcher. As with structured observations, structured interviews are especially suited to the generation of quantitative data and analysis. Again, however, calling them 'structured' interviews is no indication that they are in fact more systematic or scientific than 'directed interviews'.

As with observations, directed interviews are not as constrained in advance as structured interviews. Interview questions are not absolutely predetermined. There is some leeway for the researcher to ask questions that arise out of the conversational exchange of the interview itself, rather than have them rigidly set out prior to the interview. In this sense, what I am calling *directed* interviews have a lot in common with what are variously referred to in the methods literature as 'in-depth', 'semi-structured' or 'intensive' interviews (Bryman 2008; Denscombe 2007; Robson 2007). However, these terms are not really suitable for present purposes because they do not refer to the problem-focused nature of 'directed interviewing'. That is, in directed interviews the questions are shaped and influenced by the problem-focus of the research and the 'problem-' and 'topic-' questions that flow from it (see Chapter 3).

Apart from this obvious difference of emphasis, there are certain overlaps with semi-structured, in-depth and intensive interviewing. For example, with the latter, the interviewer does not impose questions or make assumptions about people's lives. He or she approaches the interview as a process of 'discovering' information or knowledge about a person's feelings, behaviour, attitudes, experiences, and so on. The interview is 'structured' by an interview guide (rather than a predetermined schedule) which allows the interviewer to elicit responses that the informant considers to be important. In that sense it resembles a guided conversation. The overall design of the interview guide consists of the main topics that the interviewer wishes to discuss. These main topics can be broken down into more detailed subsections, but essentially they are reminders or prompts for the interviewer.

Personal style and interviewing skills

The flexibility of directed interviewing results from the fact that when the interviewer finds that the interviewee is particularly forthcoming, revealing or informative about a topic, he or she is free to pursue the implications of this by flexibly constructing the interview around the fact. Of course, each person you interview will feel comfortable with a certain style of talk or conversation, with some being naturally very chatty, while others may be less forthcoming. Whatever the case, you will have to adjust your own style in order to obtain the best quality of information from particular individuals. In this regard, having appropriate interviewing skills will help you get the best out of particular informants. Nevertheless, because of this, interviews will never be completely standardised. Rather, they will vary in terms of how flexible and productive they turn out to be.

Indeed, the success or otherwise of such interviewing depends a good deal on how well you 'get on' with the person you are interviewing. Of course, this in turn depends on your general ability to empathise and to develop trust and rapport. A good interviewer must have a fair amount of 'emotional intelligence' (Goleman 1996; Layder 2004b). This requires that you are able to 'read' others emotions, to identify accurately the emotional state they are in, and to respond accordingly. Major clues, in this regard, tend to come from non-verbal communications – eye contact, gestures, body movements, intonation, and so on. Sometimes, maintaining rapport requires 'mirroring' a person's feelings along with empathy and sympathy. However, more often than not a safer option is to adopt a neutral, non-critical or non-judgemental attitude towards a 'sensitive' interviewee.

Of course, at the same time, it is essential to maintain a critical stance towards the 'information' interviewees impart. You must ask yourself what image of him or herself is this person trying to portray, what resentments or grudges do they hold towards others? What biases, values or judgements are implicit in how they describe their situation, the employer they work for, or their relations with colleagues are important questions to bear in mind in evaluating their responses. Unearthing inconsistencies in what an interviewee is saying and being able to detect when they are being boastful or deliberately diffident are equally crucial skills when it comes to assessing the reliability of an informant.

What are directed interviews directed towards?

The questions you ask in directed interviews, although not standardised or rigidly set out in advance, will nevertheless be directed (and thus 'structured') by your problem-focus and the research questions that follow from it. As a consequence, your interview questions will be directed towards eliciting information relevant to the research problem and thus throw light on it. In this sense, directed interviews will be framed by the same six general categories and concerns that were relevant to directed observation: settings; interactions; individuals; context; power; and temporality.

Thus, it is pertinent to re-read the earlier section on 'how and what to observe' for a general characterisation of the main categories or frames that are required in interviewing. Of course, this time you must think of the sorts of questions they raise and which questions you can ask of particular interviewees. You must keep in mind here the fact that the issue of sampling – the type and number of people you need to interview – will also play a part in how you formulate your questions and interview schedules (sampling will be dealt with in the next chapter).

As is also the case with observation, there are two types of directed interviewing – 'problem-focused' and 'refined' interviewing. The first type is influenced by the six problem-related categories just mentioned.

With regard to *settings*, directed interviews would focus on the nature of the social organisation of the research site and how it influences the social activities of those within. How does power and control operate in the setting? Are there formal positions of authority, or are they informally organised? What do informants think of this and how do they respond to the strategies and controlling ploys of others?

In relation to *interactions*, the important considerations are: what kinds of interactions (encounters) are interviewees involved in? What is their experience of encounters? Are they characterised by tension and conflict or harmony and cooperation? Why are they like this? How do the participants regulate their interactions? How do they feel emotionally? What are their experiences of dealing with others in particular situations?

As far as *individuals* are concerned, the researcher/interviewer would want to investigate how particular interviewees feel about their position in the research setting? Are they comfortable? Are their ambitions fulfilled? Do they want to get out of, or move on from, a work situation or an intimate relationship? Why? Do they have the personal resources, such as confidence and self-esteem, to cope? Are they able to deal with others?

Attention to the *context* requires the interviewer to examine the political, economic and factors that may influence individuals in the setting. How do social class, gender, ethnicity, age, and so on, impact on the day-to-day lives of those within particular settings?

Questions around *power* are to some extent covered in an examination of the nature of the setting. However, there are many other aspects of power, including personal or subjective power, the powers deriving from social background and membership of wider social groups, as well as interpersonal power embedded in social encounters. How do these different aspects of power influence behaviour and social activity?

Finally, temporality is addressed in interviews by asking questions about how things change over time? Is the setting organised in terms of its own organisational rhythms – routine events and processes, for example? How are participant's self-identities impacted? Historically, how have larger-scale social changes impacted on the setting?

The second type, the *refined* interview, is about asking questions more directly targeted at your specific problem-focus and research questions. This type of interview is especially important when viewed in conjunction with refined observation. Refined observation often reveals gaps in information and poses questions that can be investigated through interviews. Conversely, as directed interviews become more refined, they may also raise issues – gaps in information, puzzles about the meaning of behaviour and events – that can be further checked out by observation. Once interviewing and observation are in train, they feed off and into one another, and have the effect of posing new questions as well as confirming or disconfirming existing findings.

Directed conversations

Directed conversations are very useful supplementary forms of interview which are best conducted in conjunction with field observations. That is, while a researcher is actively engaged in observation, he or she naturally comes across individuals who are clearly important sources of information about what is going on. They might be people you have identified in advance as relevant or key participants. Conversely, they may be individuals that you didn't previously realise were important but who you now realise are crucial or have suddenly come to your attention. Any conversations you have with such individuals may, in fact, become important points of connection between your observations and more 'formal' interviews. This may be because the directed conversations you have might serve as preludes to later, more detailed directed interviews with them. Alternatively, they may remain 'casual' or 'passing' conversations, but the information gained from them may feed into subsequent directed interviews with other informants.

Directed conversations are *unlike* directed interviews in several respects. Directed interviews generally rest on making appointments with specific individuals whom you have chosen as part of your sample of informants. You agree with your interviewee a time and place to meet to conduct the interview, and you enter the situation armed with specific questions and topics. As such, you might also ask the interviewee's consent to let you record the interview on audio-tape, or make written notes to record what is said. Directed conversations, by contrast, occur more casually and opportunistically, that is, you make contact with potential informants by taking practical advantage of their chance 'availability' at particular times and places. Of course, you must inform them of your research interests and secure their consent to be interviewed, just as in a regular directed interview. Furthermore, this might involve some impromptu pleading and subtle persuasion on your behalf.

In this sense your relationship with such informants will be more casual or informal. Because of the chance nature of the encounter, you might not have an interview guide, a tape-recorder or a notebook with you, and so you will be reliant both on figuring out the most strategic questions to ask as well as remembering the conversational exchange as accurately as possible. Of course, in terms of questions, you will not be simply making things up on the spur of the moment, or plucking questions out of the air. The notion of a directed conversation rests on the assumption of your ready familiarity with the general interview topics (and categories of observation) that are most pertinent to your problem-focus and general research questions. If you are, it should be relatively easy for you to direct the conversation along these lines. However, your confidence may well be dependent upon how much previous experience and success you have had in conducting interviews.

Recording Interviews

In order to get an 'objective' record of what is said in an interview, it is beneficial to make an audio-tape of it. Of course, permission from the interviewee must be obtained beforehand, and sometimes – for a host of possible reasons – he or she may not want this. In this case you are left with no option but to make notes from memory as soon after the interview as possible. If consent to audio-tape is obtained, then it is still advisable to make notes to accompany the interview so that you can amplify and contextualise what goes on, over and above the actual words themselves. Things such as the physical location of the interview and how it may impinge on its content, interruptions by others, and so on, are important in understanding what is being conveyed. Notes can also be a valuable way of indicating non-verbal communication and the emotional states that play a role in clarifying the difference between *what is said* and *what is meant* in interviews.

The best place for accompanying notes is alongside transcriptions of the audio-tapes. There are several advantages in having fully transcribed interviews at your disposal. For example, they are the best form for identifying which strips of talk are the most important pieces of data or evidence in terms of throwing light on your research problems and questions. Transcriptions also make it easier to choose extracts for quotation in your research report. On the other hand, transcribing tapes is a very time-consuming activity. So unless you can afford to employ others to do this for you, it can eat up time that in all probability will be better spent on other things. It is also important not to accumulate endless piles of interview data on the assumption that the more you collect, the greater will be the benefit in the long run. This is not true. Collecting too much data, without assessing its analytic importance, is frequently the cause of confusion for a researcher – particularly for the first-time researcher.

In order to avoid problems that may arise if you amass too much data, or when you are tempted to simply collect more and more data without reflecting on its importance, it is probably best to do the following. Transcribe your initial interviews so that you have some concrete written data to work with. However, once you have thoroughly explored the problem-categories that frame your central research questions, it is wise to stop transcribing. If you need to do further interviews – to clarify points, amplify evidence, and so on – then do so without transcribing them. Retain the tapes to refer back to, if needed. From memory, make a note of the sections that are of greatest importance to help in finding them again, should you need to go back to them either for reference or to lift extracts to present in your final report.

Documentary Sources

Personal documents

As I have indicated, it is of decisive importance to use a mixture of strategies and methods – a multi-strategy approach (Layder 1993, 1997) – in order to increase the relevance and validity of research findings. Because single-method approaches are inherently one-dimensional, they are likely to give a rather constricted picture of social life. Thus documentary materials are very useful additional, or supplementary, sources of data that are best used in conjunction with observations and interviews. On their own, documentary materials can only offer a very thin, insubstantial view of social life and social processes – as would any mono-method research.

However, drawing on as many data sources as possible (or feasible) does not require you to gather excessive amounts of data. Although you may draw from two or three (possibly four) data sources, you will actually end up collecting roughly the same volume of data as if you used only one source. In this respect, each source will utilise relatively small but strongly focused data samples, but the overall sample will be the combined total from the different sources. Instead of weakening the research sample as a whole, in fact you are increasing its strength by enhancing its triangulating capacity. That is, the validity of the overall sample (and the data as a whole) is also correspondingly increased.

It is important to assess the general credibility of particular documents (Scott 1990). That is, we have to ask who has written or produced the document, what their interests are, and what message or information is being communicated or conveyed by it. In these respects, we must judge whether the document is accurate and whether it contains any biases, misleading information and assumptions. However, most important for present purposes is the 'problem-relatedness' of the document. That is, the usefulness, validity and adequacy of any document must be judged in terms of the extent to which it is capable of providing insight into the problem-focus and research questions of the project. In other words, the usefulness of particular documents is measured in terms of their capacity to illuminate various aspects of social settings, interactions, individuals, power and temporality.

Diaries, letters and memos

Unless they appear in published form, an initial difficulty in using diaries, letters and memos is that of obtaining consent to use them. Of course, if they are published, there is no problem with gaining consent, but then another equally thorny problem presents itself. This resides in the reliability of personal documents as 'objective' accounts of the events they purport to record. The writer's account will always be greatly influenced by his or her own personal point of view, ambitions, foibles and weaknesses as well as his or her strengths and virtues. That is, it is inevitable that they will put some personal gloss on the things they report because it directly reflects their self-identity and personality. If the researcher is aware of such elements entering into diaries, letters and memos, then he or she can take care to navigate around them while making good use of them as evidence.

As *personal accounts*, such documents may reveal personal attitudes, meanings and aspirations and thus may be invaluable as sources that help in throwing light on the experiences of particular individuals, particularly how self-identity and personal powers develop or change over time. They may be somewhat less reliable as accounts of 'what actually went on' or 'what happened' on the occasions or during the events under consideration. The egotism of the writer may render an account from his or her point of view, rather than a neutral one.

Research diaries – as opposed to *personal diaries* – where participants or informants are requested by the researcher to keep a record of certain incidents, events or experiences, do not pose the same dangers of distortion or the 'glossing' of events. Also, while personal diaries may well yield rich sources of data, they are usually qualitative in form. On the other hand, depending on the requirements of the researcher and the project, research diaries may be a source of quantitative data, such as the incidence and type of event that an individual is experiencing (for example, movements in and out of labour markets, see Layder et al. 1991).

Biographies and autobiographies

These suffer from similar shortcomings to those of personal diaries, letters and memos. That is, authors may embellish accounts in a way that offers a favourable impression of their own behaviour (see also Scott 1990: 174–85). But also, as I have pointed out, the personal nature of such accounts makes them likely to be unreliable representations of the contributions played by others in particular events and encounters. Nevertheless, biographies and autobiographies may provide valuable sources of data on historical developments and changes.

Newspapers and magazines

The press and various other publications can be useful as resources for research. However, they can be distinguished in terms of the reliability, accuracy and objectivity of the information they contain. Thus, for example, 'broad sheet' newspapers will frequently contain reports of research (sometimes academically based research) that is pertinent to a research project. Similarly, they may provide reports and accounts of public events or private incidents that are interesting, illuminating and reliable for research purposes. At the other end of the spectrum, the 'tabloid' newspapers cannot be relied upon as accurate sources of information or impartial views.

As far as magazines and journals are concerned, the same distinction applies. Many high-circulation 'magazines' (such as fashion, popular music or celebrity magazines) are too often heavily reliant, or even overtly based, on hearsay and gossip to be reliable as 'objective' sources of information. On the other hand, more serious journals contain noteworthy accounts that are generally factual and reliable.

However, to dismiss tabloid newspapers and popular high-circulation magazines out of hand would be to miss out on some sources of potentially interesting and important data. For example, a research project might want to seriously analyse some aspect of popular culture, such as the social or social psychological impact of fashion, popular music or celebrity culture, or the role and function of gossip in these areas of social life. In such cases, these publications may well be interesting sources of information in so far as they reveal current attitudes, influences and trends. As long as the researcher retains his or her critical awareness with regard to the veracity of various sources and journalistic pieces, then such resources become a more viable source of documentary data. In particular, it is important to be able to distinguish between the 'opinions' and 'subjective preferences' of journalists, and to be able to identify spurious 'arguments' based merely on gossip or tittle-tattle as opposed to those substantiated by accredited evidence and data on particular aspects of popular culture.

Secondary Analyses

Observational and interview data

By using data collected for other projects you might be able to supplement, reinforce or extend your own data. This would be a secondary analysis of the data in the service of your own project. For example, during your selective literature review you may come across published research that presents interesting data and analysis. It might not be on the same topic as your project, nor might you agree with the author's analysis or conclusions, but you recognise the data could be re-used to illustrate an alternative conclusion, perhaps, or that the same data could be reanalysed in a different way in relation to a different set of problems or questions.

For instance, a data set could be reanalysed in terms of the key problem issues around the six problem categories. Or you might want to reanalyse the data according to the specific topic-questions that concern you. An example from my own work concerns a study of intimacy and power (Layder 2009). I examined and reanalysed interview data with couples on the nature of their relationships. The data was originally collected on various aspects of intimacy, but I reanalysed it to illustrate the nature of power and control between couples. In this sense the data complemented the concerns and issues relevant to my own project.

Explanatory frameworks

Explanatory frameworks can also be considered as forms of 'secondary' analysis. In all probability, your selective review of existing research studies will have revealed a number of possible ways of handling, analysing and even interpreting data. Sometimes these are referred to as 'theoretical' or 'conceptual' frameworks and offer the researcher ways of organising their data. We have already encountered examples of this in Chapter 2, where Ritzer (2011) uses Max Weber's theory of bureaucratisation to study the main elements of fast-food restaurants like McDonald's. Inglis (1998) drew upon theories of status conflict in order to understand how and why The Beatles sacked their first drummer. My own study of intimacy (Layder 2009) draws upon the wider framework of 'domain theory' both to throw light on the nature of intimacy between couples and to extend the explanatory power of the theory.

Of course, this is not mandatory. You don't have to use a ready-made framework with which to analyse and organise your data. It's a matter of judgement – mainly concerning its appropriateness and relevance – whether you adopt (or even modify) an existing framework to guide you through the analysis of data. The main argument against sticking hard and fast to a preconceived framework is that it inhibits your own creativity and originality by providing pre-established categories, concepts, explanations, and so on, to analyse the data. If the point of research is to find things out, to discover aspects of the social world that weren't known beforehand, then surely adopting an analytic framework before you've begun the research simply undermines this aim. You can't know in advance what you set out to discover through research!

There is some sense in this argument. For example, if you allow an existing framework of explanation to simply 'take over', and let it *predetermine* your results, then it places a big limitation on the quality of the research. Adopting an explanatory framework in advance can hinder excellent research. However, this can also lead you to overlook the usefulness of certain concepts and explanatory devices. In fact, in some cases, a dogmatic rejection of preconceived frameworks can do the opposite of what is intended – it can stifle and stultify creativity. However, a selective and judicious use of bits of existing theories and frameworks can enhance, extend and otherwise strengthen research projects, as the examples of Ritzer's, Inglis's and my own work show. This can be done without crushing the creativity of the researcher or removing the possibility of making genuine discoveries during the research process. So while it is important to be careful and sensitive when engaging in this kind of 'borrowing' from other frameworks and concepts, it is also the case that it can often lead to very fruitful results.

Conclusion: Enhancing Validity

'Triangulation' refers to strengthening a study through the use of multiple methods to study a single problem (Denzin 1989; Patton 2001). The approach developed in this book has triangulation built into its basic assumptions (Layder 1993) in so far as the use of multiple strategies, sources and methods work towards enhancing the reliability, validity and generality of findings. Using as many sources of qualitative data, methods and strategies (observations, interviews, documents and secondary sources) as practically feasible allows the researcher to produce a dense and comprehensive coverage of the data. In turn, the denser the empirical coverage, the surer one can be about the validity of the findings and the stronger will be the evidence on which to base explanations.

Of course a project itself is defined and limited by its *problem-focus* and the core research questions its poses – and these will determine the range of your choices about strategies, methods and data sources. In all probability, you will not be able to focus on all six of the problem foci (setting, interaction, individuals, context, power and temporality) within the same project, even though it may be advantageous to bear them all in mind in a general sense. Thus you must 'selectively focus' on two or three of these 'problem categories' in any single research project.

The specific importance of qualitative data is that they are a valuable source of information on social behaviour and social processes occurring in social domains and the key problem-questions they raise. In this regard, qualitative data allow for a more in-depth analysis of information-rich 'cases' or 'units of analysis', as compared with quantitative studies with larger samples and data sets. These latter may yield a larger amount information over a broader population range, but offer little insight into underlying processes of social interaction. Qualitative data can provide insights into the meaning for the participants of particular forms of social behaviour, and how episodes or chains of interaction build up over time and the manner in which they both affect, and are influenced by, social settings and contexts. The adaptive approach can be employed either as a complement or an alternative to existing qualitative approaches such as grounded theory, case studies, action research and forms of qualitative analysis more generally (Houston & Mullen-Jenson 2011).

However, as the next chapter will show, the adaptive approach is equally compatible – and has been used in conjunction with – various forms of quantitative data. In fact, I suggest that the most important application of quantitative data is in conjunction with qualitative data and analysis. Although the issues of sampling and sample size are discussed in detail in Chapter 7, the following chapter raises some of the implications of sampling in projects that attempt to blend and integrate the traditionally different quantitative and qualitative analyses.

Checklist for Research Log

- What specific combination of qualitative methods and data sources is appropriate?

- What qualitative data is available to you?

- What sorts of 'directed observations' will you target and which observational role(s) will you adopt?

- Be aware of the distinction between 'problem-focused' and 'refined' observation.

- How will you record observational data?

- Will you use directed interviews and conversations? What skills will you need and how will you record your data?

- What sorts of documentary sources are available and relevant?

- What secondary sources and analyses will you use?

- Are you employing an explanatory framework?

- How will you triangulate qualitative data method and strategy?

6

QUANTITATIVE DATA & MIXED STRATEGIES

PREVIEW

This chapter covers the following:

- Quantitative data and secondary analysis
- Questionnaire surveys and social domains
- Constructing questionnaire surveys
- Problems with the survey as a mono-method
- Using quantitative data in multi-strategy research
- Variations in multi-strategy designs

Remember the adaptive approach can be used with quantitative data either in the context of 'mono–method' research or, *together* with qualitative data, strategy and methods in various blends or mixtures. This chapter describes some of the possibilities in this regard. It begins by describing the main forms and sources of quantitative data and how they may be used to throw light on the key problem–questions that drive adaptive research. This is followed by a discussion of the questionnaire survey in mono–method research, along with the more general advantages and disadvantages of questionnaire surveys. The rest of the chapter describes some productive ways of blending or mixing quantitative and qualitative data in small–scale research.

Quantitative Data and Secondary Analysis

Different types of quantitative data can be used for investigating the key problem–questions from a social domains perspective. These are (1) 'free–standing' quantitative data, (2) governmental or 'official' statistics, and (3) other (often professional) researchers' data.

Free-standing quantitative data

'Free-standing' data are distinguishable from the other two types by the fact that they are not produced by governmental sources or by the professional social research community. There is a range of different types within this category. For example, there are many examples of market research organisations, such as Mintel, CIPS, Markit, which endeavour to provide 'intelligence' (statistics, information and market research) on various social activities related to areas such as the food industry, the financial industry, the leisure industry, and so on. Equally, many business organisations produce their own internal research and audits, or solicit external consultations, which are often published and/or are accessible to the public. Similarly, artistic organisations linked with theatre, film and music frequently generate quantitative data through internal and external audits, statistics and research, for example, surveys of pay, salaries and working conditions.

It is always important to bear in mind questions about the credibility and reliability of such data (see later comments). Nevertheless, quantitative data of this kind can play a valuable role in adaptive research since it attempts to combine and integrate it with qualitative data. In this regard, free-standing quantitative data provides a fuller picture of social organisational features and processes (settings and contexts) that can be used to complement qualitative data which emphasises individual behaviour and/or social interaction. The mixture of data types and sources thus gives an impression of how organisational and interactional features combine in social life.

For example, Mintel provides quantitative measures of British gym ownership and gym use. The quantitative data generated by Mintel on gym ownership and gym use (C. Johnston in *The Times* 2011) could be used most profitably in conjunction with the kind of small-scale project mentioned in previous chapters. For example, in relation to the market share of the top seven gym operators (accounting for 23 per cent of clubs and 39 per cent of members), the smallest is Nuffield Health, with 51 clubs and 150,000 members, and the largest is David Lloyd Gyms, with 79 clubs and 450,000 members. Mintel also describes the threefold categorisation of gym and health club users, and potential target user groups, such as:

1 The 'Fit' category refers to men in both younger and older age groups who are wealthy/affluent and tech-savvy. From this group, 26 per cent use a health and fitness club.

2 The 'Healthy in Mind' category refers to the 25–54 age range, those who are less affluent, and parents. From this group, 16 per cent use a health and fitness club.

3   The 'Inactive' category refers to women in the 25–34 age range, parents, over 65s/retired/affluent. Of this group, 6 per cent use a health and fitness club.

Such quantitative information helps the researcher 'block-in' the background parameters of gym use (its social–organisational aspects) in the form of demographic data on the users, and the characteristics of the groups that are targeted by the operators to increase their share of the market.

Other quantitative measures provided by Mintel regarding the main activities of health and fitness club users give some indication of the nature of gyms as social settings – their internal structure and characteristics. As a result, we are also given some inkling of the kinds of interaction that might take place within the social settings of gyms, as well as the personal goals, preferences and aspirations of individual users. This kind of data can be used as a template against which qualitative data or information may serve as a validity check, or to provide analytic elaboration on the interactional dynamics underlying the bare figures. The breakdown of activities (and their 'categorisation') in percentage terms, provided by Mintel, was as follows:

percentage figure	category
70 per cent	Exercised within the gym/fitness area
48 per cent	Any swimming
44 per cent	Swimming on my own
29 per cent	Any class
27 per cent	Taken part in fitness class
23 per cent	Any indoor sport
21 per cent	Swimming with family or friends
18 per cent	Bought from café/restaurant
16 per cent	Played indoor racquet sport
12 per cent	Played another indoor sport
12 per cent	Used a personal trainer
12 per cent	Used the health and beauty facilities
9 per cent	Taken part in a relaxation class
1 per cent	Taken part in a martial arts class

Depending on which problem–questions are driving your project, quantitative information of this kind can feed into your thinking about them. For example, the figures indicate the extent to which people engage in activities that involve close cooperation/collaboration with others (those taking 'classes' or 'swimming with family and/or friends', for example) or use public/collective facilities (such as the restaurant, café or health and beauty facilities). These activities clearly relate to problem-question 2 – the nature and dynamics of social interaction and the way in which it influences social behaviour within particular settings. The quantitative data also signals individuals' priorities. This includes, for example, preferring to use the fitness centre for socialising or maintaining social bonds rather than a concern with body image, fitness or weight-control issues. The rates of more solitary activities ('swimming on my own' or exercising within the gym) indicate a concern with issues about body image, fitness or weight control and thus are more relevant to problem-question 1 – to do with personal identity and social involvement.

When used alongside qualitative data, such as directed interviews and/or observations in gyms, such quantitative measures can stimulate ideas, hypotheses and concepts about social activities within these settings. In this sense, using quantitative and qualitative data in a *complementary* fashion allows them to reciprocally influence each other and may give rise to new analytic ideas, concepts and explanations.

Official statistics

Official statistics offer another type of quantitative information that can be employed as complementary background for qualitative data on social behaviour. The Office for National Statistics produces *Social Trends* (2010), which includes key official (government) statistics covering areas of social life such as labour markets, education, crime and justice, transport, house-holds and families, lifestyles, and so on. Also, official statistics in the form of census data and registrations of births, marriages and deaths are a valuable source of background information on social settings and contexts. In general, such statistics offer a wide variety of social indicators, including the gender and ethnic composition of various labour market segments, rates of work remuneration, criminal activity, alcohol and drug consumption, waiting lists for hospital appointments, and so on.

Depending on 'what' these documents record, they may be regarded as more or less impartial (and hence reliable and valid) indicators of a factual reality. For example, birth and death rates, marriage, cohabitation and divorce are phenomena about which there is little disagreement. However, other social phenomena, such as levels of poverty or unemployment, can be measured in terms of different – sometimes competing – criteria which can make a big difference to the figures and what they 'mean' or 'show'.

Crime figures are famously subject to such disputes, depending on how the figures or rates themselves are constructed. For example, rates for particular crimes may vary because of under-reporting by members of the public or because some crimes are given a low priority by the police, and so on. Much crime, therefore, goes unrecorded. Suicide statistics are also subject to disputation for similar or parallel reasons. Where there are problems of measurement, whether with the definition of what counts as the phenomenon of interest or where there are vested interests involved, then such statistics have to be treated with caution (Bryman 2008; Denscombe 2007).

Nevertheless, the quantitative measures provided by official statistics can provide a useful platform on which to develop ideas, particularly about the settings and contexts of specific social activities. As a consequence, they may feed into ideas about the problem-focus, design and direction of research projects, especially those using quantitative and qualitative data to complement each other.

Secondary data from professional research

Published data by professional (usually university-based) researchers completes this trio of quantitative data sources. Data from such research can be found either in professional journals or in data archives (such as the UK Data Archive at the University of Essex or the Australian Social Science Data Archive). Along with free-standing data and official statistics, this kind of data can be considered as *secondary data* and can be used in conjunction with *primary data* perhaps gathered for an original small-scale project. In this regard, then, all three sources offer quantitative data suitable for *secondary analysis* – that is reanalysing the data in relation to your own research problems and questions.

Bryman (2008a: 296) has pointed out the advantages of secondary analysis, especially for undergraduate students doing small-scale research projects, but also for postgraduates doing more substantial pieces of research. First, it allows access to data sets of high quality which students would not be in a position to produce on their own because of lack of time, money and expertise. Moreover, because secondary analysis uses existing data sets, the need for data collection is eliminated and hence the researcher is able to spend more time on *analysis*. This creates the opportunity for the researcher to come up with novel interpretations of the data.

The data sets used in secondary analysis, especially those produced by professional social scientific researchers, are of a particular high quality. That is, they are usually based on large (often national) samples that have been rigorously selected and are thus 'as close to being representative as one is likely to achieve'. This is especially important since the 'representativeness' of the sample ensures rigour and validity in survey analysis. In this respect, student projects couldn't even get 'close to the coverage that such data sets attain' (Bryman 2008a: 297). Moreover, many of these data sets have been generated by highly experienced researchers, a fact which provides another check on the quality and validity of the data.

Questionnaire Survey Research into Social Domains

Many of the data sets discussed in the previous section have been generated by questionnaire surveys. There are several different ways in which quantitative data from questionnaire surveys can be used fruitfully in the context of the adaptive approach. One of these is to use a survey as the main method of data collection.

An example of this is Pruulmann-Vengerfeldt's (2006) study of the development of information technology in Estonia which is based on three large-scale surveys conducted by the Universities of Tartu and Sodertorn in 2002, 2004 and 2005. The surveys had large samples (1,500 respondents), which were representative of the whole population and were randomly selected from 150 survey points. Estonia offers a unique case for investigating the information society. It is a small country of 1.4 million people but is one of the fastest-developing economies in the former Soviet bloc and is in the process of managing the transition from a totalitarian system to an open society.

Pruulmann-Vengerfeldt is sceptical about the extent to which the development of the information society can be measured simply in terms of the adoption of technology. Instead, the author suggests that more complex forms of measurement can be achieved by using the data from the surveys in conjunction with the analysis of social domains (Layder 1997).

The domain of psychobiography (the intermeshing of individual and social life) is reflected in survey data on individuals' attitudes towards information technology in Estonia. For example, do individuals have positive or negative attitudes to the use of new machines and technology? Does access to computers and the internet makes life easier or more enjoyable? Generally, Pruulmann-Vengerfeldt found that Estonians are very technology-optimistic: they like technology-related changes and think of the internet as necessary for the betterment of the world.

According to Pruulmann-Vengerfeldt, the influence of situated activity (interaction) is related to survey data on the extent to which people with particular lifestyles (for example, 'home-centred' as compared with 'thrill and entertainment-oriented' lifestyles) engage in computer-related activities (games, chat-rooms, creating web pages, music). It was possible to identify the lifestyle groups that are more likely to adopt information technology, with the more 'traditional' lifestyles being the least responsive in this respect.

The influence of 'social settings' was measured 'through computer adoption in the workplace, the availability and use of Open Internet Access points, and the availability and use of computers among friendship groups' (Pruulmann-Vengerfeldt 2006: 5). That Estonia has definitely moved towards an information society is indicated by the 'high level use of instant messaging technologies' which suggests that computer-mediated communication has become an important setting for discussions. In the initial survey of 2003, instant messaging was of marginal importance and used by the youngest age group. By 2005 the use of instant messaging technology had reached one-third of the whole population and its use had spread through different groups.

The influence of 'contextual resources' – the overall societal context in which we work and act (including the economic and legislative environment) – can be measured by the extent of the general availability of the internet, broadband access and speed of international connections as well as the laws that support information society developments. How the Estonian media constructs the general discourses around the new technologies and Estonia as an 'information society' is also important. Pruulmann-Vengerfeldt found that the major types of discourse are 'happy' and 'optimistic' and geared towards very positive attitudes for an Estonian information society.

Constructing Questionnaire Surveys

There are obvious problems standing in the way of using national or large-scale surveys in the context of small-scale research. For such surveys to be 'representative' and the results statistically significant, they must be based on fairly large samples. But large-scale surveys like those in the Estonian study involve considerable time, money and expertise. As a result, they are just not a practically feasible option for many, if not most, small-scale projects. This simply reinforces the point about the usefulness and appeal of secondary analysis. Using existing data sets from professional researchers and organisations and reanalysing them is highly cost-effective.

Of course, this does not prevent surveys of more modest scope and scale being harnessed to small-scale research objectives. Below I set out some *general* issues and *basic* elements of the survey method. More detailed discussions, such as how to present results, or technical questions, such as multivariate analysis, tests of statistical significance, interval scales and so on, may be found in Denscombe (2007), Bryman (2008) and Bell (2010).

Surveys are based on 'questionnaires' which ask a series of standardised questions about a particular topic, or topics, the answers to which are elicited from a rigorously selected group of people. A questionnaire is devised and designed and then sent out to individuals to self-complete or to fill in during a face-to-face or telephone interview. The questionnaire itself consists of direct questions – or statements – to which the individual responds by choosing from a fixed set of alternatives (such as 'agree', 'disagree' or 'don't know'). To facilitate the process of turning these responses into numeric data, the researcher codes the answers in terms of categories decided in advance.

The most appropriate wording of questions is important, but largely boils down to common sense. The overriding issue is to achieve maximum clarity for the respondent. Thus questions should be expressed in a positive manner because negatively phrased questions will be difficult to understand. 'Leading' questions (those which tend to suggest a particular answer) obviously should be avoided where possible. It is also essential to make sure that each question sticks to one issue at a time (rather than evoking multiple responses in the individual), as is good design of the questionnaire and detailed planning of how it is to be administered. Ethical issues intrude here. Of central significance is that respondents must be freely willing to complete the questionnaire and not forced in any way.

Surveys and data sampling

Traditionally, in survey research it is assumed that the sample of people who will answer the questionnaire must be carefully selected so that they are 'representative' of the wider population from which they are drawn. In this regard, each member of this wider population must have an equal chance (or 'probability' – hence a 'probability sample') of being included in the sample. Because survey research is concerned with the population representativeness of the sample and the ability to generalise findings from the sample to the population, the response rate is crucial. A low response rate (under 70 per cent) makes it difficult to generalise with confidence from the sample to the wider population.

As far as sample size is concerned, market research companies and opinion polls use national samples of between 1,000 and 2,000 people. However, frequently small-scale research involves between 30 and 250 cases (Denscombe 2007: 28). With the latter, attention should be paid to the question of whether the sample is representative, and caution should be observed when attempting to generalise from the findings. Nevertheless, as Denscombe notes, 'provided that the limitations are acknowledged and taken into account, the limited size of the sample need not invalidate the findings' (2007: 28). However, as Denscombe also points out, samples should not involve fewer than 30 people or events; to use statistical analyses on smaller samples would be a mistake.

There are three main types of probability sample used in surveys. 'Random sampling', as already noted, requires that each sampling unit in a population has an equal chance of being included in the sample and selection can be accomplished by drawing names or numbers out of a box or by using a computer program to generate a sample using random numbers (Teddlie and Yu 2007). In 'stratified sampling' the researcher 'divides the population into sub-groups (or strata) such that each group belongs to a single stratum' (such as low-, medium- or high-income) and then selects units from those strata. Finally, 'cluster sampling' happens when 'the sampling unit is not an individual but a group (cluster) that occurs naturally in the population, such as neighbourhoods, hospitals, schools, or classrooms' (Teddlie and Yu 2007: 79).

Surveys and non-probability samples

Sometimes the use of a probability sample for a survey might not be appropriate for the kind of research project you have chosen, and Denscombe (2007: 16) notes three main reasons why this might be so. First, the researcher may not feel able to include a sufficiently large number of sample 'units' (such as individuals or events) in the study. Second, there may be a lack of information on the population to be studied, such as who or how many people or events make up the population. Third, because of this lack, it might prove difficult to contact a sample through conventional probability sampling techniques.

But there may be other pressing reasons for choosing a non-probability (or purposive) sample instead. For example, if your focus of interest is on a particular case, event or site, or involves a 'bounded' group of people, then it would be appropriate to use a more focused sample, deliberately chosen for strategic purposes. This is also true with projects that attempt to integrate quantitative and qualitative data since this usually requires a degree of flexibility in design and sampling strategies. Similarly, where there is an emphasis on *exploratory* as well as *explanatory* aims, flexibility of data collection and analysis is necessary. Finally, when focusing on the empirical links between social domains and the key problem-questions they generate, some deliberate choice of the 'best' or most appropriate segments of data (and data samples) is essential.

In all these cases the most appropriate or relevant type of sample to use is one that is *purposive* or strategically chosen. As Denscombe (2007) points out, this involves a departure from the principle that each member of the research population stands an equal chance of being included in the sample. With purposive samples 'the choice of people or events included in the sample is definitely not a random selection' (Denscombe 2007: 17). Surveys samples based on purposive principles can produce interesting and important research data, so their potential should be harnessed whenever possible (see later discussion). Of course, it is crucial that the reasons underlying the selection of such samples are rigorously argued for, and clearly stated, in order to ensure conformity to scientific standards.

Specifically for use with adaptive analysis, I have developed a particular variant of purposive sampling that I term 'problem sampling'. In the next chapter I describe this in detail and provide a fuller comparison between probability and purposive sampling. Problem sampling is uniquely tailored to the kind of research that displays some of the previously mentioned characteristics. That is, adaptive research focuses on the links between social domains (and key problem-questions) and often investigates bounded groups, events or sites. It also emphasises the integration of quantitative and qualitative data (see later examples). Finally, its flexible research designs and sampling strategies are better suited to serving its twin aims of explanation and exploration. Thus, when survey data and analysis is used in an adaptive project, problem sampling should be regarded as the most relevant selection procedure.

Problems with the Survey as a Mono-Method

There are some clear strengths of survey research. These are, first, that it produces quantitative data that can be statistically analysed 'using straightforward computer techniques' (Robson 2007: 43). Second, as Denscombe (2007: 31) points out, surveys enable a wide and inclusive coverage, which means they are more likely to produce data based on representative samples. As a consequence they are often thought to be more credible because of their greater generalisability (that is, the findings are more readily generalised from the sample to the wider population). However, it is necessary to be careful in choosing a survey as a 'mono-method' project because there are also disadvantages and weaknesses:

1 There is pressure to make the questions asked in survey questionnaires as simple and straightforward as possible because long and complex questions tend to reduce the response rates (Robson 2007). The tendency is to reduce the depth to which topics (and questions about them) can be, and are, pursued. Stated another way, there is pressure to produce rather superficial information which can only scratch the surface of the issues investigated.

2 The quantitative data associated with statistical analysis can give an inflated impression of, and a misplaced confidence in, the value of the research findings (Robson 2007).

3 Surveys rarely permit an exploration of the social environment of the phenomena being studied. Rather, they tend to 'extract' opinions, thoughts and ideas, and attitudes 'out of context', that is, away from their natural social settings and contexts. This may produce a misleadingly 'artificial' impression of the phenomena being studied.

4 Denscombe (2007: 32) points out that surveys that produce data based on a 'wide and inclusive coverage' may create the danger that researchers may 'become obsessed with the data to the exclusion of an adequate account of the implications of those data for relevant issues problems or theories'. Because the data are left to 'speak for themselves', their significance may be neglected.

5 The kind of theory that survey researchers often use focuses on discretely measurable variables (income, status, class, educational attainment, and so on) and the relationships between them. Because these variables are formally defined in advance of the research, attention is dragged away from naturally embedded social activities and processes which may be of greater explanatory importance.

6 This can lead to an analytic focus on a reality pre-defined by the researcher, rather than one which emerges from the accounts of participants or from a study of their social relationships. Thus, although survey data may be

wide and inclusive, this may be achieved at the expense of thinness of analysis and explanation. It is important to avoid this by adopting a more general analytic perspective and this is where a social domains perspective helps (as in the Prullmann-Vengerfeldt (2006) study).

7 Robson (2007: 43) argues that the fixed design approach of surveys is an advantage because it allows the researcher to accurately predict the time and resources needed to complete the data collection and analysis. This may be so, but if this is at the cost of research findings lacking depth or explanatory power, then it can no longer be deemed an advantage. A significant problem with fixed designs is that they are unable to respond and adapt to emergent developments that result from ongoing data analysis and collection. This means that findings can only confirm or question or 'test' the assumed relationship between the 'variables'. The very design of the study prevents it from unearthing new or radically different explanatory ideas.

Unless carefully handled, used as a mono-method the survey may be prone to such problems. However, using surveys in conjunction with mixed strategies and with both probability and non-probability samples, reduces the likelihood and extent of such problems.

Using Quantitative Data in Multi-Strategy Research

By adopting a 'structured but flexible' design, the adaptive approach blends 'explanatory' and 'exploratory' research objectives. Thus, it is not *limited* to issues concerned with testing and confirmation/disconfirmation. It also focuses on 'discovery' and conceptual innovation. Its flexible (emergent) multi-strategy design allows it to adapt responsively to changes in analytic ideas, concepts priorities, and so on, as a response to ongoing data collection and analysis.

A social domains perspective

Adaptive analysis is based on a view of social reality as interlinked social domains rather than uniform relationships and processes. The domains (psychobiography, situated activity, social settings and social contextual resources) have their own (internal) characteristics, but are tightly intermeshed. The multi-strategy nature of the adaptive approach, including its blending of quantitative and qualitative data, offers a means of gathering and analysing data, information and facts on domains and their interrelationships.

Integrating and blending quantitative and qualitative data

On this view, quantitative and qualitative data are blended in a complementary fashion. Quantitative data does not provide a better explanation than qualitative data any more than qualitative data is superior to quantitative data. Rather, they explain different but complementary aspects of social reality. Their analytic emphases are blended, combined and integrated through the analytic focus on social domains. That is, they are integrated in terms of what they reveal about particular social domains and how their combined effects show up in the empirical world. Specifically, they illuminate how aspects of macro and micro social reality interconnect with, and influence, each other.

Structured flexible designs and data integration

The structured flexible design aids the blending and integration of quantitative and qualitative data. Quantitative data tends to provide information on social settings and contextual resources (the 'macro' or wider organisational features of society), while qualitative methods and analysis supply data on psychobiography and situated activity (the 'micro' elements of individual agency and social interaction). Settings and contextual resources represent the wider macro environment which 'encloses' the micro elements and reflects the manner in which domains and different types of data intertwine and reciprocally influence each other.

Concurrent and sequential designs

As a general rule, quantitative and qualitative data analysis should take place concurrently. Both types of data throw light on complementary aspects of social reality (interrelated social domains). This aids the blending and integration of the different types of data. Generally, then, there is no need to ask which is the best 'order' for using particular methods or data? Do I begin with quantitative data and then move to qualitative, or begin with qualitative data and then move to quantitative? Rather, there should be a process of shuttling back and forth between the different types of data, asking the question: how does this information or data help to throw light on (explain) this other data?

However, practical problems such as availability of interviewees, access, money, time and resources – or simply not being able to do everything at the same time – may mean that different types of data and data collection must be used at different junctures, and thus in a particular sequence. If this is the case, then you must take note of any assumptions or changes in thinking and data analysis that may result from this. However, the fact that your analytic focus is trained on the links between social domains (and key problem-questions) will aid the integration of quantitative and qualitative data.

The question of the order of data collection may also arise when implementing a *planned* sequential design (see example below). In adaptive analysis this is usually associated with the sequence:

Qualitative ----------------> Quantitative ----------------> Qualitative

Figure 6.1

A preliminary qualitative inquiry serves as the basis on which questions may be formulated for a subsequent quantitative survey or structured interview. In turn, the analysis of the survey data acts as a check on the preliminary findings but is then expanded and supplemented by further qualitative data. After a deliberate 'sequential' start, it quickly 'morphs' into a concurrent design (see above), which aims at a more comprehensive picture by bringing together complementary aspects of social life (domains).

Combining explanation, exploration and triangulation

Adopting the concurrent design as your default position helps to combine exploratory and explanatory objectives, rather than treating them as separate or independent enterprises – a position taken by some proponents of mixed methods (Creswell and Plano Clark 2007; Creswell et al. 2008: 68). From the point of view of adaptive analysis, it is misleading to talk about explanatory and exploratory designs as independent 'sequential designs'. The point is to blend and integrate (Bryman 2008b: 99) exploratory and explanatory designs along with quantitative and qualitative data. The researcher should think in terms of integrated research designs in which 'slices' of data *analytically* complement and reinforce each other. In this regard it is best to conceive of the structured flexible research design as one in which qualitative or quantitative inputs interrelate with each other, creating a cumulative web of interconnections.

This links up with the notion of 'triangulation', which refers to a particular way of cross-checking findings from different points of view. Denzin (1989) has distinguished between different types of triangulation, including data, investigator, theoretical or methodological triangulation. The multistrategy design suggested here endorses these points of reference, but additionally includes a reference to social domains (Layder 1993). Particular clusters of social domains will be relevant to particular research projects because they will be driven by specific problem-questions. As a consequence, the process of triangulation must reflect this. The researcher must select relevant data segments/slices that will reveal the linkages between the domains in question.

Variations in Multi-Strategy Designs

In the following sections I discuss three research designs that bring together all the elements discussed above.

1 Using secondary data as a background resource

One option is to use existing (secondary) data sets and analyses and re-fashion them for your own (small-scale) project. For example, you might have started a project by collecting qualitative data focused around key problem-questions. You might wish to further 'strengthen' and 'triangulate' your analysis by integrating it with some quantitative data from survey research.

In this sense, while the secondary survey data you draw on may not be closely linked with a domains perspective, it must be broadly 'in tune' with such a perspective otherwise it might prove difficult to integrate the findings successfully. Additionally, many surveys are undertaken in the context of multi-method or mixed-method approaches which ensure they are more closely aligned with the multi-strategy analysis of adaptive research.

An example: smoking habits in young people

A case in point is Denscombe's (2001) study of smoking among young people aged 15–16 years. The first part of this two-phase study was a questionnaire survey based on 12 schools in the East Midlands of England 'selected to be representative of their catchment areas (social class, ethnic composition, urban/suburban/rural)'. From the '1,679 young people who took part in the survey, 1,648 usable questionnaires were returned' (2001: 162). Of these, 46.4 per cent were males and 53.6 per cent were females. In terms of ethnicity, 71.2 per cent were whites and 24.6 per cent were South Asians. The pattern of smoking revealed by the survey largely matched the national picture for the age group 'with nearly 1 in 3 being occasional or regular smokers, and with girls being more likely to be smokers than boys' (Denscombe 2001: 162). The second phase of the research comprised focus group discussions and semi-structured interviews (20 groups of 4–7 people) and served to validate the results of the survey by checking with the young people themselves.

The research explored the role that smoking plays in relation to the uncertainty around self-identity and focused on what young people regard as the personal benefits of smoking. This contrasted with a view of them as 'victims' of external influences, such as 'peer group pressure, family influences, social deprivation, and the interests of the tobacco industry' (Denscombe 2001: 159). Looking 'grown-up' or 'cool' or 'hard' were some of the reasons that young people gave for smoking, particularly the girls, which reflect the significance of smoking for impressing and influencing others. Self-feelings, such as being in control and 'taking charge of your life' in the face of known health risks, were also important, as was the paradox of the felt need 'to fit-in' as well as 'to stick-out' in terms of individuality and self-expression. In all these senses, smoking made a positive contribution to the construction of self-identity for young people.

Although the findings, methods and objectives of such a study stand in their own right, they could also be drawn on as a resource to help with small scale-projects focusing on different themes or topics and influenced by a domains perspective. Also, the use of quantitative survey data along with qualitative data from discussion groups and interviews means that it fits easily within a multi-strategy framework.

Furthermore, the 'openness' of its explanatory framework means that elements of the study could be conjoined with several of the key problem-questions. For example, the domain of psychobiography is touched upon in the concern with self-identity, power and control (being in control of one's life, self-empowerment). Situated activity is relevant to how young people perceive themselves to be seen by others in their peer group – for example with regard to looking 'cool' or 'hard', and so on.

These influences take place against the background of the school as a social setting – although its role is not really emphasised in the study. The same is true for the role of contextual resources, although the stress on the positive personal benefits of smoking is an important counterweight to the influence of external factors (the interests of the tobacco industry and social deprivation). It highlights important information about the way social domains affect particular aspects of behaviour.

General issues

Such secondary data can provide an important *supportive backdrop* to small-scale projects which focus on quite different topics and issues, such as friendship or romantic involvements in schools or universities, or questions about self-identity or emotional expression in other types of setting. In this sense, as a researcher, you are reanalysing secondary data in relation to your own project with a view to reinforcing your own findings, by drawing attention to *similarities* or *contrasts* with the secondary data. The smoking habits of 15–16 year olds and the reasons they give for them might form a supportive background for small-scale studies of many other aspects of youth culture.

2 Developing explanation and analysis

Identifying relevant secondary data not only involves technical or practical questions about whether they 'fit-in' with your own project. It is also a case of recognising their potential explanatory role in your own project. An *explanation* will, in all probability, evolve over time (sometimes drastically) as a result of ongoing data collection and any consequent finessing of ideas and concepts.

Of course, explanations should be subjected to rigorous empirical testing and counter-arguments to probe the limits of their strength and viability. If necessary, they must be altered, modified or supplanted by any alternative concepts and explanations that may emerge during the project. In this respect the structured flexible design and multi-strategy approach can help in the construction and emergence of explanations.

An example: careers research

As part of my research on careers in the acting profession, I conducted qualitative (semi-structured) interviews with actors (Layder 1993). I was trying to find out what their career experiences were and to get some overall impression of how the occupation was organised. From these interviews it became obvious that agents and casting directors (career 'intermediaries') were highly influential in shaping actors' careers, so I needed to expand my interview samples to include them. I also needed to extend my knowledge of the interactional networks and processes that determine actors' career fates.

Around the same time as conducting the interviews I made contact with the actors' union and was made aware of (and given access to) quantitative data from surveys conducted by the union documenting actors' employment and incomes. Careful analysis of this data, by comparing it with a previous survey (conducted seven years earlier), revealed that the labour market for acting work was segmented into three relatively stable income clusters which underpinned the general status and career hierarchy of the profession. At the top there was an inner circle of 'stars' earning the highest incomes, comprising around 5 per cent of the total. Below them there was a segment of middle-income actors – the 'inner circle' – comprising around 15 per cent of the total. At the base of the hierarchy were the mass of actors (80 per cent) who earned the least from work in acting and who experience regular, and sometimes lengthy, periods of not working in acting (or 'resting' as the euphemism has it).

In terms of social domains, the problem-question was: 'how do the situated activities and social links between agents and castings directors help shape the labour market in acting (the social setting of careers)?' The qualitative data from agents and casting directors and the quantitative data from the union surveys were analysed during the same time period. Each informed the other so that appropriate adjustments (in interview questions) followed from the analysis of the labour market survey data. Conversely, analysis of the interview data firmed up and added detail to my outline grasp of labour market segmentation.

The interviews began to focus on the work routines of agents and casting directors – how they chose actors for parts, their networking with each other, and so on. In short, this information revealed the way in which the work routines and interconnections between agents and casting directors tended to reproduce and perpetuate the labour market segmentation. The quantitative data suggested an economic dimension to the labour market and a rather stable structure of segments, while the qualitative data indicated the kinds of social processes that were involved in the establishment and maintenance of the stratified labour market.

Through their intersecting influences, the two kinds of data and analysis fed off each other in a complementary fashion. The overall effect was to produce an emergent explanation of the links between social domains – the interweaving of settings and the social activities that serve to reproduce them. In this sense, quantitative data is not used simply as a check or restraint on claims derived from qualitative analysis or vice versa, and neither was considered to be the 'superior partner'. Rather, the resulting synergy gave rise to an 'emergent' explanation which would have been unlikely to occur in the absence of a flexible research design and sampling strategy.

3 Planned sequential designs

Like the others, this type of design relies on a multi-strategy approach and a focus on social domains. However, it also relies on original or 'primary' data (that is, data gathered specifically for the current project) as opposed to choosing relevant secondary data (data collected by others) and reanalysing it (as with developing explanations). Further, it emphasises a particular sequence in the use of quantitative and qualitative methods while pursuing a concern with exploration as well as explanation. It does this by triangulating different types and sources of data around an analytic concern with social domains.

An example: Young people and social capital

Boeck (2011) has used a domains perspective to examine how young people generate 'social capital' (skills, resources and contacts) through their social networks. Twenty-one organisations participated in the study, including youth groups, the youth justice system, a school and a college in the Midlands area of the UK. The total sample was 547 young people aged between 13 and 29. The use of non-probability samples in both quantitative and qualitative aspects of the study demonstrates the fruitfulness of such sampling strategies, especially in relation to the deployment of a survey questionnaire.

Boeck's research design was organised in three phases. The first phase consisted of the collection of qualitative data from discussion groups (17) and in-depth interviews (16), which produced emergent themes and categories. The analysis of this data formed the basis for a second phase, which was a survey questionnaire that was sent out to 500 people. The questionnaire included both 'closed' or 'fixed-choice' questions, which yielded numeric data, as well as open-ended survey questions, which produced qualitative data. The third and final phase involved the interpretation of the combined survey (quantitative + qualitative) results and integration with the original results of phase one.

The research yielded many intriguing findings, explanations and policy suggestions concerning the best ways to enhance the social capital of young people 'at risk' of crime and substance abuse – and thus of diverting them from such activities. Boeck provides a more accurate understanding of the nature of young people's social networks and the way they are used. This was achieved via the employment of a domains perspective to give focus to the empirical data and its analysis, while using a mixed-method approach to data collection. The overall effect was to produce a subtle, multi-level analysis of a complex social phenomenon which throws light on the ways in which domains influence young people's 'bridging' and 'bonding' social networks, and how the combined influence of situated activity and social settings enhance or deplete the social capital of young people.

The research resembles a planned sequential design and pursues both exploratory and explanatory objectives. The first, qualitative, phase is used to stimulate thinking about the second, quantitative survey phase, while phase three combines the two via an analytic dialogue. But it also has a flexible design which allows it to explore analytic themes and emergent ideas. Moreover, the study also pursues explanatory objectives by showing how empirical data throw light on social domains and key problem-questions.

Final Comments

Free-standing data, official statistics and secondary data from surveys and interviews all offer rich sources of quantitative information and may be used in small-scale projects structured around key problem-questions and a social domains perspective. Although it is possible to use surveys as a 'mono-method', there are many practical problems associated with obtaining large and representative samples (time, money and resources among them). Many engaged in small-scale research (particularly undergraduates) would find these problems insuperable, so I have emphasised the efficiency and convenience of using secondary material as a source of quantitative data. Also, combining quantitative and qualitative data is a sound basis on which to construct robust research designs (those that enhance validity and are both explanatory and exploratory). Thus, I have suggested several ways in which such aims and objectives can be maximised by using mixed-strategy designs.

Checklist for Research Log Notes

- What quantitative data is available to you (free-standing, official statistics, secondary data from surveys and interviews)?

- How is such data appropriate to your main problem- and topic-questions?

- How will you employ such data in your project? Will you use it to illustrate particular features of social settings and contexts (such as gender, age, class or ethnic dimensions)? Will you use it to show how particular domains (such as situated activity and social settings) interrelate?

- How will you use the quantitative data in relation to qualitative data? For example, will you adopt a concurrent design or a planned sequential design? What are you exploring and what are you attempting to explain?

- Are you aware of the problems involved in mixing strategies, particularly combining quantitative and qualitative data? What are they with specific reference to your own project?

7

IMAGINATIVE SAMPLING

PREVIEW

This chapter covers the following:

- Problem sampling (as compared with probability sampling)
- Sampling units: the basic research unit, sub-sites and multiple sub-sites
- Strategies for sampling people, observations and documents
- Problem sampling compared with theory-based sampling
- Conceptual sampling: behavioural, systemic and bridging concepts
- Other sampling strategies: snowball and opportunistic sampling
- Sample size or sample quality?
- Sampling and the unfolding character of adaptive research

In this chapter I discuss the nature and logic of sampling in the adaptive approach. Sampling concerns the criteria used in selecting the 'sample' of people, observations and documents from which you will collect the data and evidence for your research project. Adaptive sampling differs in some ways from sampling in other kinds of research, while complementing other aspects of them. The chapter focuses on the sampling procedures most relevant to the adaptive approach, including the question of the appropriate size and the representativeness of such samples.

Problem Sampling

Stated in its most succinct form, problem sampling means choosing people, events, incidents, and so on, to serve as the data or evidence for a research project in terms of their *relevance* to key problem–questions (as described in Chapters 1 and 3).

Overall, 'relevance' is determined by analytic and empirical factors, both of which are of equal importance in providing answers to the key research problems and questions. First, in terms of analytic ideas and conceptual issues, the relevance of a sample is governed by the extent to which it contributes towards the solving or throwing light on problem–questions. However, the empirical relevance of a sample is determined by the extent to which it yields factual information, data and evidence directly pertinent to key problem–questions, and thus helps illuminate and explain the issues they raise.

Problem sampling is based on rather different principles from 'probability sampling' in quantitative analysis (particularly of surveys and experiments), in which a sample is chosen on the basis that it is 'representative' of the larger population (or 'universe') from which it is drawn. A probability sample relies on selecting a random sample that permits confident generalisation from the sample to the larger population. Every unit in the universe (the whole population under study) has the same probability of being selected in the sample.

As Yin (2009) argues, the logic of probability sampling is appropriate in survey analysis where the researcher is interested in measuring (quantitatively) the relations between discrete variables, and exerts a high degree of control over them. However, it is quite inappropriate to apply the logic of probability sampling to types of research in which the investigator has little control over events in a real-life context. Clearly, the adaptive approach is of this type. It focuses on real-life situations and the in-depth study of the complex interrelationships between individuals, interactions and their social settings and contexts.

By contrast, problem sampling relies on non-probability (or 'purposive') samples, whose logic and power derives from its focus on, and selection of, 'information-rich' cases for in-depth study. Information-rich cases are those from which one can learn a great deal about issues of central importance to the purpose of the research – thus the idea of 'purposive' or 'strategic' sampling (Patton 2001). The point of problem sampling is not necessarily to select a sample that is representative of the wider 'population' (or group of people) from which it is drawn. Such a sample is no guarantee that it is relevant to the problem-focus of a project or the key research questions that drive it. Thus in 'problem sampling', a 'representative' sample is one that represents or reflects the problem-questions that are the focus of investigation rather than the larger population from which it is drawn. In fact, it is possible that a probability sample may not contain any examples of 'units' connected with the problem and therefore may bear little relevance to the research project.

Problem sampling is applicable to both quantitative and qualitative data and analysis. This is particularly appropriate where adaptive analysis concentrates on blending and integrating both types of data. As pointed out in the last chapter, questionnaire surveys and structured interviews may be based on non-probability (purposive) as well as probability samples when the latter are not considered appropriate or feasible. Non-probability sampling, like problem sampling, is also essential with regard to flexible, multi-strategy research designs with a focus on social domains and key problem-questions. For instance, quantitative data from surveys or structured interviews may be used in parallel with qualitative data, and creatively integrated through the synergy of their reciprocal influences. In this sense, problem sampling provides a default sampling strategy that should be used when research circumstances and requirements dictate.

Sampling Units: The Basic Research Unit

When getting started on a research project, the first issue of concern is deciding which 'units' are to be sampled. The main unit in this respect – what I shall call the 'basic research unit' – is directly related to your initial choice of topic and problem-focus, for example, a fast-food restaurant, a health/fitness club, a school classroom, a friendship network, and so on. The concept of 'social setting' is helpful here in providing a useful model for your basic research unit. As we have seen, social settings provide the immediate environment of social activities and thus the main 'site' of your research will automatically be some kind of social setting.

Social settings can be distinguished by the extent to which they have 'formally' or 'informally' defined social rules, roles, positions and expectations. Although they differ in their organisational details, fast-food restaurants, health clubs, schools and universities are clearly more formal settings, in which the rules, roles, positions and expectations are set and applied (sometimes 'enforced') by the owners and/or managers who run them. On the other hand, friendship networks, gangs, cliques, families and so on, are more informally organised – the rules, roles, positions and expectations are set (defined, negotiated) by the participants themselves. Individuals who break the rules or agreements are dealt with informally through withdrawal of trust, or alliances, partnerships, and so on.

In the more 'formal' settings, the basic research unit and/or site is more clearly visible and obvious and thus more straightforwardly definable – restaurants, cafés, shops, schools, universities all have a definite presence in sheer spatial and physical terms. Informal settings tend to be more spread out and less easily identifiable as research areas or sites. For example, although there are rules (values) and expectations associated with intimacy, to research it you must accept that it is not to be found in only one 'essential' setting. In fact, various forms of intimacy can be played out in a number of settings. Friendship or romantic partnerships may take place in different areas of everyday life, such as schools or universities, neighbourhoods or family connections, at work or leisure. In such cases it is probably best to choose which setting is most suited to your research needs and purposes. Having a definite site or basic research unit will support your research efforts.

Choosing particular research units

The choice of your basic research unit or research site is of paramount importance because it places the research on a sure footing from the word go. As the distinction between formal or informal settings makes clear, the type of unit you choose suggests some basic parameters for your analysis as you go along, as well as later, when you begin to organise your findings and write up your conclusions. But there are other compelling reasons for choosing particular examples of basic research units.

Every choice you make in social research, not just this initial one, should be filtered through a comparative viewpoint. You should always be comparing your present choice with the other possible choices that are available to you and asking yourself: why am I choosing this one, as compared to other possibilities? What will it tell me about the whole class of things to which this one belongs? For example, in what sense is the setting like other similar settings? Is the school or university you wish to study similar to or different from others? You must ask yourself: how does it differ, or how can it be said to be the same or similar to others? In what sense is this fast-food restaurant similar to other fast-food outlets (both within the same company and between different companies)?

Such questions must be answered by comparing the relevant units along several criteria, for example, size, number of staff positions, policy towards customers, and so on. If you can then satisfy yourself that your chosen setting or research unit is similar to the others, it can be said to be a *typical* example. In other words, your research unit can be said to be *a representative case*. As such, you can be fairly confident that any research findings you come up with may, at least in principle, be *generalised* more widely to the whole class of phenomena. If, on the other hand, you find that your research unit is dissimilar to the others in various respects, your must take note of these as they indicate factors that will dictate the limits to which you can generalise from this unit.

Finally, if through comparison, you conclude that your research unit is quite unlike any of the relevant others, then this does not mean that your proposed research is flawed or useless. Rather, as you are aware that this is the case, you can duly note its implications as you go along and, actually, turn this into a position of strength. You can use the fact that your case is extremely atypical to argue that your proposed basic research unit has some research importance (and intrinsic interest). Its very atypical nature can, albeit in a rather roundabout fashion, throw light on the rest of the broader class to which it belongs by making the typical features stand out in relief. Furthermore, it can be argued that this case tells us something about the unique features that make it different from others.

Another reason for selecting a particular basic research unit is its relevance for explanatory or theoretical issues. In this respect you have to ask: what is the purpose of your research? Research is often divided between the kind whose main aim is to test out a tightly formulated hypothesis (theory-testing research) and that which has the aim of creating new explanations (theory-building research) (Layder 1993; Rose 1984). Although they have their good points, sticking to one of these alternatives is a narrow and rather restrictive decision. The adaptive approach combines useful elements of both approaches, while avoiding their weaknesses.

Instead of concentrating on either 'testing' a tightly formulated hypothesis/ theory or developing new theory and knowledge, the adaptive approach has more general and diffuse aims. A particular problem-focus is explored with a view to finding out what data/evidence can reveal about it. There are three possible outcomes. First, the data you collect may lead to the conclusion that existing knowledge, theories and explanations are useful as they stand – although their range of application may need to be refined. Second, the data may require modifications or reformulations of existing concepts and theories. Third, the data may suggest that entirely new insights, concepts and explanations are required to overcome the shortcomings of existing knowledge.

Thus, the selection of a particular basic research unit may rest on the general aim of throwing light on a defined problem-focus, but as the process unfolds in practice this general aim is usually achieved in more particular ways via any of the three possibilities described above.

Research sites within basic units

Sometimes it may be decided for good reasons that the main research focus will be on a site or unit *within* the basic unit rather than the basic unit itself. For example, although you may be studying a fast-food restaurant or a health club, you may decide that some defined areas within them are the most 'interesting' in terms of data collection. As a consequence, rather than attempt to cover the whole area, you may want to concentrate on a particular location and particular kinds of behaviour, for example, customer–staff exchanges at the counter, or in a staff room, or a changing room. Thus, there may be sub-sites within the basic unit that may prove more fruitful for collecting data pertinent to your particular problem-focus.

Thus, a basic research unit may be a neighbourhood, but the researcher may want to focus on a particular area, or street, or group of people within it, such as residents, friends or 'gang' members. Within a work unit such as a factory, a company, a shop, a restaurant, it may become important to focus on a particular department, office or a work team. In a school, it may be a particular classroom or break-time area. Similarly, it may become obvious that the most pertinent data can be found in studying specific events, incidents or people. These sub-units may even become more important than the basic unit, in relation to your problem-focus, research purposes and objectives.

Multiple sub-sites

An additional complication arises if there are several sites or sub-sites essential to a proper understanding of what is going on and the problem-questions and research questions you are investigating. Thus it may become necessary to sample several sub-sites in order to obtain a more complete (and accurate) picture of the research domain.

For example, professional actors' careers take place across a number of different settings, including live theatre, film, television, radio. Also, since only the more successful actors are regularly employed (in acting), large numbers of them spend a lot of time out of work, or 'resting', as the euphemism has it. So some impression of how this group of actors spends their time during fallow 'resting' periods and how it affects their motivation towards the profession is essential to understanding their work experiences. The fact that actors work in multiple sites means that a complete understanding of their careers is only possible if some attention is paid to this fact. This can be tackled, first, by interviewing a sample of actors who have experience of these different work settings (media) and, second, by conducting directed observations and interviews in more than one setting.

In the above example, the nature of the research topic itself enforces attention to multiple sites. In other cases, you may elect to sample more than one sub-site in order to gain a sense of how people's social experiences are extended in time and space, and how this, in turn, feeds back into their behaviour. So, for example, it may enhance a study of staff–customer interaction in a health club or restaurant to sample not only work periods and instances of staff–customer contact, but also to sample staff during periods of rest or leisure in order to ask them about their attitudes towards customers or to listen to their comments about specific incidents.

It is by no means always necessary to sample more than one sub-site. However, you should be aware of the relevance of possible sub-sites to an overall grasp of your problem or topic.

Strategies for Sampling People, Observations and Documents

Once your initial choices about basic sampling units have been made, the task then is to sample people (for interview), observations and documents that are pertinent to your key research questions. What types of people (and how many) should be selected for an interview and directed conversation? What criteria should be used in the selection of interviewees? What kinds of things should be targeted for directed observation? How should observations be undertaken and on what basis should they be selected? What documents should be sampled and how should they be chosen? The following discussion covers the main kinds of sampling strategies.

Problem sampling

The point of sampling basic research units, sub-sites, events and incidents is that selecting the basic sample unit has implications for the 'representativeness' of the evidence or data collected during the project. Problem sampling is thus a way of establishing the representativeness of data (collected through interviews, observations, documents and secondary data from surveys) by ensuring that they are closely linked with a defined problem-focus.

Interviewees are selected on the basis that they have information relevant to the problem-focus of the research and the key research questions. This principle applies to other sampling units, observations, documents, sub-sites, and so on, but let us for the moment concentrate on interviewees as an exemplar of problem sampling. Interviewees should be selected on the basis that they are 'representative' of one or several problem foci. To recap, the pertinent problem-foci are:

Self/Individual ---------- Interaction ---------- Setting ---------- Context

Power ---------- Time (Temporality)

Figure 7.1

Thus, if the research concern was with the way people use health clubs to deal with body-image issues, the main problem-focus would be on how individual experience and self-identity are influenced by social factors. First, the sample of interviewees must contain individuals who are grappling with a specific issue, such as controlling weight or developing fitness or musculature. But their helpfulness as informants will depend on the extent to which they feel that their self-identity is wrapped up in their body image and how others see them. That is, what they reveal about themselves reflects the problem-focus on self-identity and how it is socially influenced.

Of course there are other relevant problem-foci. For example, a person's self-identity and self-image are also significantly influenced by interaction with others both within and beyond the setting of the gym or health club. Thus, you may wish to include in your sample individuals who spend time socialising in the clubs, compared to those who use them strictly for exercise. In this manner you can explore what they talk about and how it impacts on their self-attitudes and body images. Depending on the exact point of interest,

Imaginative Sampling

a researcher might want to trace the influence of wider social factors on self-identity issues. In such a case the sample might be further refined by selecting on the basis of gender, ethnicity, class or age, in an effort to assess the extent to which such factors influence individual experiences.

Also, to further explore the influence of the wider context, the interview sample could be complemented by a documentary sample of interviewees' regular reading matter. Do their reading habits (newspapers, magazines) reflect or reinforce their views about self-identity and body images? To what extent do films, videos and adverts influence their attitudes, expectations and values?

If the research topic was friendship or romantic partnerships at university, the problem-focus would be centred on the way social relationships are influenced by the social setting (the university). To a lesser extent, you may be interested in how these in turn impact on the personal identities of those involved. Your sample of interviewees would of course be university students, but it would need to be refined in terms of gender and sexual preference in order to explore differences between men's and women's experiences in same-sex and cross-sex relationships. Your sample may also need to include individuals who participate in certain kinds of informal activities (debating societies, sport teams, quiz teams) to assess whether (and how) informal interactions (those outside the lecture room) influence friendship preferences or opportunities for establishing intimate partnerships.

In order to capture the way in which the elapsing of time impacts on the formation of intimate relationships, it would be necessary either to choose informants from (at least two) fixed age cohorts and compare them against each other, say first- and third-year students, or to study one or two age groups over a specified period of time.

Again, interviewees and observations could be supplemented by including a documentary sample of reading material – newspapers, magazines – of those already sampled. Investigating the wider social context in this manner would help in tracking down influences on the formation of intimate ties. Thus, the problem-focus of the research would be trained on questions such as 'to what extent are students' behaviour and views on romance and sexual partnerships influenced by ideas, values and images portrayed in the popular mass media?'. Conceivably, this kind of analysis could be extended to an examination of films, video and music preferences of the sample of students. Also, existing studies (along the lines of Inglis's (1997) analysis of 'romantic' lyrics of popular music – see Chapter 2) could be used to establish or help validate claims about the influence of the media in shaping students' values, opinions and attitudes with regard to intimate relationships.

Thus, depending on the exact point of interest of the research, particular problem-foci and related issues will become more or less relevant and will importantly affect the way in which the main research 'units' are sampled. Specifically, samples will be selected on the basis that they are likely to yield information (data, evidence) of maximal relevance to the problem-focus and core research questions. In problem sampling the key problem-foci – self/individual, interaction, setting, context, power and temporality – become the crucial lenses that filter the choice of informants, interviewees, observations and documents.

Problem Sampling Compared with Theory-Based Sampling

In a sense, problem sampling bears similarities with what Patton (2001: 177) calls 'theory-based' sampling, in which 'the researcher samples incidents, slices of life, time periods or people on the basis of their ... representation of important theoretical constructs'. However, problem sampling does not begin with a tightly formulated theoretical proposition and proceed to test its validity (Yin 2009). Problem sampling proceeds by identifying a general problem focus and some key research questions. Its purpose is to provide data of maximum relevance to the focus and the questions. In a sense problem sampling is theoretically informed and is designed to uncover information that has conceptual and analytic value, but in itself it is not a theory (or hypothesis) to be tested. Problem sampling has a much looser and more general theoretical role to play and is more open to the possibility of conceptual and analytic (or explanatory) discovery – to finding new perspectives on a particular problem or topic.

However, problem sampling is quite unlike what Glaser (2001) calls 'theoretical sampling', in which units are sampled in accordance with newly minted theory that emerges straight from data analysis and which constantly directs and redirects the point of interest of the research. Although open to the possibility of theory creation, problem sampling is by no means exclusively focused on, or limited by, it. Rather, it is guided on equal terms by the idea that existing knowledge of analytic problems and explanatory concepts have a crucially important role to play in research design or data collection and analysis.

Thus in problem sampling it is problem-foci – and the core research questions derived from them – that form the important driving force of the research project. They set its parameters, target relevant data and play a part in informing its findings and conclusions. However, the flexibility of research design and problem sampling is such that these initial governing assumptions never preclude the emergence or creation of new concepts, explanations or theoretical ideas as they emerge from data collection and analysis.

This is made possible by the fact that although sampling must accord with criteria worked out before data collection and analysis, this does not, and should not, mean that sample quotas are rigidly fixed throughout the research and/or despite the emergence of data or ideas suggesting that they should be extended or modified. This is also the case when blending and integrating quantitative and qualitative data because this cannot be achieved by using a rigid design and a fixed, pre-defined sample (features linked with quantitative survey analysis). In order to preserve the possibility of emergent concepts, explanations and interpretations, research outcomes must not be predetermined by a fixed sample defined in advance, such as a probability sample representing the wider population!

If data analysis suggests the relevance of alternative lines of inquiry, then it is essential either for existing samples to be topped up or for entirely new categories of interviewees or units of observation to be sampled. Adaptive analysis is not dogmatically hemmed in by the initial problem-focus and research questions. Thus while sampling is led by an initial view of problem relevance, this should not lead to a dogmatic retention of the initial framework. And while this may lead to adaptive modifications, the 'new' concepts or theory is shaped by the analytic problem that was the original focus of exploration.

Conceptual Sampling

While problem sampling is the most important, there are other strategies which may supplement or add to its overall authority. Conceptual sampling is an offshoot of problem sampling. While problem sampling is about the selection of data relevant to fairly broad domains of social life – individual, interaction, setting, context, power and time – conceptual sampling refers to areas that cut across these problem-foci. In this regard, samples may be selected on the basis of three types: behavioural, systemic and bridging concepts (Layder 1998). Such concepts may be identified at the beginning or even before a research project is underway, and may be used to construct or select samples related to them right from the start. Such concepts may also emerge during the course of the research. As a consequence, they may be used subsequently as criteria for choosing data samples later in the study, either to 'top up' existing samples or to explore alternative avenues by creating new sampling units.

Behavioural concepts

These refer to particular aspects of human behaviour and social relationships. Perhaps the most common form of behavioural concepts are those which refer to 'types of participant'. Such concepts are recognised either by the common names used by participants or by the names by which researchers identify participant 'types'. A classical example of 'participant types' is to be found in Giallombardo's (1966) study of social roles in a women's prison. The inmates themselves had developed an elaborate collection of labels to categorise the inmates – snitchers, squares, jive bitches, stud broads, tricks, cherries, and so on. These labels were based on their response to the prison situation and the quality of their interaction with staff and other inmates, including styles of sexual response. An example of researcher-identified 'types' of 'participants' or 'social actors' is Spencer and Pahl's (2006) study of friendship (see Chapter 2), in which they distinguish between four types of 'simple friendship' (including 'associates' and 'fun friends') and four types of 'complex friendship' (including 'helpmates' and 'soulmates').

Other kinds of concept may more directly indicate the quality of social relationships between the participants. For example, this is reflected in Miller's (1995) distinctions between 'honeymoon passion', 'loving attachment' and 'affectionate regard' to describe different types and/or phases of love. Other examples stressing the nature and quality of social relationships are distinctions between 'dynamic', 'episodic', 'semi-detached' and 'pretence' types of intimacy (Layder 2009).

You may come across behavioural concepts as the result of a systematic literature search and wish to investigate or explore them in your own research. This may be done to find out how or in what sense specific concepts are applicable or appropriate to your own project. You may wish to include in your sample informants who fit in with these descriptions, labels or identifications. By so doing, you are in a sense checking the validity of these concepts, either by demonstrating their usefulness to your analysis or by indicating that they need modifying or amending. On the other hand, having started out with one or several behavioural concepts, you may find that your data suggest some alternative concepts with which to explain or understand your findings. In this sense, 'new' or at least 'alternative' behavioural concepts may emerge from your research as you collect and analyse data.

Systemic or structural concepts

Behavioural concepts refer to social phenomena covered by the key problem-foci of 'self/individual' and 'social interaction' (including their relevant power and time dimensions). By contrast, systemic concepts refer to the key problem-foci of 'social settings' and 'context' (and their relevant power and time dimensions). 'Systemic' phenomena provide the 'enclosing' environment of behavioural phenomena – for example, action, feelings or the quality of interpersonal relationships – but in themselves they are not 'behavioural'. Social settings are the immediate environment in which behaviour is played out, while contexts represent wider social influences on behaviour, such as values and class position.

Systemic concepts such as 'formal organisation' or 'bureaucracy' are important for understanding hospitals, management, business companies, fast-food restaurants ('McDonaldizaton'), schools, universities, and so on. Others, referring to 'labour markets' or 'labour market segments', help in understanding how the economy, work and jobs are interrelated. In social research it is essential to use systemic concepts like these in order to refer to these crucial aspects of the social environment.

As with behavioural concepts, it is necessary to ensure that your principal data samples take account of evidence that corresponds to such concepts. For example, you may need to talk to people drawn from different labour market segments, or who work in certain kinds of formal organisation. Again, you may begin your project using concepts you have identified through a literature review and ascertain to what extent they throw light on your research questions. Alternatively, your research may suggest important revisions or modifications of such concepts in the light of the data collected.

'Systemic' concepts complement 'behavioural' concepts in the sense that in social life they intertwine with each other. Behavioural phenomena are not the same as systemic phenomena and therefore they cannot be reduced or substituted for each other. Nevertheless, they are deeply interconnected with each other. Your research should in some sense reflect this relationship between behavioural and systemic phenomena by recognising that any data samples you use are likely to contain data or evidence that refers to both these aspects of social reality.

Bridging concepts

Finally, there are concepts that attempt to depict the connection between behavioural and systemic phenomena. They refer to the combined effects of the objective world of 'systemic' phenomena and the subjective and intersubjective world of 'behavioural' phenomena (Blaikie 2009; Layder 1998). Concepts such as 'career' (Stebbins 1970) or 'emotional labour' (Hochschild 1983) and 'surveillance' (Foucault 1997) are good examples of this dual objective–subjective reference. Bridging concepts also attempt to depict the influence of social organisation on people's motivations and social involvements. In this regard, Etzioni's (1961) distinctions between 'alienative', 'calculative' and 'moral' forms of involvement in organisations are good examples of bridging concepts.

Excellent research should display some recognition of the interplay in social life between behavioural and systemic phenomena, and in this respect the use of 'bridging' concepts fits the bill. For example, although Ritzer's (2011) study (discussed in Chapter 2), concentrates mainly on the bureaucratic features of McDonaldization, he also raises the issue of whether this produces 'alienation' (estrangement, artificiality) in social relationships in and around fast-food restaurants. In this manner (as with behavioural and systemic concepts), bridging concepts like 'alienation' may be used very effectively as criteria for the selection of data samples. By sampling in terms of specific concepts – that is, selecting people, events or documents that represent them – the researcher can home-in on and more precisely target the data most relevant to tackling key research problems and questions.

Other Sampling Strategies

There are more conventional sampling strategies that may be used in conjunction with problem sampling and conceptual sampling.

Snowball or chain sampling

As Patton (2001) points out, snowball sampling is an approach for locating information-rich key informants or critical cases. The process depends on having an initial contact who is a relevant and key informant. This person is then asked: who knows a lot about (…such and such)? Who should I talk to about this? By asking this person (and then a subsequent contact) to put you in touch with others to talk to, the snowball gets bigger and bigger as you accumulate new information-rich cases and can then ask them to suggest one or two others you might talk to. Of course, you should exert some control over the selection of informants by specifying exactly what sort of person you are looking for – that is, by spelling out the criteria they should meet. Conventionally, this applies to such criteria such as gender, age, ethnicity, class and so on, and of course these might be important for your study.

However, generally speaking, snowball sampling should be used as an adjunct to problem sampling and conceptual sampling, which are the main sampling strategies for adaptive research. Thus, when using snowball or chain sampling, informants should be selected primarily on the basis of criteria used in problem sampling and conceptual sampling. If, during the collection and analysis of data, it becomes obvious that it is important to take account of unanticipated criteria for the selection of informants, then these should be adopted as soon as possible.

Opportunistic sampling

This form of sampling is most useful after the research is underway, and in connection with emergent ideas and criteria about who else to interview, and/or what else to observe. Thus, this kind of sampling is about taking advantage of unforeseen opportunities, on the spot, during data collection, thus allowing existing samples to expand or new samples to emerge during fieldwork. In a sense, opportunistic sampling addresses the fact that it is probably unwise to make all sampling decisions in advance of the actual data collection. This is simply because it pre-empts the possibility of allowing shifting nuances, emerging themes and concepts to surface during the research. Entering the research with a dogmatic, closed agenda cuts off the possible value that can be added by emergence, serendipity and genuine discovery as the project unfolds.

However, a researcher contemplating opportunistic sampling should be aware of an ever-present danger. That is, it must never be confused with, or be allowed to deteriorate into, a *convenience* sample – that is, choosing informants pragmatically on the basis of sheer convenience or practicality. Samples assembled on the basis that someone is close at hand and can therefore be a potential interviewee, or on the basis of casual observations or 'at hand' documents, will lack adequacy and validity. They will have no connection with a scientific logic of sampling and therefore lack relevance and credibility. Samples chosen on the basis of convenience represent the antithesis of purposive or strategic sampling. An opportunistic sample should always be governed by the attempt to obtain the best and most useful information on the basis of its problem-relatedness. Samples should be chosen on the basis that they are problem-driven, that is, driven by criteria suggested in problem sampling and conceptual sampling.

Sample Size or Sample Quality?

Problem sampling and conceptual sampling are examples of non-probability sampling strategies in which not everyone in the researched population has an equal chance of being included in the sample. In this sense they are not meant to accurately represent all the people within the study parameters. Rather, 'representativeness' is determined by the problem-relatedness of the units sampled, be they observations, people or documents. Thus the logic of 'purposive' sampling (as in problem sampling or conceptual sampling) cannot be judged in terms of the logic, purpose and recommended sample sizes of probability sampling (Patton 2001; Yin 2009).

In this regard sample size is less significant than the question 'when is the process of sampling finished?' There are no hard-and-fast criteria for determining sample size. Rather, it is more important to seek guidelines about when the sampling process should be terminated. Although there are no absolute rules, there are, as Patton (2001: 185) points out, some practical guidelines in terms of what you want to know, the purpose of the inquiry, what is useful and credible, and what can be done with the resources available. Patton goes on to suggest that the validity, meaningfulness and insights generated by this kind of study have more to do with the *information richness* of the cases selected, and the observational and analytical capabilities of the researcher, than with sample size.

There are, however, some quite practical criteria for determining when to stop sampling data for a specific project. The most important issue can be settled by asking yourself: have I collected enough of the right kind of information needed to answer the core research problems and questions? The most practical indication that you have reached such a position is when new information and insights are no longer appearing in the data (this is sometimes referred to as 'saturation'). When further data collection is no longer yielding anything interesting or new, then you have fully developed your categories, concepts and explanatory ideas. At such a point sampling can be terminated.

Sampling and the Unfolding Character of Adaptive Research

In an important sense, the sampling strategies discussed in this chapter are related to the flexibly unfolding character of the adaptive approach. However, it must be remembered that adaptive research always proceeds from a highly structured starting point, using existing knowledge and established concepts to act as an initial template for data collection and analysis. But the structured nature of this template is not used as a limitation on what the research may aim for as an outcome. Rather, the approach is based on an exploratory premise and thus its internal structure allows it to adapt flexibly to ongoing data collection and evolving analytic ideas.

In terms of sampling, this means that the researcher sets out with clear ideas about how the initial sample or samples will be selected (and which may include probability samples) in order to address the project's main problem-focus and core research questions. Thus, problem sampling and conceptual sampling can be set in train and will serve to support ongoing strategic research decisions. However, as the momentum of data collection and analysis develops over time, it will become clearer as to what 'direction' or outcome the research is leading towards. Thus, the exploratory starting point eventually congeals into a more definite and concentrated focus. In this regard, there are three most likely research outcomes which have clear consequences for ongoing sampling decisions and strategies. These are:

1   In relation to the evidence or data, the orienting concepts (see next chapter) are found to be useful and relevant in helping explain the main research problem and in providing answers to research questions.

2   In relation to the evidence or data, the orienting concepts are deemed to require modification, extension or elaboration.

3   The orienting concepts are found to have serious shortcomings in terms of explaining or accounting for the evidence or data.

As the research unfolds over the full span of the project it will become apparent that the overall research outcome will be reflected by one of the above possibilities.

Consequences for sampling

Each of the above outcomes has different implications and consequences for ongoing and upcoming decisions about sampling. In so far as the research heads towards outcome 1, it is likely that sampling criteria and priorities will remain fairly stable. If they do alter or depart from the initial ones, they will do so only in a fairly limited way. Conversely, in so far as the research heads towards outcomes 2 or 3, the more likely it is that sampling criteria will change more radically during the course of the research as new data samples are required to cater for new priorities and shifting (explanatory) ideas.

The question of when sampling is finished, or should be terminated, will be clearer and more apparent earlier on in data collection the more the research outcome moves towards 1. However, with outcomes 2 and 3, the issue of whether or when sampling is complete may only be settled in the later phases of the project. That is, changes in sampling practice and the collection of fresh samples may continue right to the end.

Checklist for Research Log Notes

- How and why does problem sampling fit in with the nature and objectives of adaptive research? How are these issues pertinent to your own project?

- What are sampling units? What will be the basic research unit of your own project?

- Are there important sub-sites? Is yours a multi-site project? How would these issues affect sampling procedure?

- What will be the balance between interviews, observations, surveys and documents in your sample(s)? What criteria will you use to select sample units?

- In what sense does problem sampling overlap with theory-based sampling? What are the differences between the two?

- What role will conceptual sampling play in your project? How does it relate to problem sampling? Are you using behavioural, systemic and/or bridging concepts?

- Will you need to use snowball or opportunistic samples as supplements to your main sampling strategies?

- How will you know when to terminate the sampling? What are the criteria for assessing the quality of a sample?

- How does the research outcome and the unfolding character of the research affect the decision to finish sampling?

8

DATA ANALYSIS: CONCEPTS & CODING

PREVIEW

This chapter covers the following:

- The importance of early data analysis
- Data analysis and coding categories
- Concepts, description and explanation
- Identifying, exploring and choosing orienting concepts
- The disadvantages of open (or initial) coding
- Coding, data analysis and orienting concepts
- Practical aspects of coding
- Focal points for the Research Log and sample entries
- Extending orienting concepts
- Core and satellite concepts
- Coding, data analysis and emergent concepts, including the splitting and replacement of concepts
- Innovative concepts
- The research project as an unfolding process
- The adaptive approach and data analysis
- Data analysis as a response to different research outcomes

The Importance of Early Data Analysis

You should begin to analyse your data as soon as possible after the first observations, interviews or documents. You should never put off analysis in the misguided belief that collecting more data will guarantee a better project. First, it is the overall quality of your project, not the quantity of data it is based on, that matters when assessing its excellence as a piece of social research. In turn, the overall quality of the project is greatly influenced by the nature and general quality of data analysis, not the total amount of data collected. Thus, to ensure that quality control over the analytic process kicks in from the very start and influences the whole project, it is important to begin to analyse data as soon as possible.

If you are not aware of the issues involved, and do not reflect on them at this early phase, it is easy for mistakes and errors of judgement to creep in and to be repeated innumerable times before they are spotted and corrected. More seriously, errors and weaknesses may escape recognition completely and become ingrained in the entire project. Also continual awareness of analytic issues, practices and problems is essential for keeping tabs on *emergent* aspects of the project, such as changing priorities in sampling, data collection, evolving ideas about the overall thrust of the project, or in conceptual modification and innovation.

Second, if analysis is not begun early or it is delayed because you are too busy collecting yet more data, it is more likely that you will become confused at the sheer amount of data that you accumulate. The more it gathers, the more intimidated you become and the less inclined to start the analysis. This might turn into a negative spiral which, eventually, brings everything to a halt. There is a definite parallel here with the advice offered in relation to writing early. The earlier you commit to writing, the more likely is it that your ideas will maintain clarity as you press forward.

Exactly the same is true with data analysis – the more you do it, the surer you will become that you are on the right path to achieve your objectives. However, analysis should never turn into a routine and unchanging 'habit'. Rather, it must be regarded as a responsive and adaptive process which is sensitive to the detailed implications of the data – for the ongoing analysis and structure of the project – as they are gathered. It is important for the researcher always to be alive to these possibilities, especially early in the project.

Data Analysis and Coding Categories

An essential first step in analysis is to 'code' data, or break it up and organise it into meaningful segments so that they can be identified and retrieved from their original context (notes, interview transcriptions, documents), and then either examined in more detail or used to illustrate points in your final report. In order to be able to code, you need a coding system which specifies how you will categorise data. That is, a system stating what the different categories will be, and how to identify data that 'corresponds' to them. A code is the specific label you assign to a category which in turn indicates a piece of data or a particular form of data.

Thus you read through your data sources (say, some interview transcripts or observational notes) and as you read you try to match particular extracts or descriptions of observations with particular code labels. This is the exact opposite of an 'open-coding' technique, as suggested in grounded theory (Strauss and Corbin 1998; see also Bryman 2008; Charmaz 2006). I'll say more about why presently, but it is important to say that with the adaptive approach, especially at the beginning, you are *not* trying to find *codes in the data or invent codes suggested by the data*.

Rather, you begin with a set of pre-decided code labels and attempt to match them with data. It is the issue of whether, how and to what extent they match particular strips of data that is of interest to you because this gives you a key as to whether the codes will be useful analytic tools that will help you explain what the data indicates. You are looking for several things. At the start you will probably be trying to estimate the extent to which the codes match, or do not match, the data, and whether this requires some modification or elaboration of them. Once such tasks have been completed your attention will turn to the possibility of *emergent* codes. These would be new codes to replace the ones you started with, on the understanding that they would be of more use as explanatory tools.

Coding categories

Data can be coded in relation to different code categories. That is to say, different types of social phenomena (as represented in the data) can be indicated by the use of different codes and coding categories. For example, the following categories could be used as the basis for analytic codes.

Themes: **Events**: **Words**: **Conversations**: **Feelings/Emotions**: **Concepts**: **Instances of behaviour** (such as controlling or disciplining, listening or sympathising):

As the above list indicates, there are very many possibilities as far as potential coding categories are concerned. However, for present purposes I wish to draw your attention to two points about categories that are of most importance to adaptive research.

First, while many of the above categories may be useful in various ways, *concepts* are the most important because they provide the crucial link with explanation – a link that other categories cannot or, do not, provide. This is intimately connected with the second point, which is that many coding categories are capable of referring to aspects of the social world in either a *descriptive* or *explanatory* way. Since it is the explanatory functions of coding categories that are essential for adaptive research, it is important to be able to distinguish between the two types, and to be aware of the roles they play in data analysis.

Concepts are the most closely connected to explanatory aims because they are the main component 'units' in which arguments and explanations are expressed (a prominent theme of the next chapter). In this sense concepts are almost purely explanatory or at least represent the complementary opposite of description. Other categories, such as 'themes', 'conversations' or 'emotions' can be either descriptive *or* analytic depending on how they are used by the researcher.

Thus, in a descriptive sense a 'theme' might refer to an encounter as an 'unhappy meeting' or a 'sad occasion'. Such descriptive themes are characterised by their links to particular people, times and places. On the other hand, a researcher may wish to characterise some 'themes' as *conceptual* because they may also refer to more general, analytic properties of the social world which are not bound by particular times, people and places.

Finally, some categories, such as 'events' or 'words', refer almost wholly to descriptive features of the social world. Clearly, such categories may provide a useful bedrock of empirical information about the social world, such as 'what is going on' in a particular social setting, or in recording instances of a particular kind of behaviour. In this sense, they may provide the empirical underpinning for more conceptual or explanatory analysis. In themselves, however, they are not analytic or conceptual in nature and thus do not help with the explanatory component of research. The following discussion will concentrate on how concepts can be used as coding categories and how, subsequently, they can be incorporated into explanatory arguments.

Before moving on, however, it is instructive to highlight the continuity between the issues raised above and those discussed in Chapter 4 about the distinction between research 'problems' and research 'topics'. There it was argued that research 'problems' deal with broadly conceptual, abstract and general properties of social reality, whereas 'topics' refer to, and deal with, particular, empirical matters. This directly mirrors the distinction between 'descriptive' codes versus 'explanatory' codes. Of course, it must be remembered that these distinctions deal with *complementary* aspects of the social world – and data analysis. More emphasis is placed on the conceptual/explanatory side of things here because it is the one that is most frequently neglected in discussions of data analysis.

Problems --- Topics

Conceptual codes ------------------------------- Descriptive codes

Explanation --- Description

Figure 8.1

Concepts and Explanation

Before examining more practical matters I want to spell out the relationship between concepts and explanation in order to underline the importance of conceptual codes in data analysis. There are two closely related questions that need to be answered. First, what is it that is being explained when we talk of explanation in social research? Second, what is the role of concepts in explanation?

With regard to the first question, in a nutshell, the answer is that adaptive research sets out to explain *social behaviour*. However, this definition is too general and in order to be more specific about this let me compare this to what others identify as research objectives. Glaser and Strauss (1967), Strauss and Corbin (1998) and Glaser (2001) suggest that the focus of grounded theory research is on identifying 'the central concerns of the participants' (who are under study) and 'how they continually resolve these concerns'. On a superficial reading this could be thought to be a similar to, if not the same as, explaining social behaviour.

However, it is clear that the 'concerns of the participants and their attempts to resolve them' are but one small part of the overall scenario. The grounded theory focus (and its explanatory problematic) is limited largely to the domain of situated interaction, and does not take account of the wider network of domains (and dimensions) that causally influence it. Thus the explanatory focus of the adaptive approach is more inclusive and deeper in its (ontological) reach. In a sense, the explanatory focus of the adaptive approach *begins* at the point that grounded theory *leaves* the analysis. It attempts to explain how and why the 'participants' main concerns' are the unintended outcome of a complex of psychological, interactional and social structural or systemic factors (Layder 1997), and thus proposes an underlying causal explanation. An investigation into the 'main concerns of the participants' merely scratches the surface of social life. The adaptive approach explores the underlying generative mechanisms.

Explanation relies on analytic categories which pick out general features and properties of social reality – as in social domains and their dimensions. Descriptive codes and categories cannot do this because they are couched at, and entrapped in, description. They do not go beyond the empirical world of factual information and concrete particulars. They can only produce ever more descriptions of concrete events and behaviour. Descriptive terms can never go beyond 'surface' particulars and tap into the underlying general principles and mechanisms that underpin social reality. Only conceptual/analytic categories have the capacity to go beyond empirical information and engage with the general organising principles of social reality.

It is the move from descriptive 'how', 'what' and 'who' questions to 'why' questions that signals the importance of concepts in explanation. 'Why' questions require the use of concepts to express and explain the origins and generative capacities of underlying features of social reality and social organisation. In this sense, concepts are the essential vehicles for constructing arguments, which in turn give expressive form to explanations, rather than descriptions of social phenomena.

Identifying, Exploring and Choosing Orienting Concepts

As far as identifying concepts as distinct from 'words' or 'descriptive accounts', it is best to return to the advice offered in Chapter 4 about the differences between problems and topics.

Descriptive labels (like words) provide information about the concrete particulars of a social phenomenon and are limited to particular times, people and places (rather like topics and topic-questions).

Concepts are abstract, general and analytic in nature. They classify groups of phenomena on the basis of shared principles, properties and characteristics, thus distinguishing them from other groups (of phenomena). They are independent of specific times, places and people (rather like research problems and problem-questions).

An exploratory approach

The adaptive approach requires that you begin data analysis by choosing *orienting concepts* which have proven value from the stock of established knowledge and previous research. Such concepts will help you to structure your analysis from its earliest phases, and will allow you to explore the extent to which they 'fit' and are relevant to your research data. Orienting concepts are an essential foundation for adaptive research, but their use should not be misunderstood. The advice to use orienting concepts is not a mandate for 'forcing' data into conceptual categories that are inappropriate or do not fit.

Orienting concepts should be chosen on the basis that they have an established pedigree for explaining social behaviour and processes, and not simply because they suit the preconceptions or prejudices of the researcher. Just as importantly, orienting concepts should be chosen for their power to guide the analysis, *not to determine or preconceive it*. Thus, while providing guidance and direction, they are essentially *preliminary* concepts, tentatively advanced as initial means of filtering and analysing data. As soon as data analysis is begun, their usefulness (for explaining social behaviour and processes) will start to become apparent.

The exploratory thrust of adaptive research pushes the researcher towards scrutinising and 'testing' the explanatory limits of the orienting concept (or network of concepts), in the light of ongoing data analysis and urges him or her to countenance the need for possible modifications. As the project unfolds, decisions about the aforementioned will be made on the basis of projected research outcomes. These will include identifying the relevance and applicability of the orienting concepts while simultaneously revealing potential limitations.

However, the real point of this kind of research is to explore new conceptual directions as an adaptive response to emerging data. Thus the focal point of interest is in unearthing data which challenges the explanatory power and relevance of the orienting concepts. The possibilities here include modifications, elaborations and extensions of the original concepts, but also genuine conceptual innovation – that is, the development of new concepts as they emerge from the creative confrontation between the orienting concepts and data which challenges their explanatory limits.

Choosing orienting concepts

As suggested in Chapter 4 a selective literature search is an important preparatory step for this kind of research, and this is especially the case when selecting orienting concepts. The main focus and purpose of a selective review should not be to find everything that has been written on, and researched in, a particular topic or to cover everything that is conceivably relevant to it. The 'selective' part of the review emphasises the importance of making provisional decisions about your problem-focus, your core research questions, and trawling for orienting concepts. Anything that is not connected with these three concerns should be jettisoned. If necessary, at a later date you can always come back to any of the issues you leave aside at this juncture. But where should you search for orienting concepts?

A Published research

Obviously, your first port of call for finding relevant orienting concepts is in the published research on the particular field or topic of your project – education, business, organisational leadership, nursing, friendship, intimacy, popular culture, or whatever it may be. A cursory examination of the research – possibly as described in a textbook giving an overview of the area – will provide you with a sense of the main or most important concepts that have had an impact in particular areas or topics. A suitable concept might grab your attention in the sense of making you want to explore its applicability either to new data or to experiment with the way it is used in slightly different circumstances than usual. Alternatively, you might wish to assess its relevance to entirely new circumstances or completely different issues.

B Related topics

Of course your chosen topic or area might be one about which very little research has been done – and, more rarely, none at all. In such a situation you should turn your attention to adjacent, overlapping or otherwise related topics areas or issues as potential sources of orienting concepts. For example, organisational behaviour, business, work, occupations, labour markets are all overlapping areas which often share concepts and conceptual interests, such as work satisfaction or leadership. But they also overlap with areas that, at least on the surface, may seem unrelated, such as nursing, or the medical profession in general, or universities, or religious communities, and so on.

C Generic concepts

You might select a concept (or set of concepts) of a more generic nature that are applicable to, or drawn from, a wide range of areas or contexts. For example, power-related concepts such as 'surveillance' or 'interpersonal control' or those to do with the passage of time (temporality), such as 'career' or 'behavioural routines', have the advantage that they are not tied to a particular area or topic, and are thus not restricted in their potential scope.

D Accredited theoretical frameworks

Finally, an important way of selecting orienting concepts is to draw them from an accredited body of theory or a theoretical framework. Inglis's (1998) use of 'status conflict theory' to analyse the inner workings and dynamics of a rock and roll group or Ritzer's (2011) borrowing of concepts from classical general theory, such as Weber's theory of bureaucracy and Marx's theory of alienation, to explain social experience in fast-food restaurants are good examples of this (see discussion in Chapter 2). Modern social theoretical frameworks, such as those of Giddens (1984), Archer (1995), Mouzelis (1995), or my own theory of social domains (Layder 1997, 1998, 2006), are fruitful sources of concepts (see Sibeon 2004 for an overview of these). Of course, using these as sources for orienting concepts demands no little confidence in handling highly abstract concepts, so the novice researcher might be best advised to opt for other sources.

Nevertheless, it is an important point that no matter how abstract a concept or theory may be, this should not discount their use in empirical research in general and particularly in the adaptive approach. Because we describe something as 'abstract' or 'theory' does not mean that it has no empirical relevance or applicability. The point of adaptive research is to explore and test-out the fit, applicability and explanatory relevance of certain concepts as they confront empirical data/evidence. Again, this is not to advocate the unthinking use of abstract concepts, but to creatively seek out their explanatory limits as well as their positive uses.

The Disadvantages of Open (or Initial) Coding

Thus far we have considered the use of orienting concepts to guide the analysis and coding of data. In this sense, the advice is the opposite of much qualitative data analysis in general, but in particular, it goes against the advice of grounded theorists that analysis should begin with 'open coding'. I shall have more detailed comments about these issues later in the discussion, but here I must make a general point about why I think it is best, especially at the beginning of data analysis, to avoid open coding, or what Charmaz (2006) calls 'initial coding', and instead employ orienting concepts as a preliminary way of ordering and organising data as well as guiding its analysis.

Open or initial coding are ways of generating or creating new codes from raw data at the very beginning of grounded theory research in order to create new concepts and theories from qualitative data. Grounded theorists (Glaser 2001; Glaser and Strauss 1967; Strauss and Corbin 1998) do not see any value or relevance in what they call 'preconceived' theory or concepts – that is, concepts that already exist and have been accredited *outside* a grounded theory remit. Only concepts that have been processed by the grounded theory method are regarded as valid, relevant or acceptable. In any event, creating so-called 'new' theory and concepts is the priority in any grounded theory analysis.

This is anathema to the adaptive approach, which recognises the utility and value of theory and concepts drawn from an immense diversity of sources. Especially abhorrent to grounded theorists are general social theories, which are dismissed as 'speculative' or 'armchair' theories not grounded in data and which result in the *forcing* of data into alien, ill-fitting concepts and categories – criticisms which are, incidentally, at best misplaced, and at worst plain inaccurate (Layder 1998). So, in order both to create new concepts and theories as well as to avoid speculative, preconceived theory, the grounded theory approach insists that the researcher should approach data collection and analysis without any concepts in mind since they act as 'blinders' (Strauss and Corbin 1998: 75) to seeing new codes and concepts.

Thus open coding is the grounded theorist's method of breaking up and organising data in order to look for coding categories in the service of generating grounded theory and concepts. In open or initial coding the researcher is advised to engage in very detailed coding practices, sometimes resulting in a new code per line of text (sometimes per sentence or paragraph). It is important for the researcher to be as open minded as possible at the early stages of analysis and to generate as many new ideas and codes as necessary to comprehensively reflect the data. Later, having generated all these codes, the researcher is encouraged to make connections between them, and to firm up his or her ideas about which are the most important to be taken forward as the core codes and categories. After a period of time, the researcher is in a position to be more 'selective' (Strauss and Corbin 1998) or 'focused' (Charmaz 2006) about the codes categories and concepts that should be used to analyse the data, while those that haven't proved useful should be dropped.

The adaptive approach takes a very different view of both early and later phases of coding by utilising coding categories based on orienting concepts found in the literature. But because they are *preliminary orienting devices* to be used as a departure point for critically exploring their explanatory limits, they do not act as 'blinders' to what is in the data. Quite the contrary, they point more immediately and incisively to those aspects of the data that either confirm or disconfirm their fit and relevance. They signal early on whether such concepts need to be modified or jettisoned and replaced. Moreover, they identify more accurately the empirical and conceptual space for 'new' or 'emergent' concepts, and the conditions under which they can be created and developed.

Looked at from the converse point of view, it is apparent that this kind of 'closed' coding with orienting concepts avoids some of the most obvious disadvantages of the free-form style of open or initial coding. The first of these is that the unstructured nature of open or initial coding is likely to have the effect of producing anxiety in the researcher and eroding, rather than enhancing, his or her confidence. Second, by being advised to create as many codes on a line-by-line basis, there is a likelihood of getting unnecessarily bogged down in the empirical details of the data, and hence becoming over-concerned with descriptive codes and categories at the expense of conceptual ones. Third, there is also the potential for creating too many codes which are eventually found to be irrelevant or inappropriate. This is likely to cause confusion in the researcher's mind, at the very point where he or she should be finding their feet and developing confidence in their analysis.

In short, open or initial coding is liable to cause chaos by the amassing and accumulation of raw data – a state of disorganisation that the process of coding is meant to combat in the first place. Thus, there is every chance that these coding practices might unsettle or intimidate the researcher, especially one who is relatively inexperienced. By contrast, the structured nature of coding with orienting concepts develops confidence and dispels confusion by offering direction and guidance for data analysis, without predetermining or preconceiving the outcome of the process. That is, it offers a very ordered procedure for allowing emergent issues such as modification or elaboration to take place as well as providing a secure foundation for conceptual innovation.

Coding, Data Analysis and Orienting Concepts

In summary, the adaptive approach proceeds on the assumption that coding and analysing research data – in the form of observational or interview notes and transcripts or documentary materials – are best dealt with by using pre-existing orienting concepts as initial analytic templates. As a consequence, data analysis consists of the continual assessment of the fit and relevance of these orienting concepts in relation to emerging data. This will lead to either of two broad outcomes or a combination of both.

A Modifying, elaborating or extending *existing concepts* (orienting concepts) and coding data in relation to them

or

B Once the incoming data has demonstrated that the orienting concepts have low explanatory value, the coding of data should be adjusted with a view to searching for *emergent concepts*.

With A, the researcher selects particular concepts (or several related concepts) *in advance* from a selective literature review (Chapter 4), on the basis of their relevance to current research problems and questions (Chapter 3). Data is then collected using a mixture of methods and strategies (Chapters 5 and 6) and by sampling various 'units' of data, again, for their problem-relevance (Chapter 7). Data are coded (key sections are marked or tagged with a particular symbol) to show which parts of the text 'indicate' the concepts.

Coding organises the data into 'meaningful patterns' or 'segments' which makes them more practically manageable. It also makes it easier to evaluate their efficacy for explaining the data. However, if coding and analysis indicate a weak relation between the concepts and data, the concepts are adjusted or modified and a revised coding system is adopted, before further data are gathered.

With B, the researcher begins, as in A, by using 'appropriate' concepts as a guide. The crucial difference is that, *from the start*, the concepts are regarded as temporary or 'provisional'. Data is sorted and assimilated using a coding system based on these concepts. However, if the evidence suggests the greater fit and relevance of other concepts, the originals are replaced. In this manner, concepts may *seem to* 'emerge' anew from the data, but *in fact they* are organically connected with other concepts, especially the initial 'orienting' concepts. Nevertheless, 'emergent' concepts require a revised coding system based on unfolding ideas and evidence.

A great number of research projects are a rather muddy mixture of influences of A and B. In both, however, research is geared towards *explanation* rather than *description*. In other words, the point of adaptive research is *not simply* to describe and present information on people's attitudes, or to offer an 'impressionistic' account of social life. In its search for explanation, adaptive research goes further in pursuing (and suggesting answers to) 'how' and 'why' questions, about the links between social behaviour and social organisation. For instance: Why do particular kinds of social behaviour occur? What is the influence of this or that activity on relationships or social organisation?

Data analysis using orienting concepts

Chapter 2 included examples of research using concepts that could be used in an orienting manner, such as 'alienation', 'dehumanisation', 'simple and complex friendship', 'McDonaldization', 'styles of loving', and 'episodic' and 'semi-detached intimacy'. There are countless others that could be similarly used as orienting devices, such as 'emotional labour', 'power and control', 'surveillance', 'career' and 'organisational morality', although many more can be found in the literature. Because concepts like these 'bridge', or 'tie together', behaviour and social organisation (objective and subjective aspects of social life), they *have a wide range of connections* with all six key analytic problems, although, of course, many other kinds of concepts (including 'behavioural' and 'systemic' concepts – see previous chapter) can be used as orienting concepts.

Orienting concepts such as these provide ready-made 'codes' for breaking up and organising the data into meaningful 'segments' and 'patterns' which reduces the volume of relevant data, thereby making it easier to manage and analyse. Orienting concepts indicate a particular 'take' on topics or areas of activity (such as classroom behaviour, marriage or client–professional relationships), and suggest possible explanations for observed patterns of behaviour.

The flexibility of orienting concepts means that they may be used for long- or short-term purposes. For instance, a particular concept might 'survive' the test of evidence, thus broadly reaffirming its explanatory importance, although it might 'survive' in a fundamentally modified or elaborated form. However, if a concept falls short in this regard, its relevance will diminish as data collection proceeds. Of course, although it will have already provided essential 'initial' guidance and direction for the project, once its usefulness has been outgrown, it should either be dropped or modified. There is no question of 'forcing' data into conceptual categories that do not fit.

An example: emotional labour

Hochschild (1983) originally used the concept of 'emotional labour' in her study focusing on how airline flight attendants deal with the emotional demands of the flying public. 'Emotional labour' expresses the way flight attendants use 'smiles' and 'reassurance' to allay passengers' anxieties and fears about flying. Hochschild also used the concept to explain why employers – the airline companies – encourage this behaviour. In a wider sense, the study raises the issues about 'false emotion' and whether, or how, it influences and fits alongside 'real' personal or 'private' feelings. More generally, it highlights the way emotions are variably expressed in different settings.

It might seem that the concept could be applied in a diverse range of projects and problems. But can the concept be usefully applied to other areas of work? For example, is it relevant to work settings in which the management of emotion is required as part of the job, such as school teaching, counselling or nursing or even business leadership and management? In relation to these issues, a project could focus on any of the following questions:

Is the emotional labour of flight attendants similar to or different from that required from school teachers, counsellors and nurses or even business leaders and managers?

How and why do people distance themselves emotionally from job roles?

How do professionals maintain psychological composure in the face of client demands (from customers, employees, pupils or patients)?

Does 'commercial pressure' result in more false emotion?

Is 'emotional distance' in intimate relationships different from that in other settings?

What kinds of interpersonal skills are involved in maintaining 'emotional composure'?

'Emotional labour' might help in the collection and organisation of data in a project on any of the above issues. At the same time, this data could be compared with that gathered in other (published) occupational studies. If such comparative data are not available, it is possible to imaginatively 'think through' comparisons between job settings and contexts. In either case, such comparisons could be used to assess the general usefulness of the concept. Against the background of such comparisons and assessments, the possibility is raised of 'unpacking', elaborating or extending the concept.

Emotional labour and intimacy

Alternatively, a project might explore the relevance of 'emotional labour' to non-work settings, such as friendship and couple/romantic intimacy. Certainly, 'emotional distancing' and 'deception' are commonly used by partners or friends. However, the reasons for such behaviour, and its emotional consequences (such as hurt and resentment), may differ from those in 'commercial' relationships. Thus a number of research questions could be pursued. For example:

What does it mean to speak of 'emotional labour' in intimate relationships?

When partners or friends talk about feelings, desires and secrets (including sexual desire), are they expressions of 'emotional labour'?

Why do some individuals shoulder all or most of the emotion work in a relationship while others shirk from it?

Why do partners or friends distance themselves emotionally from one another? How do they do this?

Is emotional distance used as a way of seizing power in, or maintaining control over, personal relationships?

Practical Aspects of Coding

Data analysis is partly a practical activity – coding data by actually marking bits of data and assigning labels to them. But it also involves a process of 'reflection' in which the researcher tries to figure out how to interpret the data and how it contributes to an explanation of the problem being researched. The Research Log comes to prominence at this point because it is here that the process of reflection takes place in the form of notes and memos (and/or flow diagrams). Coding and analysis go hand in hand, although they are in fact physically separate processes. That is, the researcher continually moves from one to the other, from coding to reflection, back to coding and so on, while both activities inform and feed into each other.

As a practical activity, coding involves reading and reviewing your data. This might appear in different forms, such as:

- handwritten notes on observations or interviews (or directed conversations) that were not audio recorded

- transcriptions of recorded interviews, either word processed or handwritten

- documents, published articles, books, magazines, research reports, and so on

With notes or transcriptions you should leave a blank margin (of about two or three inches) to the right (or left) of the page in which there is space to mark sections of the text. Coding then involves assigning a label (or mark or symbol) to indicate the relevance of the orienting concept to the particular section of text that has been selected. The label may simply be the initials of the concept you are using, for example, EL can stand for 'emotional labour'. Just as easily, you can use a reference number, or any symbol or mark, but it has to be one that you will *personally* recognise and remember (Glesne and Peshkin 1992).

To complete the practical act of coding, the exact section of text/data should be underlined, highlighted and/or boxed-in to signify its relevance to the code. Then the connection between the text and the code label in the margin should be clearly marked, via arrowed or dotted lines, so that it is identifiable for future reference.

When examining data you should try to adopt and maintain an 'overview' of it. That is, you should attempt to code with as general or as wide a viewpoint as possible by keeping your head up, and not get bogged down in the details of 'line-by-line' coding and analysis. Of course, by its very nature, the act of coding (the labelling, underlining and boxing) requires that you deal with specific lines of text. However, the way you choose which bits of text are relevant, should stem from a wide-angled 'overview' of the data/text rather than a restricted focus on particular bits of data. That is, your attention should be shared equally between the orienting concept, the data and wider contextual factors.

This 'wider context' itself is comprised of two things. First, the problems and research questions that drive the project should always be kept in mind when making connections between concepts and data. Second, it is important to adopt a wide-angled perspective on the interview or observation from which the data was obtained. Where and how they were conducted and any relevant aspects concerning individuals or interactions, or distinguishing features of the social setting and social context should be taken into consideration.

What to look for in the text/data

Remember you are looking for evidence of particular orienting concepts that have been defined in advance – on the basis of a selective literature review – *as likely to be relevant to your problem and topic.* This means that to some degree your perceptions of the data will already be focused and directed. You will be looking for definite connections (correlations) between a concept, or concepts, and specific pieces of data (text).

Remember, with the adaptive approach the researcher does *not begin with a completely open mind.* Using an orienting concept raises the analysis above the details of the data and forces the researcher to think in abstract general terms about how to interpret the data, and how it might help in explaining the research problems and questions.

Glaser (2001) insists that such procedures have the effect of 'forcing' the data to fit concepts which, in fact, they do not fit. But the adaptive approach does not encourage the researcher to do this. Rather, it 'forces' the researcher to think about whether there are connections between particular concepts and particular segments of data. For example, it prompts the question: Does the observation of a professional who smiles indicate a link with the concept of emotional labour? In fact a researcher might decide, on the basis of trying to match a certain kind of behaviour with a certain concept, that there is no real connection or that the connection is weak. Both are crucial for evaluating the relevance and usefulness of the concept and I shall deal with these two possibilities further on in the discussion.

Here I want to concentrate on two other possible outcomes. In the first, the researcher is convinced that there is a strong connection between the orienting concept and data. In this case he or she simply goes ahead and codes or labels the data as previously described. The second refers to the researcher's hunch or intuition that there *might be* a connection. The researcher is caught in two minds. Initially she or he is prompted by something in the data to label it as an indicator of the concept – as 'smiling' is an indicator of 'emotional labour'. But hesitancy arises perhaps because the behaviour occurs in an unusual work setting, and so its meaning is not clear. As with the first possibility, the researcher should simply go ahead and code the data, but delay the final decision by identifying it as a 'provisional' coding.

In both of the above cases you should continue to code until you have completed a fair amount of data – perhaps a whole interview or a set of observational notes. However, you should stop coding (at least temporarily) at a point where you feel the need for clarification. Or, put another way; stop coding when you begin to feel confused. There is no exact point, but a general rule is to stop sooner rather than later when confusion may become overwhelming. At this point you should leave the data coding and open your Research Log.

Research Log: memos and notes

The most useful place to document data–concept connections (that is, when you have established proof of their connection) is in your Research Log. So at this juncture you begin to use the Research Log to write notes on your thoughts and reflections on coding issues. After each entry in the log you must go back to coding once again, continually switching back and forth between the two until all the data has been coded and analysed.

At this point, the entries in the Research Log will serve as personal notes and memos, in which you reflect on the relationship between orienting concepts and particular segments of data. They are notes primarily for your own benefit, with a view to helping you sort through ideas about how closely concepts and data are linked. They will also reveal ways in which such links might aid in explaining and understanding the main research problems and questions. Without doubt, you will already have some definite or worked-through ideas. But you will also have some half-baked ones, so it is important to get the chance to clarify any of the latter by thinking reflectively about them.

In their 'free-form' state, as I have said, the notes are primarily for your own personal consumption. However, as they unfold over time and begin to take on a more settled and structured form, they will eventually serve as the basis for the 'analysis' and 'findings/conclusions' sections of your final research report. Thus, it is important to bear in mind that they shouldn't become too idiosyncratic or haphazard because in the end they will need recasting into a readable and justifiable account of your research.

Focal Points for the Research Log

1 Concepts, problem-questions and research data

The first issue in need of attention is to establish the links between data, concepts, research questions and research problems. Data, in the form of observational notes or interview transcripts, has already been pre-structured around the key problems and questions that drive the research. Hopefully this has been reinforced through the use of particular strategies and methods (of data collection and analysis) as well as sampling techniques. The first task for the log, therefore, is to discuss and reflect on the relationship between the links and influences between three key elements:

The problem-questions ------ Orienting concepts ----------- The data

Figure 8.2

For example, in a project investigating how student friends deal with each other emotionally (an aspect of emotion work), the key problem-questions might involve three intersecting social domains. These are: individual students, the setting (the college or university), and the nature of interactions between students or how they get along with one another on a day-to-day basis. The problem-focus of the study, therefore centres on (a) how the college or university setting shapes the social interactions of the students, and (b) how, in turn, emotional dealings between friends are influenced by these interactions.

The influence of this problem-focus should have seeped directly into the data sampling and collection procedures via the research design and would thus generate data heavily 'saturated' by the problem-focus. The choice of 'emotion work' as an orienting concept has to be made with reference to this wider context. So the first entry in this part of the Research Log should consist of a reflective discussion of how and why 'emotional labour' relates to this problem-focus. A typical entry might read as follows, under the heading of:

Research Log: sample entry

Note on: Student friendships and emotional responses

'Emotion work': This concept 'bridges' or ties together the interactional world of students with the social setting of the university – thus it provides a suitable (conceptual) means of understanding the links between emotion and the dynamics of friendship.

But what is the connection between 'emotion work', as expressed in social interaction, and the way in which individuals respond psychologically?

How does the social setting of a university influence the ways in which students relate to and interact with one another?

How does gender affect emotional labour? What is the extent of its influence? Do other factors, such as 'individual' psychological differences, interpersonal dynamics or the specific features of the setting, enhance or 'neutralise' the effects of gender?

If necessary, each of the above comments or notes could be broken down and discussed in further detail. However, do not feel as though you have to finalise any thoughts or comments at any one point in time. Treat the log entries as a 'running commentary' that can be added to at different phases of the research.

You also might want to begin experimenting with drawing flow diagrams that indicate the directions of influence between social behaviour and domains of social life, as well as the concepts that represent them.

2 'Measuring' concepts against/or comparing them with data

The second point for attention in the Research Log is the extent to which the orienting concept measures up to, or is 'indicated' by, particular segments of data.

The main themes of your log notes should centre on the kind of social behaviour that indicates the presence of 'emotional labour' and how examples of this behaviour can be recognised in the data. A typical note might be as follows:

What does it mean to talk about 'emotional labour' in relation to friendship?

What range of behaviours is covered by this term? Smiling, reassuring – verbally (talking things over) and/or non-verbally (physical contact, embracing comforting) – sharing and caring. Is caring and sharing behaviour different for men and women?

Are there important individual differences in emotional expression?

What is the relation between formal and informal types of situation and the tendency to express feeling/emotion – for example, a formal (teaching) situation as compared with an informal situation, such as relaxed chatting in a coffee bar?

Is the way in which the participants 'define the situation' important? How do they define the situation? What is its meaning for them and how does it affect their behaviour and attitudes towards one another?

The rest of the note might include some provisional answers to these questions, and some indication of how you will prioritise various issues. For example, you may decide to concentrate on 'how participants define informal situations' as a key factor that triggers emotional responses. Therefore, the log note will suggest how you intend to go about this – in terms of further sampling, and so on.

3 Comparison with 'alternative' concepts

A significant part of the 'test against evidence', to which an orienting concept should be subjected, is through comparison with 'alternative' concepts to see if they are able to better explain or account for the data. This kind of assessment of the orienting concept should be a constant accompaniment to the research – particularly in the data collection and analysis phase. The concepts chosen as points of comparison may be completely different from, and thus genuinely compete with, the orienting concept, or they may be more closely related ideas or concepts that seem to have greater explanatory potential or subtlety.

The alternative concepts should be drawn from previous reading and literature searches as well as from ideas that have developed from ongoing data collection and analysis. A typical log note might read as follows:

Can the behavioural phenomenon labelled 'emotion work' be better characterised as a certain type of friendship, such as 'soulmates' or 'confidantes' (Spencer and Pahl 2006)? Do these latter compete with 'emotion work' to explain the same phenomena? Or can they be used in conjunction with emotion work, in the sense that they refer to discrete and parallel phenomena?

Similarly, how does the concept of 'emotional terrorism' (Miller 1995) compare with that of emotion work? Do they compete with each other or are they complementary?

Again, the note might go on to suggest possible answers to these questions. However, at this stage they will remain provisional in nature because subsequent entries might amend them in the light of incoming data or evolving analytic ideas.

Back to coding

The actual length or fullness of the Research Log notes will depend on factors unique either to your own way of working or to the nature of the project itself. But there is absolutely no reason why they should be any particular (predetermined) length. You must set your own agenda in this respect, although you might reserve your fullest notes for the later phases of data collection and analysis. Regardless of how the notes pan out, they should be done in an alternating sequence with coding. Once the first Research Log entry is completed, you should go back to coding data.

But, again, if the coding begins to generate confusion, you must stop and return to the log in order to clarify your thinking. In a positive sense confusion may arise because of emerging ideas about coding labels, orienting concepts or alternative strategies of analysis. Here the advice is the same: stop coding and return to the Research Log. This will enable you to sharpen up your ideas, compare and evaluate the options you have, the choices you must make, and the direction you must take.

Extending Orienting Concepts

The above discussion has concentrated on using an orienting concept in a fairly conventional manner, but another possibility is when ongoing data collection and analysis requires that the definition of an orienting concept be extended. A second alternative occurs when data collection and analysis confirms the core importance of the orienting concept to the project, but also requires a set of supporting (or 'satellite') concepts. The necessity of either, or both, of these possibilities may become apparent at any point. However, they imply rather different implications for the future direction of the research.

Initially, a particular orienting concept may offer an interesting perspective on the research problem or topic. However, at some point – if not before, then certainly during data collection – it may become clear that it cannot adequately cope with particular aspects of the data.

For example, originally 'emotional labour' was applied to the work situation of flight attendants. In fact, the 'labour' part of the term suggests that it might be of use in relation to other kinds of work. However, perusal of the literature on other areas, such as teaching or nursing, or, indeed, the sampling and collection of data on these areas, might reveal significant differences between these work situations. For example, the extent to which commercial considerations impinge on nurses' or teachers' job performance would appear to be much less than with flight attendants. As a consequence, the problem of insincerity (or the inauthentic expression of emotion) would seem to be much less pronounced.

Therefore, before using the concept in relation to these jobs, some extension of its terms of reference (involving a redefinition of the behaviour referred to) would be required. Adjustments of definition and their corresponding empirical indicators should be incorporated into the coding system.

A Research Log entry should document any of the above changes involved in extending orienting concepts.

Core and Satellite Concepts

From its own inner momentum a research project often generates more and more relevant concepts. In such a case the original orienting concept may remain at the 'core' of the analysis. However, as analytic ideas change in tandem with subsequent data collection, it may become clear that other supporting or subsidiary concepts are necessary.

With 'emotional labour', and depending on the exact focus of the research project, several related concepts may become salient. For example, the concept of 'company' or 'employer pressure' (for emotional labour) would be pertinent to a comparison between teaching and flight attendants. To what extent is there pressure from employers for flight attendants to engage in emotional labour as compared with teachers? Similar considerations apply to the concept of 'client pressure' (for emotional labour). Is client pressure important for understanding the differences between pressure from passengers (flight attendants) and pressure from pupils or students (teachers)? Also, asking questions about the consequences of emotional labour may lead to other important supporting concepts, such as 'emotional overload', 'emotional burnout', 'true and false emotion' or 'impression management' (Goffman 1971).

In such a case 'emotional labour' could be understood as the 'core' concept at the centre of a potential web of other supporting concepts, such as 'emotional overload', 'client demands' and 'employer demands', and so on. This web of interrelated concepts will form the basis of an explanatory narrative for the project.

It is important to document the emergence of satellite concepts in the Research Log. You should spell out their interrelations both with the core concept and with each other. In this manner, you create a 'reference map' of concepts that may be important for any additional sampling and data collection. Of course, such a proliferation of concepts requires that your coding system is expanded to include them.

Coding, Data Analysis and Emergent Concepts

The discussion now moves from coding orienting concepts to searching out or developing 'emergent' concepts. On the surface, this might seem to involve the exact opposite of what is required for orienting concepts. However, closer scrutiny reveals that this is not the case. Concepts can only 'emerge' out of the synergy that arises from the confrontation between the ongoing collection of new data and its analysis via concepts. In this very important sense, emergent concepts do not (and cannot) emerge solely from data!

In this respect, the adaptive approach is markedly different from 'grounded theory', which insists that the researcher clears his or her mind of any preconceived concepts or ideas to enable 'new' ones (and theory) to emerge directly from data. However, even if it was possible to erase all concepts from a researcher's mind (which is very doubtful), it still remains the case that 'newly minted' concepts (or theory) cannot emerge solely from empirical data. The meaning and validity of 'new' concepts and the empirical phenomena to which they refer are determined equally by the nexus of relationships *they already have* with other concepts. In this sense, just as a word in a dictionary is defined by another set of words, so the meanings of concepts are in large part defined in relation to other concepts. So while the empirical grounding of emergent concepts is important for their adequacy and validity, their links with other related concepts are of equal importance. Certainly, their validity or adequacy cannot be solely evaluated in terms of their empirical grounding in data.

The adaptive approach acknowledges the importance of existing concepts in the production of 'new' ones, and therefore the search for them cannot begin with 'open coding'. Instead, the process *begins* in broadly the same way as coding with orienting concepts. However, there is one major difference! Orienting concepts are used to crank start the research process and as such should be regarded simply as *provisional guides* for the early phases of data collection and analysis. If a more appropriate or adequate concept emerges, the initial orienting concept will begin to diminish in significance, either immediately or rather more slowly, eventually to be replaced by the alternative concept.

There are three main ways this might happen. First, it may occur through a process of modification by 'splitting' or 'fragmenting' from the orienting concept. Second, the orienting concept may be completely dispensed with and replaced with another orienting concept that more adequately represents newly collected data. In such a case the replacement concept 'emerges' as a result of the researcher's hand being forced by the data which indicates exactly the sort of concept that is needed. The replacement may be an extant concept, an innovative one, or a combination of the two. Third, a concept may emerge that has no link either with the orienting concept (or one that has split from it) or with a replacement concept.

Emergence via splitting

The search for an emergent concept may begin with a strong reliance on an orienting concept to provide initial ideas and guidance for the collection, coding and analysis of data. Remaining with the example of 'emotional labour', imagine that after a selective but rigorous literature review it was decided that 'emotional labour' could offer initial guidance for a project focusing on the dynamics of interpersonal relationships in friendship or romantic intimacy.

The researcher begins to code and analyse data around the concept of emotional labour. However, the concept may raise certain problems because the 'labour' part is clearly related to work, but its relevance to intimacy is not readily apparent. In this sense, the researcher might decide that 'emotional labour' may lack sufficient subtlety when applied to intimate relationships. Further data collection confirms that it fails to capture the subtle nuances of communication between couples.

The researcher searches for a more appropriate way of 'talking about' such emotional exchanges, and a number of possibilities present themselves. Concepts such as 'styles of emotional management' or those of 'emotional distance' and 'emotional availability' may present themselves as more suitable candidates for understanding what is going on in intimate communication.

As data increasingly underlines the importance of these concepts, they become the main focus of coding and data analysis. Correspondingly, the original orienting concept (emotional labour) declines in significance. However, it is because the emergent concepts bear some relation to 'emotional labour' that they can be said to have 'split off' from, and thus emerged out of, it. Nevertheless, they also break new ground conceptually and thus take data analysis in another direction.

Research Log memos and notes should document the changes in conceptual emphasis of the research towards the 'new' (emergent) concepts. This should be undertaken with reference to the three 'discussion points' outlined in the previous discussion of working with orienting concepts. To recap, these points focus on:

a   research problems and questions

b   the fit between data and concepts

c   the relative merits of 'alternative' concepts.

In the cases of splitting, the memos and notes should concentrate primarily on (a) and (b) (since (c) is somewhat irrelevant). That is, they must document how the emergent concepts can offer a more accurate/comfortable alignment with the core research problems and questions. Also, they should emphasise how emergent concepts were generated by problems caused by a lack of fit between the orienting concept and ongoing data analysis.

Emergence via replacement by an alternative

Replacing the original orienting concept with an alternative due to a lack of supporting data/evidence will more than likely require a fairly radical reorientation and disruption of the project. For example, in the light of incoming data it may be decided that a project (provisionally) guided by the core concept of 'emotional labour' would be better analysed in terms of the concepts of 'power and control'. In this sense, power and control can be said to 'emerge' as the core conceptual foci (even though they are already 'established' concepts).

In such a case, the evidence demands a fundamental rethink and reorientation of the core concepts on which the research design and analytic framework is based. This, in itself, would also require some reorganisation of sampling procedures, including changes in target samples and sampling strategies. In one sense, the whole process implies a fundamental interruption of the research process in order to implement the necessary reorientation. Such a situation requires a good amount of unanticipated additional effort to deal with the problems it poses.

However, rather than respond to it as if it signalled the endpoint or failure of the project, it is much more constructive to see it as an opportunity to rescue a piece of research that has, for whatever reason, veered off-track. So while there is undoubtedly some upheaval involved, it also offers the chance to take advantage of the flexibility of the adaptive approach. In this sense, the research can be reoriented around a more appropriate concept, and thus may yet again have the chance to arrive at a successful conclusion.

Research Log

In response to the radical or total replacement of an orienting concept your *Research Log* will be a little more complicated by the necessity for documenting the reasons for its replacement and the ensuing reorganisation of the project around an alternate concept or set of concepts. However, clearly, the memos outlining the reasons for the rejection of the original concept will centre on the issues raised in points (a) and (b). The reflective discussion of the suitability of the 'emergent' alternate concept will hinge around the issues raised in point (c) – how alternative concepts compare with the original in terms of their explanatory potential.

Innovative Concepts

Finally, conceptual emergence may entail the complete replacement of the original orienting concept, but not by an established one. Rather the 'emergent' concept is 'freshly created' by the researcher as a response to analytic problems posed by specific data. Of course, as noted before, the meaning and referents of any 'new' concept depend, in part, on other (extant) concepts which define it. In that sense, such 'emergent' concepts have both empirical and conceptual origins.

However, although the aim is to search for emergent concepts, the researcher does not approach data collection and analysis with a 'blank' mind and 'open coding' (creating as many fresh codes as possible). Rather, he or she begins with a selectively chosen orienting concept (or several of them) to direct and channel data collection and coding. Only when the researcher comes up against data that cannot be assimilated in terms of these directive 'channelling' concepts, does he or she make the decision to creatively develop a concept that solves the analytic problems posed by the data. But to reiterate, the data itself does not simply 'suggest' or 'offer up' a new, more 'appropriate', concept. Such concepts are generated in equal measure by a web of links with other concepts.

Let me use Miller's (1995) concept of 'emotional terrorism' as an example. However, it is appropriate to point out the following is not Miller's account, but my own analysis of Miller's concept. The concept of 'emotional terrorism' is created from two strands. First, Miller was confronting a data-fit deficit problem. His data on the behaviour and relationships of married couples was not consistent with concepts such as 'marital love' or 'romantic love' which are excessively positive, if not idealised, images. Miller's data suggested the predominance of power struggles and co-dependence in modern marriage/intimate relationships – what he calls 'unpeaceful co-existence'. This contradiction indicated the 'empirical space' for a concept such as 'intimate terrorism', which recorded the more negative aspects of modern intimacy. But the meaning of the concept derives from its ironic juxtaposition of 'intimacy' (implying harmonious co-existence) and 'terrorism' (suggesting an opposite state of antagonism and exploitation). Thus the unique force of the concept is created out of the drawing together of these two meanings. This is also intensified by the implied rejection or critique of the idea that only the presence of 'mutual satisfaction' or 'romantic love' is capable of keeping relationships going.

The same empirical and conceptual influences are at work in relation to the concept of 'episodic intimacy' (Layder 2009). The 'space' for the concept arose because empirical data on relationships between couples (Marshall 2006; Miller 1995; Reibstein 1997) suggested that there were different forms of couple intimacy not captured in concepts like the 'pure relationship' (Giddens 1991, 1992), which claim to characterise intimate relationships in the modern world. Episodic intimacy is one of several concepts designed to capture something of the empirical variation and subtlety in modern intimacy.

However, creation of the concept depended not only on what problems of explanation are revealed by the evidence, but also on its relation with other concepts. For instance, it challenges the idea that intimate relationships can be adequately 'summarised' by a highly generalised concept such as the 'pure relationship'. The 'episodic' part of the concept implies that in the real world many couple relationships are not continuously at the same level of intensity (of emotional involvement and commitment) – they vary depending on the moods, arguments and disappointments of the individuals concerned. Thus, it is not appropriate to think of intimate relationships as unimodal, fixed or stable, but rather as fluid and labile.

The Research Log

In this case, log memos and notes will debate, reflect on and document the way in which the emergent concept is produced. Thus, the focus will be on the 'data-fit problem', which signals the need and subsequent search for a more adequate and appropriate concept. This involves identifying the data that cannot be assimilated in terms of existing or established concepts. Another equally important focus will be on outlining how the concept is developed and formed in tandem with data collection, coding and analysis. Part of this will entail demonstrating how the concept relates to other concepts and the extent to which it explains aspects of data that cannot be explained by alternative concepts.

The Research Project as an Unfolding Process

The foregoing discussion has concentrated on the links between the collection of data, the process of coding and its conceptual analysis. The primary concern has been with describing two main ways in which such linkages may be forged – working with existing orienting concepts, and searching for emergent concepts. However, with both, the researcher begins with orienting concepts to ensure that the project is based on firm and clear foundations that are rigorously scientific in nature. The concern with concept–data linkages ties the research to explanatory objectives underpinned by the corroboration of empirical evidence.

In the case of the search for emergent concepts, the requirement of starting with orienting concepts has a secondary advantage. It avoids the confusion that inevitably arises from a lack of structure if research is begun without any preconceived ideas and with the intention of open coding (as advised in grounded theory). Starting with no clear ideas about what it is you are looking for is a recipe for confusion and blind stabbing in the dark.

By contrast, beginning with orienting concepts offers guidance and direction for the researcher. Because of their provisional status as 'holding' or 'modelling concepts', against which data can be measured or tested for feasibility, orienting concepts are never forced on data, and neither is data 'forced' into their conceptual mould. Thus, the researcher is not limited by or constrained to accept any concepts or strategies if they are not up to the explanatory task that they are meant to perform.

The Adaptive Approach and Data Analysis

A guiding structure – but flexibly adaptive

Adaptive research is highly structured at the start, in the sense that it relies on the use of orienting concepts (and the wider set of assumptions in which they are embedded) to act as a guide and a directive for the analysis of data. However, this starting 'structure' is not fixed and unchangeable. Rather, it is open to the unfolding nature of the research and, thus, to adaptive responses to emergent data and analytic ideas which cannot be accommodated by, or assimilated into, the original structure.

At the start, the researcher has no idea of what to expect, in terms of the extensiveness of the adaptive responses that may be required. In fact, this is an open question, the answer to which depends on what turns up in data collection, the extent of gaps in knowledge that are revealed, and whether (and how) analytic ideas evolve during the course of the project. There is, therefore, a wide span of possible outcomes for such research. These range, on the one hand, from a situation in which:

A. The analytic component of the research may remain largely as originally defined, but not wholly because of the essentially exploratory nature of the research. Instead of testing out or verifying a relationship between two or more variables, adaptive research sets out to explore a problem-focus in more general terms. That is, it investigates various explanatory aspects of a specific problem-focus rather than test a specific hypothesis. This exploratory character ensures that at least some novel research outcomes will be generated (such as new or unexplained data, or unexplored topics, areas or contexts), which may require the modification, extension or elaboration of orienting concepts. In this sense, the approach's openness to 'emergent possibilities' makes it likely that at least some discovery, or addition of challenging data, or innovations in conceptual analysis will occur.

B. At the other end of the spectrum, the analytic framework of the research might move away from its original (orienting) starting point to such an extent that it becomes largely (though not wholly) unrecognisable. In this case the 'not wholly' caveat refers to the fact that the imprint of the original orienting starting point is never completely erased. This is because the structured framework on which the research starts out generally ensures that adaptive responses are most usefully calibrated and assessed in terms of their *departure* from orienting assumptions. So, although such adaptations are in a significant sense 'innovative', of necessity they also bear some relationship to their point of departure – in extant knowledge. In this manner it may add to the cumulative thrust of social scientific knowledge.

Data Analysis as a Response to Different Research Outcomes

Most research projects will fall somewhere between A and B described above. However, depending on the nature of the data collected and the corresponding evolution of analytic ideas in relation to a specific project, there are three most likely research outcomes.

1 Elaboration

The orienting concepts and supporting assumptions require elaboration or the additional support of a network of 'satellite' concepts in order to adequately analyse the data. In this respect, coding and analysis of data will shift in accordance with the changes in conceptual framework.

2 Emergence

Through pressure from accumulating evidence or data, the orienting concepts and supporting assumptions outlive their usefulness and give way to innovative concepts and assumptions that are better able to deal with problems raised by incoming data and changing analytic ideas. Again, coding and data analysis will change in response to conceptual innovations.

3 Elaboration and emergence combined

A combination of elements represents the most productive and sophisticated outcome for adaptive research since both elaboration and emergence are interweaved within the same project. Research that produces a 'mixed outcome' can legitimately claim that it contributes to social scientific knowledge in two ways. First, it contributes through confirming or verifying some aspects of an existing corpus of knowledge, while simultaneously extending and elaborating on this knowledge. Second, it also contributes to social scientific knowledge through 'innovation' (via emergent concepts). In this sense, the research expands the current boundaries of knowledge by providing new (original) perspectives, concepts and analytic assumptions.

Final Comment

This chapter has described how concepts and data – or concepts and their empirical indicators – are related via the process of coding and analysis. The focus on the role of concepts in coding and data analysis emphasises the *exploratory and explanatory basis* of adaptive research. That is, data analysis should not be thought of as simply sorting and organising data as if it was a means of revealing the findings or conclusions of the research. Such a vision of analysis would miss out the crucial link between concepts and data and would remain entrapped at a descriptive (rather than explanatory) level.

The first step in moving beyond description towards explanation is to understand the relation between concepts and the data that are, in fact, their empirical indicators. Only once this step has been taken is it possible to examine how research projects achieve internal coherence in the form of a network of inter-related concepts which underpin the explanatory part of the research. The next chapter turns to examining the way in which concepts are importantly linked to wider research arguments to form an overall explanatory narrative.

Checklist for Research Log Notes

- Reflect on the importance of early analysis and avoiding over amassing of unstructured data.

- Begin to make decisions about codes, code categories and code labels. Make sure you know the difference between (and can thus identify) descriptive and conceptual coding categories. Take care that you have enough conceptual codes at your disposal to support your anticipated explanation(s).

- Familiarise yourself with the links between descriptions, concepts and explanations by reflecting on how they relate to your own project.

- Make notes on the question of which orienting concepts you will use, and how your project will explore their explanatory potential.

- Assess the most likely sources from which you might select your orienting concepts: published research on the area or topic; an 'adjacent' area; generic concepts; theory and theoretical frameworks.

- Begin to think through the logic of coding with orienting concepts and how this differs from 'open' or 'initial' coding. Become aware of the advantages of coding with orienting concepts, including its flexibility in terms of unfolding research outcomes.

- Reflect on the nature of coding, using your own orienting concepts and drawing parallels with the discussion of 'emotional labour', work and intimacy in this chapter.

- Familiarise yourself with the practical aspects of coding. How, in practical terms, will you code your interview transcripts, observational notes, documents, and so on? What will you look for in the text? How will you identify the links between concepts and data.

- Remember the three focal points for the Research Log: (1) establishing the links between problem-questions, orienting concepts and data; (2) measuring concepts against, and comparing them with, data; (3) comparing alternative concepts. How do these relate to your own project? Re-read the discussion of sample entries for the Research Log in this chapter.

- Begin to anticipate how your project will unfold. Will you need to extend, add to or modify your orienting concepts? What sort of data will suggest which option is most appropriate for your project? Do you need to adopt a core and satellite model for your orienting concepts? Are there areas of your project that might yield or benefit from the search for, or development of, emergent concepts?

- Be aware of the possibilities for the development or discovery of emergent concepts in your project. For instance: (a) emergence via 'splitting' from orienting concepts; (b) emergence by replacement of alternative concepts; and (c) the emergence of innovative concepts.

- Try to anticipate the final research outcome. You are not irrevocably committing yourself to anything here. You can always change your mind in accordance with the manner in which your project develops. But being aware of the 'direction' of the project at any point in time helps in the management and practical aspects of the coding and analysis of data.

- How much conceptual elaboration and how much conceptual emergence do you anticipate or expect? Do you expect or intend to reach a research outcome that combines conceptual elaboration and emergence?

9

WRITING THE RESEARCH REPORT: ARGUMENTS & EXPLANATIONS

PREVIEW

This chapter covers the following:

- Using the Research Log as a basis for the final research report

- Writing style and presenting the final report: two writing styles you must avoid and one you must adopt

- Some key definitions: argument, concepts, explanations and explanatory narratives

- The six basic elements of the research report

- Using mini-arguments to build a meta-argument

  1 Outlining the purposes and objectives of the project
  2 Presenting the research design: problems and topics
  3 Describing methods and strategies of data collection
  4 Sampling criteria and strategies
  5 Concepts, coding and data analysis
  6 Conclusion: arguments and explanations

Writing generally, and writing up the final research report in particular, should not be delayed until 'everything else' has been completed. Throughout the book I've consistently emphasised the importance of beginning to write as soon as possible, along with other research preparations, such as formulating your problem or deciding what methods of data collection to use (see Creswell 2009; and Wolcott 2001 for similar ideas about 'early' writing). This goes hand in hand with the idea that the best writing always goes through several *drafts*.

Undergraduates do not usually adopt this habit for essay writing, but it is one that should be acquired for presenting reports on original research. You must be willing to change or tinker with your ideas (and the words you use to express them) in order that you can come up with the best formulation.

Your first attempts to put thoughts down on paper – as they are recorded in your Research Log notes – should be regarded as *preliminary drafts* that will be successively polished and finalised as the research progresses. This present chapter appears here as one of the 'concluding' chapters not because it is the first time you should think about writing, but rather because the research report should be regarded as the 'final draft' of what you have been attempting to do in your Research Log.

As suggested in Chapter 4, you should adopt a technique of writing 'back to front' when filling in your Research Log. You do this by imaginatively 'anticipating' what the later phases and conclusions of your project will be, so that you have some idea of what the interim chapters or sections will contain. In this sense you are trying to 'foresee' what your research will entail and how it will work out before actually carrying it out. This allows you to develop a template for writing up successive drafts of the research right from the word go, but which can be modified as the exact shape of the research begins to unfold.

The 'back-to-front' logic of writing is also essential to the development of research arguments and explanations (see also Booth et al. 2003; Fisher 1993; Mosely et al. 2005; Toulmin 1958). As a result, much of this chapter will be devoted to the question of how to structure and develop your research arguments in the context of your final report. In this respect, methods texts often give the impression that the quality of social research is solely measured in terms of technical and practical matters such as how, and how much, evidence was gathered, and how data was analysed and interpreted. Of course these are important, but in large part the validity of social research is judged in terms of the quality of the framework of reasoning that underpins it. In turn, the quality of this chain of reasoning is reflected in the way it moves from an initial set of assumptions (questions, claims) through to a conclusion (or set of findings) by constantly referring back to a body of evidence (empirical data).

Using the Research Log as a Basis for the Research Report

If you have been diligent in filling in your Research Log, at this point it should consist of notes documenting your research experiences. It will take the form of rather separate groupings of notes corresponding to such activities as identifying your problem, topic and research questions, choosing methods of data collection, sampling strategies and forms of data analysis. Clearly, in this form they do not represent your project as a closely integrated sequence of phases. As they stand, your Research Log notes will have been drawn together rather loosely, certainly not in any systematic fashion.

This chapter concentrates on what is involved in pulling together the different elements of the research process and in constructing your overall research argument. The final report is thus an expanded, polished and modified version of what is contained in your Research Log notes.

Writing Style and Presentation

Before describing how the research elements fit together, it is necessary to consider the style and presentation of research arguments. What kind of style is best suited to the writing of a research report? In a general sense, research reports should be characterised by the clarity of their structure, the lucidity of the writing, a professional standard of presentation (including standard spelling, punctuation and referencing), the avoidance of plagiarism (making sure that it is your own work) and originality (see Denscombe 2007; Robson 2007, for detailed accounts). Here, however, I want to deal with issues of style and presentation that speak more directly to the quality of the research and its organisation. In what ways can style and presentation help or hinder the communication of your overall research argument?

Later, I describe a style of presentation that I encourage you to adopt – although this doesn't mean that you shouldn't express yourself. I'm referring to a pattern of presentation that will produce the most effective form of communication rather than attempting to restrict your *individual* style. In order to portray this style as clearly as possible, I'll first describe a couple of other styles that you should definitely avoid.

The magician style

A magician impresses an audience by disguising the sleights of hand and misdirection he or she uses when performing a trick. The 'trick' itself, such as to plucking a coin out of thin air, is left to the very end so that the audience is surprised and impressed to maximum effect. In a similar way, students often write essays by withholding their 'conclusions' (or ultimate arguments) right until the very end in the belief that the more of a surprise it is, the more impressive it will be! This essay habit is often used in writing up course work projects such as small-scale research. The 'surprise' element is frequently increased by deliberately avoiding a clearly signposted argument. Typically, the first paragraph (section or chapter) fails to state what the writer is going to argue and what conclusion(s) he or she is attempting to arrive at.

But this magician style of exposition is totally inappropriate for either essays or research reports! The reader/assessor will not be impressed by a 'surprise' ending. The ending or conclusion should follow logically from your initial statement of purpose, and then through a reasoned argument backed by evidence. If you have not provided a clear route map and signposts, the 'surprise' ending will make no sense and you will receive a lower grade.

The additive style

Although a slight improvement on the magician style, the 'additive' or 'the next thing I did' style should also be avoided. Unlike the magician, who attempts to conceal and disguise his or her methods, with the additive style everything is clearly revealed. However, this takes the form of a linear sequence – first this, and then this, and then this, and so on. But as with the magician, the argument (and the chain of reasoning linking it to a conclusion) is left as a kind of 'surprise' that pops up at the end. This may provide an 'interesting journey' and it certainly is a good thing to be transparent about what you are doing, but it is inappropriate to treat each element or phase of the research as if it were simply 'added on' to the others. The additive style makes the mistake of assuming that the importance of each of the research elements is measured in terms of its capacity to 'stand alone'. This is not true. Individual elements are measured in terms of their relationship to all the others considered as a combined whole.

Furthermore, the conclusion should not be attached at the end as if it were a bolt-on extra. Rather, the concluding statement must be *prefigured* in (and thus, in some sense, predictable from) the initial assumptions of the research and should be traceable through all its stages of development. It should not appear as a 'surprise' at the end of the research. The reader should be aware of it, right from the beginning.

These two styles compared

The additive style does not intentionally disguise the conclusion, but does so inadvertently by choosing to describe the process in a myopic, step-by-step fashion. However, the magician style intentionally conceals the ending by setting out, as if it were, a secret to be guarded and only revealed at the very end. Effectively, neither style reveals the final objective or purpose at the beginning, or even during the exposition. Both delay ultimate disclosure until the very end to ratchet up the 'surprise' element.

Both styles of presentation seem to be influenced by the narratives of popular culture, particularly of books and films. Thus, when describing the plot of a novel or a film, a person will say 'I won't tell you what happens' – either how it ends or in the build-up – 'because it will spoil it for you'.

While this may be true for fictional or semi-fictional narratives, it is inappropriate for research reports which must be scientifically rigorous in their presentation.

Transparency and full disclosure

The style I would recommend requires full transparency and disclosure as early in the writing as possible. This completely reverses the logic and presentational style of the other two.

Conclusions: must be transparent right from the start. The reader must know (be informed of) the end point or intended end point – the goal, purpose, objective – right from the first chapter.

Arguments: must display consistency, coherence and rationality. Any claims must be supported by appropriate evidence as well as adequate 'warrants' – the logical reasoning that links the two.

Explanations: you must clearly identify the problems that you are attempting to throw light on or resolve, and set them out in the form or an explanatory narrative – a 'storyline' – that threads through all the chapters/sections and unfolds as they unfold.

Processes: the links between all research elements must be made explicit. Each section of the research must be rational and logically consistent, but you must also show that together they form a tightly coordinated and coherent whole. Each section (and element) must contribute to the overall research argument and the unfolding explanatory narrative.

In sum, 'full disclosure' requires that your intended ending or concluding argument/explanation must not be 'disguised' or 'held back' until the end as an (inappropriate) surprise. Instead it must be made clear ('given away') right from the beginning. If you do not do this, then your supervisor, teacher or lecturer cannot properly judge the validity of the overall argument of your research report. As a consequence, of course, he or she will award a lower mark.

You should attempt to lead the reader through the logic of your decision-making throughout the project. That is, you should attempt to show how this logic leads to a reasoned conclusion. But you should say at the beginning what sort of ending/conclusion you are working towards. That is, you should be absolutely transparent about your aims, goals, purposes and objectives right from the start. Only then can the reader judge whether you have properly succeeded in accomplishing what you set out to do, by taking the particular route you have taken.

Some Definitions

Arguments

Arguments are the vehicles which carry an explanation from its beginnings to its conclusion. An explanation is always expressed in the form of an argument or series of arguments. Arguments contain *claims* backed by *evidence* and a *chain of reasoning* that spells out the links between the claim and the evidence.

Concepts

Concepts are the specific tools for expressing arguments. They are the most important constituent units of arguments. Concepts are abstract and general ideas that group or classify objects in terms of their common aspects. (See previous chapter for a discussion of their importance for the coding and analysis of data.)

Explanations

Explanations are specific lines of reasoning (involving arguments and concepts) that outline the relationship between a pattern of social behaviour and the social context in which it occurs. They provide answers to the following sorts of questions: (a) What is the nature of this behaviour? (How can we recognise it and what effects does it have?); and (b) Why does it occur? What social and psychological factors give rise to it? Explanations (and concepts) go beyond description – they are abstract and general and not defined (or limited by) *particular* times and places.

Explanatory narratives

Explanatory narratives are specific chains of reasoning that link research concepts and evidence together into a coherent and unfolding narrative (storyline) that eventually leads to an overall explanation of the social phenomenon in question.

The Basic Elements of the Research Report

Chapter 4 demonstrated how to create a proposal or plan of the project by writing up the basic research elements (using the Research Log). At this juncture, we want to consider the same key elements after the research has unfolded in actual practice. The same key elements are pertinent, but here they are treated as part of a concluding report about how the various phases of the research actually panned out. That is, they are part of a 'retrospective' report on how the methods of data collection were chosen, how the sampling, collection and analysis of the data was undertaken, any problems encountered, and so on. Let us remind ourselves of the key elements.

The key elements of research

1 Statement of purpose and objectives

2 Research proposal and design

3 Methods and strategies of data collection

4 Sampling strategies

5 Findings: concepts and data analysis

6 Conclusion: arguments and explanations

(All six of these elements are integrated and combined to form the final research report – which might be for a course work project, a thesis, a book or an article.)

Although there are six elements, this does not mean that they will automatically translate into just six chapters (of a book or PhD thesis), or into six sections or sub-headings (of an article or Master's thesis). Depending on the exact circumstances, you might decide to split some of these elements into two (or more) chapters or sections. For example, you might have two sections on different aspects of methods or strategies, or two (or three) presenting findings or some aspect of data analysis, and so on. The actual number of chapters or sub-headings will depend entirely on the unique characteristics of your particular project.

However, in writing up your final report you must make reference to *all these key elements*. By doing this, you are establishing an 'audit trail' (Denscombe 2007) and a road map for those who evaluate your work. The six elements also form the focus and anchor for the chain of reasoning that underpins the research. It is important that these elements – chapters or sections – support and reinforce each other to form an interlocking set of arguments.

As always, the Research Log is crucial. Steadfastly keeping a record of your experiences through memos, notes and reflections on the problems you encountered and research decisions you made throughout the project allows you to systematically document this process. Thus the Research Log records of the chain of reasoning as it unfolds.

From Mini-Arguments to the Meta-Argument

The chain of reasoning takes the form of a series of mini-arguments which cumulatively build up to create a meta-argument. Each one of the key elements of research can, and should, be regarded as a mini-argument held together by an internally coherent argument or theme. Of course, the mini-argument of each chapter will differ in terms of its content and theme, but the message of the arguments must be passed along a 'conveyor belt' of connecting themes and concepts so that every step in the research process is explicitly documented. In this sense, the overall coherence of your research project is expressed in the way the individual chapters interrelate with each other.

Also, and very importantly, only in this manner is it possible for you to create an overall or meta-argument – a chain of reasoning that runs from the first to the last chapter, building cumulatively all the way. I shall come back to the idea of building a meta-argument after I've dealt with each of the key elements as a mini-argument in its own right.

Building Mini-Arguments

1 Purpose and objectives

The first mini-argument should be organised around a statement of the objectives and purposes of your research and its intended 'contribution to knowledge'. You must come up with the most compelling reasons why your project is significant and necessary. Thus you must argue for the importance of your research in relation to an existing body of research, information and ideas. By so doing, you will be measuring the viability and relevance of your own project in relation to what has already been done.

As suggested in Chapter 4, this is best accomplished through a selective literature review which enables you to pick out ideas, concepts, methods and strategies that are likely to be relevant to your project. It also allows you to pinpoint the way in which your own project builds on, rectifies or goes beyond existing research findings. Finally, immersion in the relevant literature helps you to think about the distinction between problems and topics and how to formulate your core research questions.

Apart from a selective literature review, you are also attempting (albeit sketchily) to identify the anticipated route you will take through both the practical (data collection) and conceptual (data analysis) phases of the project. You are also 'pointing' the argument in a particular direction, and thus 'anticipating' a specific end-point or conclusion (which, overall, is referred to as the meta-argument).

You must demonstrate that you are aware that research is not a 'one step at a time' process (as in the 'additive' style). You should show that you have a fairly firm idea of the research problems and questions you wish to tackle, and how you will resolve or answer them. In the end, your job is to produce an overall research argument, that is, an argument that binds the six elements together.

So this mini-argument is part of an organic entity – the whole research report (thesis or article). It must link strongly and seamlessly with the argument in the next element/section as well to the rest of the research report by providing a condensed 'sketch' of the entire meta-argument (the complete 'arc' or 'span' of elements/sections 1–6).

In sum, with this element the argument is different from those in sections 2–5 because it contains two mini-arguments joined together, whereas the others have only one. The first kick starts the whole research report by setting up its basic premises and assumptions. The second, in a condensed and preliminary fashion, outlines the anticipated route you will take on the way to your explanatory conclusions.

The strength of the mini-argument of this first chapter or section does not rest on a discussion of actual data or empirical material. The report is not yet a discussion of the evidentiary basis of the project. That is, it is not about how your evidence leads to and supports your conclusions – although these are important background considerations. Rather, the mini-argument is primarily a discussion of the various procedures you use to collect and analyse data in relation to your specific research problems and questions. You should also mention at this point any ethical issues that are pertinent to your project and any effects they may have had on how the research was conducted.

2 Research design: problems and topics

The issues: a recap

Here, the mini-argument focuses on a specific issue: developing and outlining a project plan or 'research design'. Remember, adaptive research is problem-driven. Thus the initial plan or design of the project is structured by its problem-focus and core research questions. Chapter 3, in particular, highlighted the importance of the distinction between *problems* and *topics* and the way in which they generate *different*, but *complementary*, kinds of research questions. In effect, decisions about the exact problem-focus and the core research questions are the most pivotal the adaptive researcher has to make. This is because the problem-focus shapes and moulds the core research questions.

The research design (or plan) follows fairly logically from the core research questions. It outlines the methods and strategies, sampling procedures and forms of data analysis most likely to yield evidence that will throw light on these questions.

The first task, therefore, is to establish the problem-focus of the project as distinct from its topic-focus. This must be done in advance of all other considerations. However, there is no 'best' starting point. Your interest might have been stimulated by a particular topic or topic-question (for example, 'Why and how do college friendships end?' or 'Why do men or women (of certain ages) use health clubs or gyms?'). Conversely, your initial research interest may have been prompted by a problem-question (for example, 'In what sense do personal relationships change over time?' 'Is modern intimacy different from that in previous eras?' 'How does status within a group affect the behaviour of individual members?').

Where you get your initial point of interest from is of no particular consequence. What is important is that once you have identified your initial interest – either problem-question or topic-question – you must pair it with its 'equivalent opposite'. That is, if your initial interest happens to be an analytic problem, you must pair it with a topic-focus or question. On the other hand, if your initial point of interest is a topic-focus or question, you must pair it with an equivalent problem-question.

You cannot begin to produce a research design for an adaptive project until you have successfully coupled an analytic research problem with an equivalent empirical research topic.

Once this is done you must concentrate on your problem-focus. What problem-questions you will focus on? You must then work out the relation between the problem-questions and the topic-questions. This entails:

1 Sorting out how problem-questions define the range and focus of topic-questions.

2 Deciding on the best amalgam of problem- and topic-questions to form the basis of your core research questions.

3 Deciding which data collection strategies will produce the most relevant evidence – that is, evidence that throws light on your research questions.

The argument

This argument involves more than logic, ideas and reasoning. Unlike the previous mini-argument, this one must refer to the evidentiary basis of the project. That is, it is essential that you specify the kind of research questions that in your judgement will yield the sort of data or empirical evidence that would help resolve or explain the analytic problems and questions that drive the project.

In turn, of course, this raises the question of the sorts of methods, strategies, data collection, sampling and analysis that are best suited to harnessing such data or evidence. In this sense your mini-argument should indicate how the core research problems and questions mesh with the subsequent data collecting phases in a way likely to yield the best results.

Clearly, you must use your reasoning and argumentative skills at a fairly high level – especially in dealing with the relationship between problems, topics and research questions. As detailed in Chapter 4, such skills include the ability to move between different levels of thinking and to express this in writing your research report. You need to be able to move routinely between problem and topic issues – as well as from topic to problem issues – throughout the research. This requires shifting from general, conceptual and analytic language and thought processes to those that are more specific, concrete and descriptive. Since such skills are essential for producing 'explanatory', as opposed to merely 'descriptive' or 'applied' research, then you cannot afford to be without them.

So how do you acquire, and then keep in touch with, these skills? One way is to closely familiarise yourself with the examples and advice offered in Chapters 2 and 3 and then refer back to them when necessary. Another way is through the experience of actually using them. In this regard you should regularly ask yourself such questions as: what is my problem? What is my topic? How are they related? Such 'self-interrogation' will help you distinguish between problem and topic issues on an ongoing basis.

There is no way round learning these skills because they reappear all the way through adaptive research. Continually applying them is what keeps the research firmly focused on its explanatory objectives and prevents it reverting back into a simple descriptive mode. These skills are also essential for creating your overall or 'meta' research argument. In the light of their all-round importance, it is worth investing time and effort *before* you collect any data in acquiring the ability to switch between conceptual and descriptive levels of thinking and writing.

In conclusion, then, by defining your problem and topic, and being clear about how they influence your research questions, you are in a position to construct your research design and general 'plan of action', so to speak. In this respect, you need to firm up what you sketched out in general terms in discussing your 'anticipated' sequence of research phases. That is, your research design will consist of a discussion of the key elements 1–6, but this time your comments will be more *directly* linked to your *specific* project. Thus, you must give a more detailed (although still preliminary) indication of what will be involved for each of the key elements in relation to your own project and in the light of your discussion of your specific problems, topics and research questions.

Finally, it is essential to provide thematic continuity between this research element and the next. Thus, as long as you are clear about how you constructed your research plan or design, you are automatically setting up the next element by raising the issue of the most appropriate methods and strategies of data collection.

3 Methods and strategies of data collection

With this research element your argument has to be organised around two major points. First, you must say why you focused on particular *types* of data – and the reasons why you judged them to be the most appropriate for your project. Second, you must give your reasons for selecting certain methods and strategies of data collection and why you thought they were likely to deliver the most useful and pertinent data. Of course, in attempting to deal with both issues you need to describe the links between them. Your mini-argument, therefore, has to persuade the reader that there is a comfortable and reasoned fit between your core research questions, your targeted data, and the methods used to gather them.

You must avoid the suggestion that the links are based on sheer expediency, practical convenience or are simply 'thrown together'. You must show that your choices about methods and data were shaped by the core research questions in a carefully reasoned manner. Of course, practical expediency may play a limited role (for instance, certain individuals may not be available for interview, or particular documentary evidence may not be accessible). In general, however, decisions about methods and strategies of data collection must not be made on the basis of convenience or availability. There must be a basic foundation of principled judgements about why certain methods and strategies were thought to be the most appropriate given your core research questions and problem-focus.

The adaptive method relies generally on a multi-method approach. Therefore, your argument must specify why you thought that the specific spread and pattern of methods and strategies you chose – including both qualitative and quantitative forms – would be the most likely to achieve the best results in relation to your research problems and questions.

For example, for a project investigating the nature of friendship at university/college, you might need to justify your decision to focus on particular 'types' of students – what age range, which gender or mixture of genders, what ethnicity, what kind of family background, and so on, depending on your exact focus of research interest. You might need to state the reasons behind your decision to interview your sample of students, the style of interviewing you adopted, along with your data recording techniques (audio-recording or notes made during or after interviews). You must also state the reasons why you thought (or decided against) supplementing the interviews with observations, documentary evidence, survey data or secondary analyses. You must say if, and why, you chose a particular balance of quantitative and qualitative data.

Furthermore, you must document which dimensions of social organisation – individual, interaction, setting, context, power, temporality – informed the focus of your interviews, observations and documents, and why. Here, your research report should map out the exact links between your problem-focus, research questions and methodological strategies.

In so doing, you should identify your problem-focus – such as the relationship between self-identity and social interaction, or between social interaction and social setting. But you must also demonstrate how this problem-focus connects with the specific topic issues, for instance, whether friendships are influenced by the temporal organisation of college life. In such a case, you might have been interested in whether friendships are more typically initiated or terminated at specific times in the academic year (such as at the beginning or end of semesters) or whether more friendships are generated during the first year of university/college life than in later years.

In dealing with issues of methodology and strategy, you must say how problem and topic issues are linked, but this time how they connect with practical aspects of data collection. Here the evidentiary basis of the research takes centre-stage. You are specifying the way in which your data and collection methods provide you with the kind of evidence that allows you to throw light on or resolve your research problems and questions.

Clearly, the logic of your argument and its evidentiary basis could be found wanting in certain respects. For example, if your evidence is not sufficiently strong to support certain conclusions about the nature of friendship, then the mini-argument about methods and strategies of data collection will be flawed. The same would be true if the evidence is not of a certain *type*. For example, you cannot make authoritative statements about the way in which friendships vary over time if you have not focused on, or controlled for, temporal sequencing – that is, if you haven't studied friendship over specified periods of time or at specific points in time.

Likewise, you cannot make claims about the effects of gender or class on friendships at college unless these 'factors' have deliberately been targeted in your interviews, observations and documents and/or secondary data, or unless you have controlled for them in your data samples (see the next section on sampling). You cannot make quantitative claims (such as about rates of friendship formation) in the absence of appropriate numerical data, any more than you can claim to have given an account of friendship *experiences*, unless you have qualitative data to back this up.

4 Sampling strategies

This mini-argument should focus on justifying how you selected your data samples, be they people (interviewees), events (observations), documents (official or personal) or even 'analytic units'. As with the other arguments, you must outline the link, on the one hand, between the objectives of your study, its problem-focus and research questions and, on the other hand, your research conclusions. Thus the logic of your sampling procedures – how and on what basis you selected your data samples – must consistently mesh with your initial assumptions, as well as your findings and conclusions.

Problem sampling and probability sampling

As discussed in Chapters 6 and 7, the flexible research designs of adaptive analysis may be used with both probability and non-probability samples. In fact, projects that blend and integrate quantitative and qualitative data involve combinations of probability and non-probability (or purposive) samples. However, because of the exploratory character of adaptive analysis in combination with its focus on the analysis of social domains, an overall flexible sampling strategy is required. Thus, with regard to projects that attempt to integrate quantitative and qualitative data, problem sampling should be used as the default strategy.

Problem sampling: the argument

Problem sampling is appropriate for adaptive research because it deals with social life in 'naturally occurring' circumstances, in which social domains dissolve into and 'interpenetrate' one another. Problem sampling is also more suited to its 'exploratory' objectives. In problem sampling, people, events, situations, documents and domains of social reality are included in data samples on the basis of their problem-relevance. That is, their relevance to the main problem-focus of the research and its core questions. For example, you might choose to study particular research sites and sub-sites (locales) because they are most likely to yield information on the problem-focus and its associated research questions.

Your argument should include the reasons why you have selected particular social domains, people, events, episodes of interaction, or documents in your sample(s). You must say why you used particular selection criteria as preliminary sampling guidelines. The argument should indicate how you thought your initial samples would be relevant to your problem-focus.

However, despite its highly structured starting position, adaptive analysis remains open to new lines of inquiry and to the development of new modes of explanation. Thus, it is important that sampling responds adaptively to the flow of incoming data and what it reveals about the problem-focus and research questions. Thus, the research report must also document the way in which emergent ideas and concepts became incorporated into your project via adaptive sampling procedures. Thus, if a particular concept is modified or 'emerges' as a response to data collection and analysis (see next section), you must say how this came about and the way in which you adjusted your sampling to reflect this.

You may also have used 'conceptual sampling' (or snowball or opportunistic sampling) to supplement the more general problem sampling. If you have, you must state your reasons for using supplementary samples.

More generally, you should be clear about how both the size and the content of your sample(s) follow the ongoing development of your analytic ideas. What domains, people, events or documents were sampled according to their emergent relevance to your problem-questions? How is their emerging relevance revealed in the ongoing data analysis? In this sense, the overall size of your sample (remembering that you may have sampled settings, events and domains as well as people) is less significant to the validity of your findings and procedures than is the question of its problem-relevance. In this respect, the question of when you decided to stop (further) sampling is important, and the reasons for doing so must be documented (see Chapter 7).

Of course this mini-argument about sampling strategies must be self-sufficient and internally coherent. But it must also provide a robust bridge between the preceding mini-argument about methods and strategies of data collection and the one that follows it, focusing on concepts coding and data analysis. This may seem 'clear and obvious' in one sense, but it would be dangerous to take this for granted. The argument must be made explicit by describing the reasoned links between the data gathering methods you used and how you sampled particular types of data (including events, situations, time periods, locales). But this connection must be carried through to include your decisions about how to analyse data, including the use of particular concepts and coding data in terms of them.

In sum, this mini-argument represents the middle segment of your 'meta-argument'. As such, it is very important because it conveys the heart of your overall research argument. It is the bridge or main connector that holds all your arguments together at this crucial juncture and is necessary to carry them through to a reasoned and coherent conclusion.

5 Concepts coding and data analysis

General issues

Adaptive research has exploratory and creative objectives and investigates social situations, settings or activities with the aim of producing new insights or understandings. However, unlike 'grounded theory', it does not reject or ignore existing concepts and knowledge. Instead, the adaptive method adopts a dual approach. Established concepts and knowledge are freely used and their relevance and adequacy are 'tested' against appropriate data or evidence. At the same time, adaptive analysis remains open to conceptual discovery (emergent concepts) and thus to the possibility of generating new explanatory insights and understandings.

More generally, adaptive research explores a set of empirical questions (often reflected in topic-based, 'factual' information) in the light of an analytic, problem-focus on the principal domains and dimensions of social life, selectively chosen from psychobiography, interaction, social settings, social contexts, power and temporality. It does this with a view to generating novel conceptual insights supported by empirical evidence. Its ultimate aim is to help explain or understand particular social processes or social phenomena.

The argument

This mini-argument should outline the reasoning underlying your data analysis and how this informs the conclusions of the research. There are two related aspects to be considered. First, the use of 'orienting' concepts as guides for data analysis to provide stability, clarity and direction in the initial phases of the research. The second aspect concerns the exploratory character of adaptive research and the possibility of discovering 'emergent' concepts.

First, you must document your use of 'orienting' concepts by indicating how you chose them from a selective literature review, and why you thought they would offer insights into your research problems and questions. You must show how your main orienting concepts served as a provisional 'analytic' and 'coding' frame that allowed you to match up concepts with particular bits of data (empirical indicators). You must show how you used your orienting concept(s) *only as guides* for analysis, noting any efforts you made to avoid 'forcing' data to conform to them.

Second, as regards 'emergent' concepts, you must carefully and thoroughly document how you dealt with 'anomalous' data – that is, data that didn't 'fit' easily with, or couldn't be properly explained by, particular orienting concepts (or supporting networks of them). As a consequence, you must mention any modifications, extensions, elaborations or refinements of orienting concepts that were required as a response or adjustment to the anomalous data.

You must note and give reasons for any changes in coding made in response to the appearance of unanticipated data and consequent shifts in emphasis on, or importance of, particular concepts and their role in data analysis. This is especially crucial with coding since it plays such an important part in matching up concepts with data. You must document any changes in the relevance, significance and balance of both 'established' and genuinely 'emergent' concepts and any corresponding changes in the coding system made in relation to them.

It is important to be aware that this mini-argument about concepts and analysis represents a shift in the emphasis of your overall meta-argument. Up to this point you have been outlining the logic of your methodological choices (data collection and sampling) in relation to your initial assumptions problems and questions. However, here the argument should begin to engage with the question of how to *explain* your findings/evidence.

You should spell out how your main concepts form an important part of your explanation. Concepts should be regarded not only as indicators of data – for example, as the 'sympathetic smiling' of flight attendants is an empirical indicator of the concept of 'emotional labour'. Concepts are also tools for expressing explanatory arguments. That is, an explanation of, say, the relationship between a pattern of social behaviour and its social context is expressed by deploying concepts in the form of an argument. For example, the concept of 'emotional labour' helps to explain a consistent pattern of sympathetic and empathetic behaviour by flight attendants towards passengers.

Thus your discussion of concepts, coding and analysis is a crucial link in the chain of reasoning that eventually leads to your explanatory conclusions. It describes how these conclusions not only grow out of initial problems and research questions, but also through practical procedures of data collection.

Here the importance of being able to shuttle between levels of analysis reappears. As with the distinction between problems and topics, the question of the relation between concepts and data requires the same shifting between thought levels and processes – in this case, between analytic thinking and handling factual data (evidence).

Finally, this mini-argument must dovetail neatly with the more general concerns discussed in the next and final section, which, in effect, summarises your overall meta-argument. At this point the cumulative impact of your argument should be very strongly apparent. It is, therefore, doubly important that the clarity of your arguments is reinforced by your grasp of the connection between analytic and empirical thinking.

6 Conclusion: arguments and explanations

Here the task is to provide a reverse version of the first mini-argument (in section 1). In this you were not only required to state your initial assumptions and objectives, but to project forwards and describe the *anticipated* trajectory of the research. However, in this final section you are attempting to do the opposite. You are looking back and reflecting on how the main body of the research turned out, in terms of the phases and developments *that actually occurred*. In this sense, you are stating your conclusions (in the form of an explanation) by looking back over the project, reflecting on how it unfolded, and revealing the logic and the chain of reasoning on which the conclusions are based.

First, you must state your main conclusion in the form of an explanation of your findings and data. This should be expressed in terms of the relationships between your core concepts and categories and what they reveal about the evidence (data/evidence) you have gathered. The exact form of your explanation will be unique to your project. It will depend on the particular circumstances of the research, the main concepts you used (or generated) and how both these factors interlinked with the collection and analysis of data. However, in general terms there are three main possibilities.

For example, let's say your main explanatory concept was 'emotional labour' (originally used in a study of flight attendants) and you were investigating whether, or to what extent, the concept applies to teaching work. That is, in general terms your research was posing the question 'does the concept of emotional labour help to explain some aspects of the behaviour of teachers in the school setting?' Again, depending on the exact aspect of the teacher's work activities you concentrated on (interaction with pupils in the classroom, after-school activities, assignment of homework, written reports) and which particular situations you investigated (classrooms, sports events, special events, staffroom discussions, parents' evenings), your explanation could take one of the following forms:

1   You might argue that your evidence/data leads you to the conclusion that the concept of 'emotional labour' explains typical patterns of behaviour exhibited by teachers in specific circumstances. In other words, you are arguing that your evidence supports the idea that 'emotional labour' explains why particular behaviour occurs, and why it takes the form it does. It goes without saying that you must demonstrate this conclusion with specific examples of teacher behaviour and teacher–pupil interaction drawn from your evidence (such as extracts from your data).

2   You might argue that while the concept of 'emotional labour' fits behaviour patterns in some work settings, your data highlights several aspects of teacher behaviour that cannot be adequately explained in terms of the concept in its present form. Further, your evidence leads you to suggest that certain 'extensions' or 'elaborations' of the concept might offer better explanatory purchase on the behaviour you have documented. So, for example, you might suggest that concepts such as 'feeling encouragement' or 'affective coaching' could provide more adequate ways of explaining your data. Of course, you must state how and why this is the case and illustrate the reasons with examples from your data.

3   Your data might suggest that particular aspects of teacher behaviour (or leadership behaviour in business organisations) is best explained by a concept that 'emerged' from your 'immersion' in the data – including its collection and analysis – and which has little to do with the original concept of emotional labour. For instance, you might decide that what you have documented and observed is more aptly explained by concepts such as 'benign power' or 'benign control'. In this case, the concept of emotional labour would recede in importance for your arguments and conclusions.

However, your conclusion should not be expressed as a complete rejection or denial of the usefulness of 'emotional labour' in a broader sense, as it applies to other contexts and situations. Rather, your conclusion should be expressed as follows: while 'emotional labour' remains useful for understanding behaviour in other settings and situations, your ongoing data collection and analysis led you to conclude that your 'emergent' concept or concepts more adequately explained those patterns of behaviour recorded in your data.

With emergent concepts there are two possible additions to your conclusion. First, you might decide to retain 'emotional labour' as part of a network of background concepts that support your main finding – while the 'emergent' concepts, whatever they are, take on an equal importance for your explanatory conclusions. Alternatively, having had your research attention redirected away from emotional labour as the 'core' or 'central' concept, you might decide that your emergent concept should take centre-stage in your conclusions. This is an example of 'adaptive evolution' in analytic thinking during the research. Such a conclusion is perfectly valid as long as you have systematically documented its progress (in your Research Log) from the point that it began to develop all the way through the project.

However, again, remember that such a conclusion is not to be confused with the idea that you have proved or demonstrated the irrelevance of the concept of emotional labour for understanding or explaining behaviour in other settings or situations. In this respect, and this applies more generally to all concluding statements, your conclusions and claims should be judicious and circumspect. Furthermore, in all circumstances, concluding statements must be supported by appropriate evidence and strong 'warrants' – coherent chains of reasoning that connect evidence and explanatory claims and conclusions.

Meta-argument and explanatory narrative

Although your final section should present a *distinct* conclusion, you must be careful to avoid a *discrete* conclusion – as if it were separate from the rest of the report. This is because you should also be summarising the overall flow of your mini-arguments and showing how, altogether, they have unfolded as a meta-argument during the course of the project. While each chapter or section of the final research report should be capable of standing up as an argument in its own right, it must also be integrated with all the others to form an organic whole.

The trajectory of this argument is the explanatory 'spine' or 'narrative' of your thesis, article, or whatever form your research report takes. However, in this concluding section you are tracing the chain of reasoning backwards, reviewing and reflecting on your argument as it actually unfolded in time. In this sense the resulting meta-argument should make sense in relation to the initial assumptions and mini-arguments as they appear at the beginning, as well as to your explanatory conclusions. In either case, the logic, coherence and cumulative effect of the meta-argument should remain firm. The chain of reasoning that underpins your explanatory narrative must ensure that each section is smoothly integrated and consistent with each of the others so that there is an overall interdependence of all the elements.

Checklist for Research Log Notes

- Remember that your Research Log notes can provide the basis for (initial drafts of) your research report. To make your notes usable in this manner it is important that they are not too idiosyncratic in style and content.

- Examine your general writing style and your presentational style. It is best to avoid the 'magician' style or the 'additive' style. You should adopt a style based on the principles of full and transparent disclosure.

- In writing the final report be certain about its basic organising principles. Be sure you know what arguments, concepts, explanations and explanatory narratives are, and the roles they play in ensuring that the research report is ordered and coherent.

- Be aware of the six basic elements that are applicable to all social research and ask yourself how they will feature in your project and what you will say about them in your research report.

- The first chapter or section of the report should outline your research purpose and objectives. You must state why your project is important and what it contributes to existing knowledge. However, you should also give some impression of the route you will take, what research tools you will use and why you will conduct the research in a particular manner, including the main ethical considerations.

- The second section, the research design or 'plan of action', needs to set out your problem-focus, as distinct from your topic-focus, and how they combine to influence and shape your core research questions.

- The third section, or chapter on methods and strategies of data collection, requires that you outline the specific spread and pattern of methods and strategies you have used and how they relate to your initial assumptions, objectives and research questions. You must explain why you chose the methods and strategies you employed and why you thought they would produce the kind of evidence appropriate to your research questions (and support your anticipated findings and explanatory conclusions).

- The fourth section concerns sampling. You must state how (on what basis) you selected or chose people, events, time periods, domains of social life, and so on, to observe, interview or examine, in order to support your initial assumptions and answer core research questions. You must also document how sampling issues and adaptive responses unfolded during the course of the project (if indeed they did) and how they contributed to your conclusions and findings.

- In the fifth section, you must take care to show how you used orienting concepts – and coding categories used in conjunction with them – to organise and analyse your data. You must also outline the balance between conceptual modification and innovation that underpins the findings and conclusions of your specific project.

- In the sixth and perhaps most crucial section, you must be aware of the 'optimal' structure and organisation of the final research report. Each chapter or section (dealing with a key research element) will form a distinct mini-argument in its own right and must stand up in its own terms. However, each mini-argument must also integrate and interlock with all the others to form an overall meta-argument or explanatory narrative.

10

GUIDELINES & CHECKLIST FOR ADAPTIVE RESEARCH

This final chapter is an overall checklist for the main issues covered in the book. The checklist can be used at different points in the research process – that is, before starting a project, during its execution, or after you have completed it. The list is a series of prompts, pointers, advisories or 'reminders' of the key issues that are pertinent to adaptive research either generally or in relation to specific questions. The checklist is split into three main sections.

The first deals with general features of the adaptive approach, including: the role of scientific rigour and the importance of concepts in the search for explanation; the habit of early, regular writing and redrafting; and the importance of maintaining a continuous Research Log.

The second section deals with more specific issues of adaptive method, including: choosing an appropriate topic; the need for a 'selective' but rigorous literature review; problem-questions and topic-questions; research design: mixed strategies and methods; sampling; concepts and data analysis; arguments and explanations.

The final section considers how the unfolding and evolving nature of adaptive research can help the inexperienced researcher overcome potential difficulties. It includes: preparing yourself for the ups and downs of research; how to deal with unforeseen problems; how to turn adversity into a potential strength.

General Issues

A scientific approach

- Be aware of the cumulative nature of scientific knowledge and the need to explore the links between your own research and existing findings and knowledge.

- Familiarise yourself with the differences between *description* ('who', 'when' and 'where' questions) and *explanation* ('how' and 'why' questions), and the role they will, or might, play in your project. While a scientific approach depends on a bedrock of descriptive information, it always goes further, to ask 'how' and 'why' questions in order to come up with explanations of social phenomena.

- How will you achieve the right balance between description and explanation in your project?

- Science relies very heavily on the role of empirical evidence in support of its propositions and explanations. What exactly is the relationship between evidence – in the form of the data you collect – and explanation? Will your research findings/conclusions be properly supported by the evidence you gather?

- How will you ensure the scientific rigour and adequacy of the practical and strategic research decisions made during your project?

The early writing habit and the Research Log

- Be aware of the advantages of writing very early on in the research process. Make sure you adopt an appropriate writing style (see Chapter 9) in which *transparency* and *full disclosure* are the guiding principles.

- Get into the habit of redrafting notes and memos about your research decisions and experiences by continually filling out a Research Log. Generally, organise your log in terms of the key elements of the research process. Refer to the checklists at the end of each chapter to help you with entries for the Research Log.

- Use the Research Log notes as 'early drafts' of the more 'formal' documents you are required to produce, such as your proposal, your research design and, importantly, your final research report.

Specific Issues of Adaptive Method

Choosing an appropriate topic

- Can you be objective about your topic? Do you have strong feelings, biases or prejudices about it?

- Does the topic or area genuinely capture your interest? Will it keep you motivated enough to (a) finish the research, and (b) help you overcome problems and uncertainties?

- What ethical issues does the topic raise? Are they resolvable?

- Is the topic manageable and relevant? Are there problems of scale? Can they be resolved? Are there problems of accessibility?

- Will there be enough evidence/data available for you to form an adequate initial sample? Will there be enough data (of the right kind) to help you answer your research questions?

Research problems, topics and questions

- A selective literature search/review will help you identify research *problems* as distinct from research *topics* and core research *questions*.

- Which of the key problem-questions (discussed in Chapters 1, 2 and 3) are most relevant to your project?

- Which problem-question will form your primary focus? Are others of secondary or overlapping relevance?

Research questions and research design

- Be aware of the problem-driven nature of research questions and what this means for research practice.

- In what ways are your core research questions influenced by your research problems and your problem-focus?

- What will you include in your research design, and how do you expect it will help you to plan your project?

Mixed strategies and methods

- How can qualitative data, methods and strategies throw light on your research problems and questions?

- Which aspects of your project would benefit from the support of quantitative data (from existing surveys and audits)?

- How can you use both qualitative and quantitative data in a complementary fashion?

- Be aware of the ways in which mixed strategies and methods can contribute to flexibility in research design. What are the advantages of such flexibility?

Sampling

- What is problem sampling? How will it enable you to select your initial sample – of observations, events, interviewees, documents and secondary data?

- What other sampling techniques might be relevant?

- Do you anticipate additions or adjustments to your samples and sampling strategies as the research unfolds?

Concepts, coding and data analysis

- Familiarise yourself with the role that concepts play in explanation and social research.

- Which orienting concepts will you use to provide initial guidance and direction for data analysis?

- How will such concepts help you code data for subsequent analysis?

- Be ready to explore and 'test' the fit and relevance of orienting concepts in relation to the data and evidence that you collect. Ask yourself what this signifies for the appropriateness and range of applicability of such concepts across different settings and contexts.

- As the research unfolds and data collection and analysis proceed, be aware of the possibilities for conceptual modification, elaboration or development.

- Ask yourself whether conceptual innovation – the cultivation of 'emergent' concepts – is appropriate or relevant in the light of data collection and analysis. In what sense would the emergent concept or concepts help in formulating your explanatory argument?

- How do concepts throw light on your research problems and help answer your core research questions?

Writing the research report

- Make sure you adopt the most effective style of writing and presentation. As long as you have diligently attended to your Research Log throughout the project, your log notes should provide you with a good initial basis for your final report. Of course, you need to polish and redraft sections of the report to give an overview of the way in which the research actually worked out.

- Be aware of the relationship between concepts, arguments and the explanatory narrative in your final report. Remember that while each 'individual' section must possess its own coherent mini-argument, collectively the sections must add up to an overall meta-argument or explanatory narrative.

The Unfolding and Flexible Nature of Research Outcomes

- Adaptive research is not a rigid, linear approach. It responds – adapts – to the changing circumstances of the project as well as to what the emerging data or evidence indicates or reveals about the concepts used to analyse and explain them.

- Ask yourself, if everything went smoothly and according to plan, what phases would you expect your project to pass through and what research outcome would you anticipate?

- Are you psychologically prepared for dealing with predictable problems? What would they be? What about unanticipated problems?

- A reassuring feature of the adaptive method allows the researcher to flexibly reconfigure the research objectives in the light of emerging evidence/data.

- Because of this flexibility, a seeming wrong turn or mistake, at least potentially, can be rescued and refashioned as an emergent outcome of the research. Thus apparent adversity can be transformed and overcome by a creative, adaptive response.

REFERENCES

Ahmed, M. and Hamilton, F. (2009) 'They say you can't buy friends ... now you can have them for £125 per 1,000.' *The Times* 31 December.

Allan, G. (1989) *Friendship*. Hemel Hempstead: Harvester.

Archer, M. (1995) *Realist Social Theory: The Morphogenetic Approach*. Cambridge: Cambridge University Press.

Baert, P. (2005) *Philosophy of the Social Sciences*. Cambridge: Polity Press.

Baron-Cohen, S. (2004) *The Essential Difference*. London: Penguin.

Becker, H. (1963) *Outsiders*. Glencoe, IL: Free Press.

Becker, H. (1986) *Writing for Social Scientists*. Chicago: University of Chicago Press.

Bell, J. (2010) *Doing Your Research Project* (5th edition). Milton Keynes: Open University Press.

Bergman, M. (ed.) (2008) *Advances in Mixed Methods Research*. London: Sage.

Blaikie, N. (2009) *Designing Social Research* (2nd edition). Cambridge: Polity Press.

Boeck, T. (2011) Young People and Social Capital: An Exploration. PhD Thesis, De Montfort University, Leicester, UK.

Booth, W., Colomb, G. and Williams, J. (2003) *The Craft of Research* (2nd edition). Chicago: Chicago University Press.

Brain, R. (1976) *Friends and Lovers*. London: Hart-Davis, MacGibbon.

Bryman, A. (2008a) *Social Research Methods* (3rd edition). Oxford: Oxford University Press.

Bryman, A (2008b) 'Why Do Researchers Integrate/Combine/Mesh/Blend/Mix/Merge/Fuse Quantitative and Qualitative Research?' in M. Bergman (ed.), *Advances in Mixed Methods Research*. London: Sage.

Burgess, B. (1984) *In the Field*. London: Allen & Unwin.

Cameron, D. (2007) *The Myth of Mars and Venus: Do Men and Women Really Speak Different Languages?* Oxford: Oxford University Press.

Cashmore, E. (2006) *Celebrity Culture*. Abingdon: Routledge.

Charmaz, K. (2006) *Constructing Grounded Theory: A Practical Guide Through Qualitative Analysis*. London: Sage.

Collins, R. (2005) *Interaction Ritual Chains*. Princeton, NJ: Princeton University Press.

Creswell, J. (2009) *Research Design: Qualitative, Quantitative and Mixed Methods Approaches* (3rd edition). London: Sage.

Creswell, J. and Plano Clark, V. (2007) *Designing and Conducting Mixed Methods Research*. Thousand Oaks, CA: Sage.

Creswell, J., Plano Clark, V. and Garret, A. (2008) 'Methodological Issues in Conducting Mixed Methods Research Designs', in M. Bergman (ed.), *Advances in Mixed Methods Research*. London: Sage.

Czarniawska, B. (2007) *Shadowing and Other Techniques for Doing Fieldwork in Modern Societies*. Univesitetsforgalet: Copenhagen Business School Press.

Denscombe, M. (2001) 'Uncertain Identities and Health and Risking Behaviour: The Case of Young People and Smoking in Late Modernity', *British Journal of Sociology*, 52(1): 157–77.

Denscombe, M. (2002) *Ground Rules for Good Research*. Buckingham: Open University Press.

Denscombe, M. (2007) *The Good Research Guide* (3rd edition). Maidenhead: Open University Press.

Denzin, N. (1989) *The Research Act* (3rd edition). Englewood Cliffs, NJ: Prentice-Hall.

Duck, S. (1992) *Human Relationships* (2nd edition). London: Sage.

Durkheim, E. (1982) *Suicide*. Cambridge: Polity Press.

Economic and Social Research Council (ESRC) (2005) *Research Ethics Framework*. London: ESRC.

Etzioni, A. (1961) *The Comparative Analysis of Complex Organisation*. New York: Free Press.

Fisher, A. (1993) *The Logic of Real Arguments*. Cambridge: Cambridge University Press.

Flanders, N. (1970) *Analysing Teacher Behaviour*. Reading, MA: Addison-Wesley.

Foucault, M. (1997) *Discipline and Punish: The Birth of the Prison*. Harmondsworth: Penguin.

Giallombardo, R. (1966) 'Social Roles in a Prison for Women', *Social Problems*, 13: 268–88.

Giddens, A. (1984) *The Constitution of Society*. Cambridge: Polity Press.

Giddens, A. (1991) *Modernity and Self Identity*. Cambridge: Polity Press.

Giddens, A. (1992) *The Transformation of Intimacy*. Cambridge: Polity Press.

Glaser, B. (2001) *The Grounded Theory Perspective: Conceptualization Contrasted with Description*. Mill Valley, CA: Sociology Press.

Glaser, B. and Strauss, A. (1967) *The Discovery of Grounded Theory*. Chicago: Aldine.

Glesne, C. and Peshkin, P. (1992) *Becoming Qualitative Researchers: An Introduction*. New York: Longman.

Goffman, E. (1971) *The Presentation of Self in Everyday Life*. Harmondsworth: Penguin.

Goffman, E. (1983) 'The Interaction Order', *American Sociological Review*, 48: 1–17.

Goleman, D. (1996) *Emotional Intelligence*. London: Bloomsbury.

Gray, J. (1992) *Men Are from Mars, Women Are from Venus*. New York: HarperCollins.

Hart, C. (2009) *Doing a Literature Review*. London: Sage.

Hochschild, A. (1983) *The Managed Heart*. Berkeley, CA: University of California Press.

Homan, R. (1991) *The Ethics of Social Research*. London: Longman.

Houston, S. and Mullen-Jensen, C. (2011) 'Towards Depth and Width in Qualitative Social Work: Aligning Interpretative Phenomenological Analysis with the Theory of Social Domains', *Qualitative Social Work*, June: 1–16.

Inglis, I. (1997) 'Variations on a Theme: The Love Songs of the Beatles', *International Review of the Aesthetics and Sociology of Music*, 28(1): 37–62.

Inglis, I. (1998) 'Pete Best: History and His Story', *Journal of Popular Music Studies*, 11: 103–24.

Johnson, C. (2011) 'It's no stretch for budget gyms to flex their muscles: Business Briefing', *The Times: Business Briefing*, 22 August.

Kane, E. (1990) *Doing Your Own Research*. London: Marion Boyars.

Layder, D. (1993) *New Strategies in Social Research: An Introduction and Guide*. Cambridge: Polity Press.

Layder, D. (1997) *Modern Social Theory: Key Debates and New Directions*. London: University College Press (Taylor & Francis).

Layder, D. (1998) *Sociological Practice: Linking Theory and Social Research*. London: Sage.

Layder, D. (2004a) *Social and Personal Identity: Understanding Yourself*. London: Sage.

Layder, D. (2004b) *Emotion in Social Life: The Lost Heart of Society*. London: Sage.

Layder, D. (2006) *Understanding Social Theory* (2nd edition). London: Sage.

Layder, D. (2009) *Intimacy and Power: The Dynamics of Personal Relationships in Modern Society*. Basingstoke: Palgrave Macmillan.

Layder, D., Ashton, D. and Sung, J. (1991) 'The Empirical Correlates of Action and Structure: The Transition from School to Work', *Sociology*, 25(3): 447–64.

Lee, J. (1977) 'A Typology of Styles of Loving', *Personality and Social Psychology Bulletin*, 3: 173–82.

Magee, B. (1997) *The Philosophy of Schopenhauer*. Oxford: Oxford University Press.

Marshall, A. (2006) *I Love You but I'm Not In Love with You*. London: Bloomsbury.

Martin, P. and Bateson, P. (1993) *Measuring Behaviour: An Introductory Guide* (2nd edition). Cambridge: Cambridge University Press.

Miller, M. (1995) *Intimate Terrorism: The Crisis of Love in an Age of Disillusion*. New York: W.W. Norton.

Mosely, D. et al. (2005) *Frameworks for Thinking*. Cambridge: Cambridge University Press.

Mouzelis, N. (1995) *Sociological Theory: What Went Wrong?* London: Routledge.

Office for National Statistics (2010) *Social Trends*. London: Palgrave.

Patton, M. (2001) *Qualitative Research and Evaluation Methods* (3rd edition). Thousand Oaks, CA: Sage.

Pruulmann-Vengerfeldt, P. (2006) 'Exploring Social Theory as a Framework for Social and Cultural Measurements of the Information Society', *The Information Society*, 22: 1–8.

Punch, K. (2008) *Introduction to Social Research* (2nd edition). London: Sage.

Reibstein, J. (1997) *Love Life: How To Make Your Relationships Work*. London: Fourth Estate.

Ritzer, G. (2011) *The McDonaldization of Society* (6th edition). Thousand Oaks, CA: Pine Forge Press.

Robson, C. (2007) *How To Do a Research Project*. Oxford: Blackwell.

Rojek, C. (2001) *Celebrity*. London: Reaktion Books.

Rojek, C. (2011) *Pop Music, Pop Culture*. Cambridge: Polity Press.

Rose, G. (1984) *Deciphering Sociological Research*. London: Macmillan.

Rowlands, M. (2009) *Fame*. Stocksfield: Acumen Publishing.

Sawyer, K. (2003a) *Group Creativity: Music, Theatre, Collaboration*. Mahwah, NJ: Lawrence Erlbaum Associates.

Sawyer, K. (2003b) *Improvised Dialogues: Emergence and Creativity in Conversation*. Westport, CT: Greenwood Press.

Scott, J. (1990) *A Matter of Record*. Cambridge: Polity Press.

Sibeon, R. (2004) *Rethinking Social Theory*. London: Sage.

Smith, J. (2001) 'Fit and Flexible: The Fitness Industry, Personal Trainers and Emotional Service Labour', *Sociology of Sport Journal*, 18(4): 379–402.

Smith, J. (2008) 'Leisure and the Obligation of Self-Work: An Examination of the Fitness Field', *Leisure Studies*, 27(1): 59–75.

Smith, J. and Stanway, K. (2008) 'Looking Good: Consumption and the Problems of Self-Production', *European Journal of Cultural Studies*, 11(1): 63–81.

Smith, K., Todd, M. and Waldman, J. (2009) *Doing Your Social Science Dissertation*. London: Routledge.

Spencer, L. and Pahl, R. (2006) *Rethinking Friendship: Hidden Solidarities Today*. Princeton, NJ: Princeton University Press.

Stebbins, R. (1970) 'Career: The Subjective Approach', *Sociological Quarterly*, 11: 32–49.

Strauss, A. and Corbin, J. (1998) *The Basics of Qualitative Research: Techniques and Procedures for Developing Grounded Theory* (2nd edition). London: Sage.

Tannen, D. (1992) *You Just Don't Understand*. London: Virago.

Tannen, D. (2002) *I Only Say This Because I Love You*. London: Virago.

Teddlie, C. and Tashakkori, A. (2009) *Foundations of Mixed Methods Research*. Thousand Oaks, CA: Sage.

Teddlie, C. and Yu, F. (2007) 'Mixed Methods Sampling: A Typology with Examples', *Journal of Mixed Methods Research*, 1(1): 77–100.

Toulmin, S. (1958) *The Uses of Argument*. Cambridge: Cambridge University Press.

Way, N. (2011) *Deep Secrets: Boy's Friendships and the Crisis of Connection*. Cambridge, MA: Harvard University Press.

Weber, M. (1964) *The Theory of Social and Economic Organisation*. New York: Free Press.

White, P. (2009) *Developing Research Questions: A Guide for Social Scientists*. Basingstoke: Palgrave Macmillan.

Wolcott, H. (2001) *Writing up Qualitative Research* (2nd edition). Thousand Oaks, CA: Sage.

Yin, R. (2009) *Case Study Research: Design and Methods* (4th edition). London: Sage.

INDEX

Index